REGENTS RENAISSANCE DRAMA SERIES

General Editor : Cyrus Hoy
Advisory Editor : G. E. Bentley

TAMBURLAINE THE GREAT

Parts I and II

CHRISTOPHER MARLOWE

Tamburlaine the Great
Parts I and II

Edited by

JOHN D. JUMP

UNIVERSITY OF NEBRASKA PRESS · LINCOLN

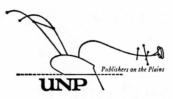

Copyright © 1967 by the University of Nebraska Press
All Rights Reserved
Library of Congress Catalog Card Number: 67–10666

MANUFACTURED IN THE UNITED STATES OF AMERICA

Regents Renaissance Drama Series

The purpose of the Regents Renaissance Drama Series is to provide soundly edited texts, in modern spelling, of the more significant plays of the Elizabethan, Jacobean, and Caroline theater. Each text in the series is based on a fresh collation of all sixteenth- and seventeenth-century editions. The textual notes, which appear above the line at the bottom of each page, record all substantive departures from the edition used as the copy-text. Variant substantive readings among sixteenth- and seventeenth-century editions are listed there as well. In cases where two or more of the old editions present widely divergent readings, a list of substantive variants in editions through the seventeenth century is given in an appendix. Editions after 1700 are referred to in the textual notes only when an emendation originating in some one of them is received into the text. Variants of accidentals (spelling, punctuation, capitalization) are not recorded in the notes. Contracted forms of characters' names are silently expanded in speech prefixes and stage directions, and, in the case of speech prefixes, are regularized. Additions to the stage directions of the copy-text are enclosed in brackets. Stage directions such as "within" or "aside" are enclosed in parentheses when they occur in the copy-text.

Spelling has been modernized along consciously conservative lines. "Murther" has become "murder," and "burthen," "burden," but within the limits of a modernized text, and with the following exceptions, the linguistic quality of the original has been carefully preserved. The variety of contracted forms ('em, 'am, 'm, 'um, 'hem) used in the drama of the period for the pronoun *them* are here regularly given as 'em, and the alternation between *a'th'* and *o'th'* (for *on* or *of the*) is regularly reproduced as *o'th'*. The copy-text distinction between preterite endings in *-d* and *-ed* is preserved except where the elision of *e* occurs in the penultimate syllable; in such cases, the final syllable is contracted. Thus, where the old editions read "threat'ned," those of the present series read "threaten'd." Where, in the old editions, a contracted preterite in *-y'd* would yield *-i'd* in modern spelling (as in "try'd," "cry'd," "deny'd"), the word is here given in its full form (e.g., "tried," "cried," "denied").

Punctuation has been brought into accord with modern practices. The effort here has been to achieve a balance between the generally light pointing of the old editions, and a system of punctuation which, without overloading the text with exclamation marks, semicolons, and dashes, will make the often loosely flowing verse (and prose) of the original syntactically intelligible to the modern reader. Dashes are regularly used only to indicate interrupted speeches, or shifts of address within a single speech.

Explanatory notes, chiefly concerned with glossing obsolete words and phrases, are printed below the textual notes at the bottom of each page. References to stage directions in the notes follow the admirable system of the Revels editions, whereby stage directions are keyed, decimally, to the line of the text before or after which they occur. Thus, a note on 0.2 has reference to the second line of the stage direction at the beginning of the scene in question. A note on 115.1 has reference to the first line of the stage direction following line 115 of the text of the relevant scene.

CYRUS HOY

University of Rochester

Contents

List of Abbreviations

Brooke	C. F. Tucker Brooke, ed. *The Works of Christopher Marlowe*. Oxford, 1910.
Cunn.	F. Cunningham, ed. *The Works of Christopher Marlowe*. London, 1870.
Dyce	A. Dyce, ed. *The Works of Christopher Marlowe*. London, 1850.
Dyce 2	A. Dyce, ed. *The Works of Christopher Marlowe*. London, 1858.
Ellis-Fermor	U. M. Ellis-Fermor, ed. *Tamburlaine the Great*. London, 1930.
Heninger	S. K. Heninger, Jr. *A Handbook of Renaissance Meteorology*. Durham, N.C., 1960.
Kirsch.	L. Kirschbaum, ed. *The Plays of Christopher Marlowe*. Cleveland, 1962.
Kocher	P. H. Kocher. "Marlowe's Art of War," *Studies in Philology*, XXXIX (1942), 207–225.
McKerrow	R. B. McKerrow, ed. *A Dictionary of Printers and Book-sellers in England, Scotland, and Ireland, and of Foreign Printers of English Books 1557–1640*. London, 1910.
MLN	*Modern Language Notes*
O1	First Octavo of 1590.
O2	Second Octavo of 1593.
O3	Third Octavo of 1597.
O4	Fourth Octavo of 1605 (Part I) and 1606 (Part II).
Ortelius	A. Ortelius. *Theatrum Orbis Terrarum*. Antwerp, 1570. Many subsequent revised editions.
Parr	Johnstone Parr. *Tamburlaine's Malady and Other Essays on Astrology in Elizabethan Drama*. Alabama, 1953.
PMLA	*Publications of the Modern Language Association of America*

Rob.   G. Robinson, ed. *The Works of Christopher Marlowe.* London, 1826.

Seaton   E. Seaton. "Marlowe's Map," *Essays and Studies by Members of the English Association*, X (1924), 13–35.

Tilley   M. P. Tilley. *A Dictionary of the Proverbs in England in the Sixteenth and Seventeenth Centuries.* Ann Arbor, 1950.

Introduction

DATE

In the autumn of 1587, a serious accident interrupted a performance given by the Lord Admiral's men. Philip Gawdy described
it in a letter to his father dated November 16, 1587:

> Yow shall vnderstande of some accydentall newes heare in this
> towne thoughe my self no wyttnesse thereof, yet I may be bold
> to veryfye it for an assured troth. My L. Admyrall his men and
> players having a devyse in ther playe to tye one of their fellowes
> to a poste and so to shoote him to deathe, having borrowed
> their callyvers one of the players handes swerved his peece being
> charged with bullett missed the fellowe he aymed at and
> killed a chyld, and a woman great with chyld forthwith, and
> hurt an other man in the head very soore.[1]

In *Tamburlaine*, Part II, V.i.107–159, the Governor of Babylon is
hung in chains upon his city walls and shot to death. This may well
have been the episode that gave rise to the accident Gawdy reports.
If so, since the Prologue to Part II confirms our natural assumption
that the dramatist wrote Part I first, the earliest productions of both
parts of *Tamburlaine* presumably belong to 1587, the year in which
Marlowe left Cambridge.

But perhaps Gawdy was referring to a performance of some other
play, now lost. Even if this could be shown to be the case, there
would be no need to shift *Tamburlaine* to a very much later date. In
the epistle "To the Gentlemen readers" prefixed to Robert Greene's
Perimedes The Blacke-Smith (1588), the words "daring God out of
heauen with that Atheist *Tamburlan*"[2] constitute an unmistakable
reference to it, and very likely to Tamburlaine's defiance of Mahomet
and burning of the Koran and other "superstitious books" in Part II,

---

[1] E. K. Chambers, *The Elizabethan Stage* (Oxford, 1923), II, 135.

[2] *The Life and Complete Works of Robert Greene*, ed. A. B. Grosart (printed
for private circulation, 1881–1886), VII, 8.

V.i.171–200. *Perimedes The Blacke-Smith* was entered on the Stationers' Register on March 29, 1588.[3]

Clearly, all that we can say with certainty is that Part I was written before the spring of 1588. But it seems very likely that both parts were written by that time. Nor are we being unduly rash if we accept Gawdy's letter as referring to a performance of *Tamburlaine*, Part II, and date both parts 1587.

AUTHORSHIP

None of the early editions names the author of the play. This being so, it is remarkable that scholars and critics are virtually unanimous in ascribing *Tamburlaine* to Marlowe. The external evidence for this ascription is slight and inconclusive. The passage in Greene's epistle prefacing *Perimedes The Blacke-Smith* (1588) from which the reference to *Tamburlaine* has already been quoted can be interpreted in such a fashion as to associate Marlowe with the play; and the same is true of Thomas Heywood's Cock-pit prologue (1633) to *The Jew of Malta*. But neither passage has necessarily to be read in this way. The earliest unambiguous statements of Marlowe's authorship occur in Francis Kirkman's play list appended to his edition of *Nicomede. A Tragi-Comedy, translated out of the French of Monsieur Corneille, by John Dancer* (1671), in Anthony à Wood's remarks on Thomas Newton in his *Athenae Oxonienses* (1691),[4] and in Gerard Langbaine's *Account of the English Dramatick Poets* (1691).[5] Statements made as belatedly as these, however, cannot alone be decisive.

Fortunately, the internal evidence is strong. The play itself seems in every respect to point to Marlowe as its author—in its thought and feeling; in its imagery, syntax, diction, and verse rhythm; and in its striking anticipations of a number of passages in later plays that are universally accepted as his—so much so that practically everybody now takes Marlowe's authorship for granted.

SOURCES[6]

Marlowe took much of his material for Part I from the descriptions of Tamburlaine's character and career provided by certain sixteenth-

[3] E. Arber, ed., *A Transcript of the Registers of the Company of Stationers of London; 1554–1640 A.D.* (London, 1875–1894), II, 227b.

[4] (London, 1691–1692), I, col. 288.   [5] (London, 1691), pp. 344–345.

[6] Most of the material in this section derives from the full and careful study of the sources of *Tamburlaine* in U. M. Ellis-Fermor, ed., *Tamburlaine the Great* (London, 1930), pp. 17–52, 286–303.

century historians. Two of these scholars were especially important to him: Pedro Mexia, a Spaniard, whose account of Tamburlaine in his *Silva de Varia Leccion* (Seville, 1543), I.xiii and II.xxvii, had become available also, with various modifications, in Italian, French, and English by the time Marlowe wrote; and Petrus Perondinus (Pietro Perondino), an Italian, who used the universal language, Latin, in his *Magni Tamerlanis Scytharum Imperatoris Vita [Life of Tamburlaine the Great, Emperor of the Scythians]* (Florence, 1553).

Mexia assembles a good deal of information, reliable and unreliable, from a variety of sources. Most of the chief incidents later introduced by Marlowe into Part I have a place in his narrative. Admittedly, his eclecticism results in a portrait of Tamburlaine that lacks coherence. But his imagination is successfully stirred when he considers how Bajazeth fell, and how Tamburlaine's empire decayed after his death so that men lost sight of his great achievements. In Mexia, these thoughts inspire reflections upon the precariousness of worldly pomp and riches and fame.

Marlowe appears to have read Mexia's story in the English translation made by George Whetstone from the French and included in his *English Myrror* (London, 1586).[7] He presumably read Perondinus in the original Latin. Perondinus has a much clearer and more consistent conception of Tamburlaine's character than has Mexia. He imagines him as a pitiless, destructive, and irresistible barbarian, dominated by an insatiable thirst for power.

Marlowe simplified and condensed what he found in the writings of these men. He cut out anything that might distract his public from the spectacle of Tamburlaine's rapid ascent to supreme power, and he admitted no check to that ascent. He degraded Tamburlaine's principal opponent, Bajazeth, transforming him from a courageous leader into an undignified braggart leading a numerically stronger army to disaster. He added Zenocrate to the plot, using her to reveal an important aspect of his protagonist. In all this, his aim was evidently to make Tamburlaine stand out in his splendor, his insolence, and his indomitability.

While writing Part I, Marlowe apparently meant that to be the whole play. He covered in it so much of the career of Tamburlaine as recorded in his sources that, when public demand induced him to write Part II,[8] he had to turn elsewhere for supplementary materials.

[7] T. C. Izard, *George Whetstone* (New York, 1942), pp. 215–217; and "The Principal Source for Marlowe's *Tamburlaine*," *MLN*, LVIII (1943), 411–417.

[8] Part II, Prologue, ll. 1–3.

From a work on the history of Hungary, *Antonii Bonfinii Rerum Ungaricarum Decades Tres* (Basle, 1543), he took the story of the Christian monarch who made a pact with the Turks, broke his oath, and suffered defeat when his Mohammedan foe called on the Christian God to punish his treachery. Historically, this defeat occurred in the battle of Varna (1444). Marlowe moved it approximately forty years back in time and substituted Sigismund and Orcanes for Vladislaus and Amurath II. For the story of Olympia and Theridamas, he was chiefly indebted to Ariosto's *Orlando Furioso*, XXVIII and XXIX, in which Isabella suffers persecution by Rodomonte. He borrowed much of the lecture on fortification which Tamburlaine delivers to his three sons in Part II, III.ii.53–92, from Paul Ive's *Practise of Fortification* (London, 1589), II; to do so in 1587 or 1588, he must have read this work in manuscript. He developed some of the other main elements in Part II from details in his original sources: Whetstone's *English Myrror*, for example, supplied him with Sigismund, King of Hungary; Bajazeth's son Calapin (Callapine); and Orcan (Orcanes).[9] Two major incidents, finally, seem to have been invented by Marlowe himself: the cowardice of Calyphas, and the death of Zenocrate.

Throughout his play, Marlowe made use of one of the finest of sixteenth-century atlases, Abraham Ortelius' *Theatrum Orbis Terrarum* (Antwerp, 1570). In the present edition, the note on Part II, I.iii.186–205, shows him relying upon this for Techelles' account of his African campaign.

The knowledge that Marlowe assembled materials from so many and so varied sources has encouraged some critics to declare that Part II is more fragmentary than Part I, that no consistent "criticism of life" unites its various elements and achieves expression through a sufficiently homogeneous work. Against this, others argue that Part II has its own unity and significance and that, once these have been appreciated, it can be seen that Marlowe's imagination has been powerfully creative in fusing materials from almost disconcertingly miscellaneous sources. Clearly, source-studies alone will not tell us whether Part II is a single coherent whole or not. On the contrary, the view we take of Marlowe's handling of his raw materials will itself depend upon our interpretation and evaluation of his finished work.

[9] Izard, *George Whetstone*, p. 216.

TAMBURLAINE, PARTS I AND II

The two parts of this play are concerned with the career, partly historical and partly imaginary, of a man who sets out to conquer the world. In furtherance of this aim, he resorts to methods which, if less horrifying than those that have been employed for the purpose in the twentieth century, are certainly horrifying enough to bring twentieth-century methods to our minds. In itself, such a career can only seem detestable, and our prior expectation may well be that a play concerned with it will show it as detestable. But is this how Marlowe shows it in *Tamburlaine*?

R. W. Battenhouse[10] says that it is. He argues that *Tamburlaine* shows wickedness growing until it destroys itself. No doubt, many readers would like Marlowe to have written the "grandly moral" work Battenhouse describes. But most readers believe that he wrote something rather different.

Probably all who know the play would agree that one of its key speeches is Tamburlaine's famous justification of his restless striving for power:

> Nature that fram'd us of four elements,
> Warring within our breasts for regiment,
> Doth teach us all to have aspiring minds.
> Our souls, whose faculties can comprehend
> The wondrous architecture of the world
> And measure every wand'ring planet's course,
> Still climbing after knowledge infinite,
> And always moving as the restless spheres,
> Wills us to wear ourselves and never rest
> Until we reach the ripest fruit of all,
> That perfect bliss and sole felicity,
> The sweet fruition of an earthly crown.
>
> (Part I, II.vii.18–29)

The resolute careerist who delivers this apologia had humble enough beginnings. But Mycetes, in scorning him as a "paltry Scythian" (Part I, I.i.53), was merely illustrating his own foolishness. His brother Cosroe more justly appreciates Tamburlaine's valor and "accomplish'd worth" (Part I, II.i.34) and accepts from his counselor

[10] *Marlowe's "Tamburlaine": A Study in Renaissance Moral Philosophy* (Nashville, 1941).

Menaphon a description of the Scythian's physical appearance that goes so far as to compare him with the Greek hero, Achilles. An extraordinary eloquence accompanies Tamburlaine's manly beauty. Of his two superb speeches of invitation in Part I, I.ii, one effectively initiates the conquest of Zenocrate and the other both initiates and completes that of Theridamas. Courteous in his treatment of the captured Zenocrate, expressing more than once his regard for his followers, and receiving in return their devoted loyalty, Tamburlaine is an impressive and attractive figure in these earlier acts of Part I. He is confident that Fate and Fortune are on his side, even under his control.

When he utters the lines quoted, he has just made himself master of Persia by first backing Cosroe, the pretender to Mycetes' throne, and then destroying him after their joint victory. It hardly needs saying that this is an act of bad faith and treachery. Yet, strangely enough, neither Cosroe nor any of his supporters charges Tamburlaine with it in these terms. Cosroe accuses him of "presumption" (Part I, II.vi.2) and "ingratitude" (Part I, II.vi.30) and, when mortally wounded, denounces him as "Barbarous," "bloody," and "insatiate" (Part I, II.vii.1, 11). As a result, Tamburlaine has only to defend himself against the charge of ruthless ambition.

He first claims that ambition is sanctioned by classical authority. "What better precedent than mighty Jove," who supplanted his father, Saturn, as lord of heaven? Then, in the lines quoted, he argues, first, that Nature teaches us the same lesson, and second, that our spiritual beings likewise direct us to aspire. Each of these arguments is embodied in a single suspended sentence, the second sentence tracing the ampler and more powerful periodic curve. But the eventual completion of the second main clause with the line, "Wills us to wear ourselves and never rest," does not, despite our expectations, signalize the climax of the speech. An additional subordinate clause mounts even beyond it, by way of a series of nouns in apposition, "fruit," "bliss and . . . felicity," and "fruition," to the true climax, "The sweet fruition of an earthly crown." Throughout the passage, the upward thrust of aspiration is reflected in the very syntax of the sentences.

Within these, the individual blank-verse lines never cease to be separately audible. Rhythmically, they are fairly regular, and most of them are end-stopped. By closing several with polysyllables, Marlowe invites for them a sustained and resonant delivery. As a result, the lines remain relatively self-sufficient five-foot units, as well as members of the more complex periodic structures already analyzed. Their firm iambic tread gives an assurance and a cogency to this rhetorical justification of vaulting ambition as something sanctioned by ancient myth, by the strife that is constant among the elements, and by the strenuous spirit of inquiry into the earth and the cosmos that was especially active during the Renaissance period.

But at its climax the speech proposes for the aspiring mind an object that has disappointed one after another of Marlowe's more idealistic readers. "Scythian bathos," protests Havelock Ellis.[11] In the age of Marlowe, however, intelligent men did not commonly think the exercise of political and military power an unworthy employment for the highest human abilities. Very few contemporary playgoers can have felt surprise at his introduction of crowns, the traditional symbols of supreme power on earth, as the natural objects of the aspiring mind and consequently as the central symbols of his play.

What is really surprising is his evident readiness to condone in Tamburlaine the use of any methods that will secure power for him and to tolerate from Tamburlaine any deeds that will impressively demonstrate his possession of it. He quietly neglects the fact that Tamburlaine shows himself a liar and a traitor when obtaining the Persian crown; his energy goes into providing Tamburlaine with an apologia for his ambition so persuasive that dissent is unimaginable, at all events while the words are sounding in our ears. In the same way, he does his utmost to present the massacre of the Virgins of Damascus, not as the atrocity that in itself it indubitably is, but as an impressive demonstration of the conqueror's firmness of mind in discharging the responsibilities of power. As far as possible, he shifts the blame for the Virgins' deaths to the Governor of Damascus, whose reckless obstinacy prevented the surrender of the town before the invader's tents had been altered "to the last and cruell'st hue" (Part I, V.i.8). When Tamburlaine sets eyes on the Virgins, he voices pity for them; and, when he sadly but sternly orders their deaths, they are slaughtered off-stage in the time it takes him to utter eight verse lines—in other words, before we have fully imagined what is happening. As soon as Techelles reports that the massacre is over, Tamburlaine distracts us by delivering his most famous

11 *Christopher Marlowe*, ed. Havelock Ellis (The Mermaid Series, London, 1887), p. xxxv.

tribute to Zenocrate's beauty. From beginning to end, the incident is so manipulated as to magnify our admiration for Tamburlaine and to minimize our pity for his victims.

Much the same may be said of the presentation of Tamburlaine's maltreatment of Bajazeth. As Emperor of Turkey, Bajazeth was boastful and complacent; as Tamburlaine's prisoner, he grows bitter and desperate. Since the Turks at that time constituted a serious threat to Christendom, Marlowe was doubtless assuming that his audiences would rejoice at Bajazeth's degradation and admire the greatness of the conqueror who could bring him low. In particular, he seems to have expected them to feel delight at the vicious and sadistic taunting of Bajazeth in the banquet scene, Part I, IV.iv.40–58. Zenocrate herself, the most humane member of Tamburlaine's immediate circle, confirms that the agonies of Bajazeth and Zabina "make a goodly show at a banquet" (Part I, IV.iv.56–57). But in Part I, V.i, Marlowe allows Bajazeth to achieve, in the speeches leading to his suicide, a dignity lacking both to his arrogant pronouncements before his defeat and to his malignant railings after it. These speeches inspire in us a respectful pity for the monarch who has fallen from his high estate. Marlowe allows Zenocrate to voice this pity, as it were on our behalf, in her great strophic dirge with its refrain-line, "Behold the Turk and his great emperess" (Part I, V.i.354, etc.). He has even allowed her, immediately before this, to express pity for the Virgins of Damascus. But he is determined not to let pity gain the upper hand. So the laments are quickly corrected by a further victory for the mighty Tamburlaine.

Clearly, Marlowe's purpose is to prevent conventional moral judgments, and humanitarian and Christian feelings, from compromising the almost unbounded admiration that he wishes to excite for his hero's prowess. This prowess, the Renaissance "virtù" that gives a man greatness, is for Marlowe the highest of human attributes, and his play exists to celebrate it—so much so that one function of the foolish Mycetes is to make compassion ridiculous:

> Accurs'd be he that first invented war!
> They knew not, ah, they knew not, simple men,
> How those were hit by pelting cannon shot
> Stand staggering iike a quivering aspen leaf
> Fearing the force of Boreas' boist'rous blasts.
>
> (Part I, II.iv.1–5)

"Fascist" is a word that J. B. Steane [12] is willing to use of *Tamburlaine*. The anachronism is almost excusable.

Several times in Part I and the first half of Part II, Tamburlaine is described, or describes himself, as a "scourge," or "scourge of God." The description occurs rather more frequently in the last two acts of Part II and is rendered in visual terms when Tamburlaine is drawn in his chariot by the captive kings, *"in his right hand a whip with which he scourgeth them"* (Part II, IV.iii.0.2–3).

In so far as he is a "scourge of God," Tamburlaine is a divinely appointed instrument for punishing the sins of men. Of his victims, Mycetes is unworthy of his office; Cosroe is a usurper; Bajazeth and his son Callapine, as Turks, are enemies of Christendom; and the Governors of Damascus and Babylon persist in foolhardy opposition to the irresistible providential instrument. All of these suffer for their sins and follies and cause innocent persons, such as the Virgins of Damascus, to suffer with them. But, while it is clearly true that Tamburlaine is a "scourge of God," it is equally true, and more important in the play, that he is an embodiment of Renaissance "virtù," an exponent of the aspiring mind.

Critics occasionally argue that Tamburlaine's ambition receives a number of setbacks in Part II and that his defiance of Mahomet and burning of the Koran and other "superstitious books" (Part II, V.i.172) bring down on him a divinely inflicted punishment. The rest of us, however, are entitled to suspect that these critics wish to make the work more moral than it really is. Admittedly, Tamburlaine's fatal sickness develops shortly after his challenge to Mahomet; but there is nothing to suggest that it has been caused by that challenge. Equally, certain incidents in Part II serve to define the limits of Tamburlaine's power; but they are hardly what we should normally understand by "setbacks." In Part II as in Part I, Tamburlaine goes on from strength to strength. He defeats the victors of the struggle between the Turks and the perfidious Christians; he harnesses the captive kings to his chariot; he takes Babylon; and, by his mere appearance in the field, he routs Callapine's Turkish army for a second time.

But he cannot instil his own prowess into all three of his sons. While two of them are worthy enough, the third, Calyphas, is a cowardly degenerate. Marlowe seizes the opportunity, as he did in

[12] *Marlowe: A Critical Study* (Cambridge, England, 1964), pp. 82, 83.

the case of Mycetes, of discrediting humane and Christian sentiments by ascribing them to him:

> I know, sir, what it is to kill a man.
> It works remorse of conscience in me.
> I take no pleasure to be murderous,
> Nor care for blood when wine will quench my thirst.
> (Part II, IV.i.27–30)

After Calyphas has dawdled in his tent instead of facing the enemy, Tamburlaine executes him with his own hands. This is one more instance of his ruthless exercise of power. But his inability to make Calyphas a worthy son is a reminder that in some directions that power is distinctly limited.

The death of Zenocrate is another such reminder. Since the first act of Part I, she has been the object of that love of beauty in Tamburlaine which coexists with his craving for power. He acknowledges that every warrior who aspires to the highest manly achievements "Must needs have beauty beat on his conceits" (Part I, V.i.182). But he cannot prolong Zenocrate's life. All he can do is to keep her corpse with him, "Embalm'd with cassia, ambergris, and myrrh" (Part II, II.iv.130), and by so doing pretend to have defeated death.

Nor can he prolong his own life. He can "strive and rail" (Part II, V.iii.120) against the gods, he can review his conquests and instruct his worthy sons on how to manage his empire after him, but eventually, having gazed on Zenocrate for the last time, he must die.

Before this, his lieutenant, Theridamas, has likewise come up against the limits of his power in attempting to compel the love of his prisoner, Olympia.

In Part II, then, the self-assertive, ambitious man confronts the limits imposed upon his power by the natures of the persons involved and the mortality to which all are subject. Within these limits, however, Tamburlaine continues to carry everything before him and is at his most victorious immediately before his death. Nor does he tire of demonstrating his power by the perpetration of atrocities, as witness the fates of the Turkish kings and the Governor of Babylon. Embodying these conflicting tendencies, Part II is more complex than Part I. We are not surprised that Marlowe should have drawn on a greater variety of sources for it than for its predecessor. Some readers prefer its greater complexity and, perhaps, maturity to the relative simplicity and single-mindedness of Part I.

The two parts were apparently designed for production in theaters of very different sorts. In Part II, the Captain commanding Balsera and the Governor of Babylon stand upon their respective city walls to parley with enemies below; in the scene of her death, Zenocrate is discovered on her bed, and an arras is drawn before her when Tamburlaine and the rest retire. In planning these scenes, Marlowe must have counted on a theater with an upper stage and a discovery-space. But he counted on nothing of the sort when writing Part I. Even the siege of Damascus is managed without the use of an upper stage. Part I could have been successfully performed on a simple platform stage, but the full resources of a well-equipped London theater would have been needed for Part II.

Marlowe seems to have intended that one of the strengths of his play should be that it gives opportunities for many striking and even sensational tableaux. Bajazeth is brought on in a cage and is compelled to serve as Tamburlaine's footstool; Tamburlaine feasts his lieutenants and has a *"course of crowns"* (Part I, IV.iv.104.1) served to them; Callapine is crowned Emperor of Turkey; Tamburlaine consumes a town by fire in his mourning for Zenocrate; the captive kings draw the chariot of the triumphant conqueror; and the sacred books are publicly burnt.

In other ways, too, the appeal to the eye is strong. Bajazeth enters *"in great pomp"* (Part I, III.i.0.2); the Soldan of Egypt enters *"with streaming colors"* (Part I, IV.iii.0.1); and repeatedly the stage directions remind us of the impressive trains attendant on the various leaders. Each time that Tamburlaine's patience runs out, his tents and ensigns change from white to red and from red to black. Equally symbolic are the numerous crowns, and the various weapons, and even the fires, that have their essential place in the action.

Ceremonial scenes are frequent. Marlowe evidently expected that an extremely formal, even symmetrical, grouping of the actors would characterize the production of these. This is implied, for example, by his meticulously balanced distribution of speeches to those concerned in the preliminaries to the battle in Part I, III.iii. Immediately after Bajazeth's entry, he and Tamburlaine speak alternately, three time each; Bajazeth's three lieutenants address him in turn, and he replies; Tamburlaine's three lieutenants address him in turn, and he replies; Bajazeth addresses Zabina, and she replies; Tamburlaine addresses Zenocrate, and she replies; Bajazeth and Tamburlaine threaten each other and leave; Zabina and Zenocrate speak alternately, twice each; Zabina addresses her maid,

Ebea, who replies; Zenocrate addresses her maid, Anippe, who replies; and Zenocrate and Zabina pray in turn for victory (ll. 61–200).

When all has been said about the appeal to the eye, however, it remains less important than the appeal to the ear. The play echoes with the sound of drums and trumpets and with the din of battle. Even more, it rings with the music of Marlowe's incomparable verse. Passionate and formal, lyrical and rhetorical, this verse does not merely show Marlowe to have been a gifted poet; it is easily his most useful tool as a playwright. We must not overlook its variety. In the world of Tamburlaine, as Harry Levin [13] has helped us to perceive, a character's eloquence is a sign of his "virtù"; Tamburlaine and Bajazeth, Cosroe and Mycetes, Callapine and Calyphas achieve widely different kinds and degrees of eloquence. But what we most readily recall are the great set speeches of the characters who possess abundant "virtù"—especially those of Tamburlaine himself who does, after all, speak more than one-third of the entire play. We remember these speeches for their clarity and force; for their bold hyperboles; for their richly evocative classical imagery; for their emphatic colors—reds and golds, blacks, whites and silvers; for their lavish, almost Spenserian, verbal melody; for their sonorous, almost Miltonic, use of proper names, often strange and exotic proper names; for their frequent approximation to strophic form and their occasional adoption of haunting refrain-lines; and for the various metrical and syntactical attributes discussed earlier. In short, we remember them for the superb, youthful elation which they irresistibly communicate. We may legitimately have our doubts about the ethics of the play in which Marlowe's Tamburlaine is held up for our almost unbounded admiration; but we can have no doubts about our immediate, spontaneous sympathy with the eager aspiration that was so important a part of what Marlowe was trying to express through him.

STAGE HISTORY

If Philip Gawdy's letter of November 16, 1587, quoted at the beginning of this Introduction, does indeed refer to *Tamburlaine*, it is our earliest record of a performance of the play. Philip Henslowe's information is more explicit. From him we learn that between August 28, 1594, and November 13, 1595, the Lord Admiral's men

[13] *Christopher Marlowe: The Overreacher* (London, 1954), pp. 62–66.

acted Part I fifteen times and Part II seven times.[14] The play must have enjoyed great popularity not only during this short period for which profitable performances are on record but also both before and after it. So much is clear from the numerous references to *Tamburlaine* in the literature of the age. Peele, Lodge, Greene, Nashe, Shakespeare, Dekker, Jonson, Marston, Heywood, Beaumont and Fletcher, Massinger, Ford, and Suckling are no more than one-half of the writers who provide these.

Inventories of the properties and costumes belonging to the Lord Admiral's men in 1598 include items used in the staging of *Tamburlaine*: "Tamberlyne brydell," "Tamberlynes cotte with coper lace," "Tamberlanes breches of crymson vellvet," and very likely "j cage."[15] Edward Alleyn (1566–1626) appears to have played Tamburlaine in these early performances. Such is almost certainly the meaning of an ambiguously punctuated passage in Heywood's Cock-pit prologue (1633) to *The Jew of Malta*.

The play presumably dropped out of the repertories during the first half of the seventeenth century. At all events, it seems never to have been acted between 1660 and the twentieth century. Independent tragedies by Charles Saunders (1681) and Nicholas Rowe (1701) helped to keep alive the memory of its hero; but Marlowe's work was almost completely forgotten.

During the twentieth century, university dramatic societies on both sides of the Atlantic have revived it; and in 1964, the year in which occurred the four-hundredth anniversary of Marlowe's birth, the British Broadcasting Corporation presented on sound radio an impressive production of both parts, with Stephen Murray in the title role. This was the B.B.C.'s third broadcast of *Tamburlaine*.[16]

The first production in the professional theater since the seventeenth century took place in London in 1951, when the Old Vic company performed an abridgement of the two parts into a single play. Tyrone Guthrie directed this. Donald Wolfit was Tamburlaine, Jill Balcon Zenocrate, Leo McKern Bajazeth, and Margaret Rawlings Zabina. "Guthrie flung his great army of characters, his machines of death and cages of torture, across the whole stage and apron of the Vic"—so much so that a *Catholic Herald* headline

---

[14] *Henslowe's Diary*, ed. R. A. Foakes and R. T. Rickert (Cambridge, England, 1961), pp. 23–33.

[15] *Ibid.*, pp. 319–322.

[16] Information supplied by the B.B.C.

carried the mock-protest, "What! No Elephants?"[17] In the *Manchester Guardian*, September 26, 1951, Philip Hope-Wallace wrote that Guthrie was "probably right to make his production strenuous to the point of suffocation; the apron stage is continuously heaped with writhing bodies and the horrors are never shirked—rather the reverse, gloatingly protracted . . . . One comes away battered and blood-boltered." Hope-Wallace admired Wolfit's "thwacking, lusty performance" and commended "the relish with which he depicts the cunning, cruelty, and jovial arrogance of the Scythian Scourge." The reviewer in the London *Times*, September 26, 1951, agreed with him: "It is as a vibrant figure of pure theatrical flamboyance that Mr. Donald Wolfit plays Tamburlaine . . . . It is at rough grandeur that he aims, giving the base-born conqueror a street-arab delight in cruelty and in all the dazzling appurtenances of power."

Guthrie directed the play again in New York in 1956. There has been no subsequent production in the professional theater.

A NOTE ON THE TEXT

The following entry was made in the Stationers' Register on August 14, 1590: "**Richard Jones**. Entred vnto him for his Copye *The twooe commicall discourses of* TOMBERLEIN *the Cithian shepparde* vnder the handes of Master ABRAHAM HARTEWELL, and the Wardens."[18] The first edition of the play, a black-letter octavo, has a title page that describes the work at some length but fails to name its author:

> Tamburlaine/ the Great./ *Who, from a Scythian Shephearde,/* **by his rare and woonderfull Conquests,/** became a most puissant and migh-/ tye Monarque./ And (for his tyranny, and terrour in/ Warre) was tearmed,/ **The Scourge of God./** *Deuided into two Tragicall Dis-/* courses, as they were sundrie times/ **shewed vpon Stages in the Citie/** of London./ **By the right honorable the Lord/ Admyrall, his seruantes./** Now first, and newlie published./ [lace ornament]/ LONDON./ **Printed by** Richard Ihones: **at the signe/** of the Rose and Crowne neere Hol-/ borne Bridge. 1590.

Despite the statement that Richard Jones printed the book, it seems more likely that Thomas Orwin did so for him. A single compositor

---

[17] Audrey Williamson, *Old Vic Drama 2* (London, 1957), pp. 77–80.
[18] E. Arber, ed., *A Transcript*, II, 558.

evidently set the whole of it, and the pages appear to have been composed by formes rather than seriatim.[19]

While the sheets were passing through the press, a number of corrections were made in the text. Of the two extant copies of the 1590 octavo, that in the Henry E. Huntington Library has the outer forme of sheet A in a corrected state, and that in the Bodleian has the outer forme of sheet B in a corrected state. The corrections are very few and concern only details of spelling and punctuation.

Three more octavo editions soon followed: in 1593 (O2); in 1597 (O3); and in 1605 and 1606 (O4), Part I and Part II on this occasion being issued separately. The play was not published again until the nineteenth century. Of the early editions, O2 and O3 are reprints of O1 of 1590, and O4 is a reprint of O3. Each reprint corrects some obvious errors in its copy-text, and each of them introduces rather more fresh errors of its own. None of them contains anything new for which special authority can be claimed.

The printer's copy for O1 is unlikely to have been a theatrical manuscript. The octavo's stage directions, though far from meager, too often lack the precision and explicitness regarding entrances that a prompter needed. This can be seen in the many places in the present text where, despite a generally conservative editorial policy, square brackets reveal that the stage directions, and especially the entries, have had to be supplemented. From this, we may surmise that O1 is a print of the text as it stood before the prompter revised it for theatrical use. Very likely he made this revision on a fair transcript of it, leaving Marlowe's original manuscript, his "foul papers," to be sold in due course to the publisher of 1590.

Whether this was the case or not, the fact remains that the modern editor of *Tamburlaine* must take his text from O1. For present purposes, certain changes have been made in it without record in the textual notes: spelling and punctuation have been modernized, abbreviations have been expanded, the most obvious misprints have been corrected, mislined verse has been emended,[20] and speech prefixes have been regularized. Since O1 normally neglects to use the word *"Enter"* to

[19] W. W. Greg, *A Bibliography of the English Printed Drama to the Restoration* (London, 1939–1959), I, 171–172 (items 94, 95); R. F. Welsh, "The Printing of the Early Editions of Marlowe's Plays" (Duke University dissertation, 1964), pp. 8–31.

[20] O1 contains only six cases of mislineation clear enough to compel emendation. It omits the line divisions in Part I, I.ii.154–155 and V.i.245–246, and Part II, III.iv.67–68 and IV.ii.71–72; and it divides Part I, I.i.188, after "then.", and IV.iv.26–27, after "curses" instead of "these."

introduce the names of the characters entering at the beginning of a scene, this word has been silently added in square brackets wherever appropriate. When an entry refers to a character by some such term as "*his wife*" or "*the Turke*," or merely by a pronoun, the proper name has been silently added in square brackets. In several places where O1 omits speech prefixes, evidently meaning us to ascribe the speeches in question to characters whose entries are announced immediately prior to them, the speech prefixes have been silently inserted. O1 sets out its scene-headings in Latin ("*Actus. 1. Scæna. 1.*", etc.); in making its scene-divisions, it vacillates between the English system and the French system; but it omits some headings entirely, and it includes wrong serial numbers in others. This whole apparatus has been silently replaced by scene-headings introduced in accordance with the English system and printed in the style usual in the Regents Drama Series. This has meant, on the one hand, introducing the five new scene-divisions which occur in the present text before Part I, II.iv, II.v, and II.vii, and Part II, II.iii and III.iv; and, on the other hand, deleting the five scene-divisions which occur in O1 after Part I, V.i.63, and Part II, I.i.77, I.iii.111, I.iii.127, and III.v.57.

All other emendations are recorded in the textual notes, where the source of each preferred reading is acknowledged and each rejected reading is quoted. In addition, the textual notes display all substantive variants from O1 that have been found in O2, O3, and O4. Variants arising from the most obvious misprints have been ignored, however, as have also differences in verse-lineation and nearly all those between elided and unelided forms. When a single reading is ascribed to two or more of the octavos, it should be understood that the readings of the octavos named are identical in substance, but not necessarily in the accidents of spelling, punctuation, etc. For the readings which introduce the textual notes, the accidents are those of the present edition; outside the lemmas, they are those of the earliest of the octavos in which any particular reading occurs.

In accordance with the general policy of the Regents Renaissance Drama Series, editions after 1700 are referred to in the textual notes only when an emendation originating in some one of them is received into the text. Many of these emendations affect only the stage directions. In such cases, what is acknowledged in the textual notes is an indebtedness for the sense of the emendations; for present purposes, the wording may differ from that employed by earlier editors.

JOHN D. JUMP

University of Manchester

TAMBURLAINE THE GREAT

Part I

To the Gentlemen Readers and Others that Take Pleasure in Reading Histories

Gentlemen, and courteous readers whosoever: I have here published in print for your sakes the two tragical discourses of the Scythian shepherd Tamburlaine, that became so great a conqueror and so mighty a monarch. My hope is that they will be now no less acceptable unto you to read after   5
your serious affairs and studies than they have been lately delightful for many of you to see, when the same were showed in London upon stages. I have purposely omitted and left out some fond and frivolous gestures, digressing and, in my poor opinion, far unmeet for the matter, which I   10
thought might seem more tedious unto the wise than any way else to be regarded, though haply they have been of some vain, conceited fondlings greatly gaped at, what times they were showed upon the stage in their graced deformities. Nevertheless, now to be mixtured in print with such   15
matter of worth, it would prove a great disgrace to so honorable and stately a history. Great folly were it in me to commend unto your wisdoms either the eloquence of the author that writ them or the worthiness of the matter itself. I therefore leave unto your learned censures both the   20
one and the other and myself, the poor printer of them, unto your most courteous and favorable protection, which

2. the two] *O1–3*; *this O4.*
2. discourses] *O1–3*; *discourse O4.*
5. they] *O1–3*; *it O4.*
6. they have] *O1–3*; *it hath O4.*
7. were] *O1–3*; *was O4.*
12. haply] *O1–3*; *happilye O4.*
13. times] *O1, O3–4*; *time O2.*
15. mixtured] *O1–2*; *mingled O3–4.*

19. them] *O1–3*; *it O4.*
20. leave unto] *O1–3*; *leaue it vnto O4.*
20–21. both . . . other] *O1–3*; *not in O4.*
21. of them] *O1–3*; *thereof O4.*
22. protection] *O1–2*; *protections O3–4.*

8–9. *I . . . gestures*] Without this statement, few would have suspected that anything was missing from *Tamburlaine.* Perhaps the publisher merely cut out some passages of low comedy which had been inserted, by Marlowe or another, after the completion of the play.
9. *fond*] foolish.
12. *haply*] perhaps.
13. *fondlings*] foolish persons.
20. *censures*] judgments.

if you vouchsafe to accept, you shall evermore bind me to
employ what travail and service I can to the advancing and
pleasuring of your excellent degree.   25

Yours, most humble at commandment,
R. J., Printer

23. accept] *O1–2*; *doo O3–4*.   26. humble] *O1–3*; *not in O4*.

27. *R. J., Printer*] Richard Jones, who was at work throughout Marlowe's
lifetime and for some years after his death (McKerrow). But see "A Note
on the Text."

[CHARACTERS OF THE PLAY

MYCETES, KING OF PERSIA
COSROE, *his brother*
CENEUS ⎫
ORTYGIUS ⎪
MEANDER ⎬ *Persian lords*   5
MENAPHON ⎪
THERIDAMAS ⎭
TAMBURLAINE, *a Scythian shepherd*
TECHELLES ⎫ *his followers*
USUMCASANE ⎭   10
BAJAZETH, EMPEROR OF TURKEY
KING OF ARGIER
KING OF FEZ
KING OF MOROCCO
ALCIDAMUS, KING OF ARABIA   15
SOLDAN OF EGYPT
GOVERNOR OF DAMASCUS
AGYDAS ⎫ *Median lords*
MAGNETES ⎭
CAPOLIN, *an Egyptian*   20
A SPY
MESSENGERS, *including* PHILEMUS
BASSOES, LORDS, CITIZENS, MOORS, SOLDIERS, *and* ATTENDANTS

ZENOCRATE, *daughter of the Soldan of Egypt*
ANIPPE, *her maid*   25
ZABINA, *wife of Bajazeth*
EBEA, *her maid*
VIRGINS *of Damascus*]

---

12. *Argier*] Algeria.
16. *Soldan*] sultan.
19. *Magnetes*] O1 has the speech prefix "*Mag.*" at I.ii.17 and 80 but nowhere gives the name in full. The editors have tacitly agreed upon the form adopted here.

Tamburlaine the Great

The First Part of the Two Tragical Discourses of Mighty Tamburlaine, the Scythian Shepherd, etc.

THE PROLOGUE

From jigging veins of rhyming mother wits,
And such conceits as clownage keeps in pay,
We'll lead you to the stately tent of war,
Where you shall hear the Scythian Tamburlaine
Threat'ning the world with high astounding terms   5
And scourging kingdoms with his conquering sword.
View but his picture in this tragic glass,
And then applaud his fortunes as you please.

[I.i]

[*Enter*] Mycetes, Cosroe, Meander, Theridamas, Ortygius, Ceneus, [Menaphon,] *with others.*

MYCETES.

Brother Cosroe, I find myself aggriev'd,
Yet insufficient to express the same,
For it requires a great and thund'ring speech.
Good brother, tell the cause unto my lords;
I know you have a better wit than I.   5

The First Part of] *O2; not in O1,*   *tragicall Conquests of Tamburlaine*
O3–4.   *O3–4.*
the ... Tamburlaine] *O1–2; The*   [I.i]
                                          0.2. Menaphon] *Rob.; not in O1–4.*

---

1. *jigging . . . wits*] a disparaging reference to popular plays written in rough rhyming verse that did not lend itself to serious utterance.
2. *conceits*] devices.
[I.i]
2. *insufficient*] unable.   5. *wit*] understanding.

COSROE.

    Unhappy Persia, that in former age
    Hast been the seat of mighty conquerors,
    That in their prowess and their policies
    Have triumph'd over Afric and the bounds
    Of Europe, where the sun dares scarce appear   10
    For freezing meteors and congealed cold,
    Now to be rul'd and governed by a man
    At whose birthday Cynthia with Saturn join'd,
    And Jove, the sun, and Mercury denied
    To shed their influence in his fickle brain!   15
    Now Turks and Tartars shake their swords at thee,
    Meaning to mangle all thy provinces.

MYCETES.

    Brother, I see your meaning well enough,
    And through your planets I perceive you think
    I am not wise enough to be a king.   20
    But I refer me to my noblemen
    That know my wit and can be witnesses.
    I might command you to be slain for this.
    Meander, might I not?

MEANDER.

    Not for so small a fault, my sovereign lord.   25

MYCETES.

    I mean it not, but yet I know I might;
    Yet live, yea live, Mycetes wills it so.
    Meander, thou my faithful counselor,
    Declare the cause of my conceived grief,
    Which is, God knows, about that Tamburlaine,   30

9. Afric] *O1–2*; *Affrica O3–4.*   19. through] *O3–4*; thorough *O1–2.*
15. their] *Rob.*; his *O1–4.*

---

   8. *policies*] statecraft.

   11. *freezing . . . cold*] sleet and snow. In Elizabethan English, "meteors" was used for atmospheric phenomena of every kind.

   13–15. *At . . . brain*] The malignant conjunction of Saturn and Cynthia (the moon) at the time of Mycetes' birth has made him feeble-minded and unstable. Had Jove (Jupiter), the sun, and Mercury been more favorably placed, they might have fitted him for rule by making him magnanimous, judicious, and resourceful; but their influence was denied to him. See Parr, pp. 24–31.

   16. *thee*] i.e., Persia.

That like a fox in midst of harvest time
Doth prey upon my flocks of passengers,
And, as I hear, doth mean to pull my plumes.
Therefore 'tis good and meet for to be wise.

MEANDER.

Oft have I heard your majesty complain   35
Of Tamburlaine, that sturdy Scythian thief,
That robs your merchants of Persepolis
Trading by land unto the Western Isles,
And in your confines with his lawless train
Daily commits incivil outrages,   40
Hoping, misled by dreaming prophecies,
To reign in Asia, and with barbarous arms
To make himself the monarch of the East.
But ere he march in Asia, or display
His vagrant ensign in the Persian fields,   45
Your grace hath taken order by Theridamas,
Charg'd with a thousand horse, to apprehend
And bring him captive to your highness' throne.

MYCETES.

Full true thou speak'st, and like thyself, my lord,
Whom I may term a Damon for thy love.   50
Therefore 'tis best, if so it like you all,
To send my thousand horse incontinent

38. Trading] *O2*; Treading *O1*,   40. incivil] *O1–2*; vnciuill *O3–4*.
O3–4.

---

32. *passengers*] travelers.   34. *meet*] fitting.

36. *Scythian*] According to the maps of Abraham Ortelius, which Marlowe used, Scythia was the district along the northern shore of the Black Sea, just west of the Crimea. But the name was often applied to a larger area in central and northern Asia. Ortelius (1527–1598) was a geographer of Antwerp, whose atlas, *Theatrum Orbis Terrarum*, went through many editions from 1570 onwards. For Marlowe's use of it, see Seaton and Ellis-Fermor.

37. *Persepolis*] the ancient capital of Persia.

38. *the Western Isles*] Britain.   39. *confines*] territory.

40. *incivil*] savage.

45. *vagrant ensign*] nomadic banner.   47. *Charg'd*] entrusted.

50. *Damon*] He and Pythias, by their willingness to sacrifice themselves for each other, provided one of the most famous examples of faithful friendship in the ancient world.

51. *like*] please.   52. *incontinent*] immediately.

To apprehend that paltry Scythian.
How like you this, my honorable lords?
Is it not a kingly resolution?   55

COSROE.

It cannot choose, because it comes from you.

MYCETES.

Then hear thy charge, valiant Theridamas,
The chiefest captain of Mycetes' host,
The hope of Persia, and the very legs
Whereon our state doth lean as on a staff   60
That holds us up and foils our neighbor foes:
Thou shalt be leader of this thousand horse,
Whose foaming gall with rage and high disdain
Have sworn the death of wicked Tamburlaine.
Go frowning forth, but come thou smiling home,   65
As did Sir Paris with the Grecian dame.
Return with speed, time passeth swift away,
Our life is frail, and we may die today.

THERIDAMAS.

Before the moon renew her borrowed light,
Doubt not, my lord and gracious sovereign,   70
But Tamburlaine and that Tartarian rout
Shall either perish by our warlike hands
Or plead for mercy at your highness' feet.

MYCETES.

Go, stout Theridamas, thy words are swords,
And with thy looks thou conquerest all thy foes.   75
I long to see thee back return from thence,
That I may view these milk-white steeds of mine

58. chiefest] *O1–3*; chiefe *O4*.

---

56. *choose*] be otherwise.

66. *the Grecian dame*] Helen of Troy, whom the Trojan prince Paris stole
from her husband, Menelaus.

67–68. *time . . . frail*] Mycetes seems to be thinking of the proverbs
"Time flees away without delay" and "Flesh is frail" (Tilley, T 327 and
F 363).

71. *Tartarian*] Tartar. In Ortelius' maps, Tartary covers a large part of
northern and central Asia; Marlowe uses "Tartar" and "Scythian" interchangeably. See note on l. 36, above.

74. *thy . . . swords*] "Words hurt more than swords" was proverbial
(Tilley, W 839).

All loaden with the heads of killed men,
And from their knees even to their hoofs below
Besmear'd with blood; that makes a dainty show.   80

THERIDAMAS.

Then now, my lord, I humbly take my leave.   *Exit.*

MYCETES.

Theridamas, farewell ten thousand times.
Ah, Menaphon, why stayest thou thus behind
When other men press forward for renown?
Go, Menaphon, go into Scythia,   85
And foot by foot follow Theridamas.

COSROE.

Nay, pray you let him stay. A greater task
Fits Menaphon than warring with a thief.
Create him prorex of all Africa,
That he may win the Babylonians' hearts,   90
Which will revolt from Persian government
Unless they have a wiser king than you.

MYCETES.

"Unless they have a wiser king than you."
These are his words, Meander, set them down.

COSROE.

And add this to them, that all Asia   95
Lament to see the folly of their king.

MYCETES.

Well, here I swear by this my royal seat—

COSROE [*aside*].

You may do well to kiss it then.

MYCETES.

—Emboss'd with silk as best beseems my state,
To be reveng'd for these contemptuous words.   100
O where is duty and allegiance now?
Fled to the Caspian or the Ocean main?
What, shall I call thee brother? No, a foe,
Monster of nature, shame unto thy stock,

87. you] *O1–2; not in O3–4.*   89. all] *O4; not in O1–3.*
87. task] *Rob.; not in O1–4.*   98. S.D. *aside*] *Kirsch.; not in O1–4.*

89. *prorex*] viceroy.
99. *beseems*] suits.

−10−

That dar'st presume thy sovereign for to mock!   105
Meander, come, I am abus'd, Meander.

Exit [*with* Meander *and others*]. *Manent* Cosroe *and* Menaphon.

MENAPHON.

How now, my lord? What, mated and amaz'd
To hear the king thus threaten like himself?

COSROE.

Ah, Menaphon, I pass not for his threats.
The plot is laid by Persian noblemen   110
And captains of the Median garrisons
To crown me emperor of Asia.
But this it is that doth excruciate
The very substance of my vexed soul:
To see our neighbors that were wont to quake   115
And tremble at the Persian monarch's name
Now sits and laughs our regiment to scorn;
And that which might resolve me into tears,
Men from the farthest equinoctial line
Have swarm'd in troops into the Eastern India,   120
Lading their ships with gold and precious stones,
And made their spoils from all our provinces.

MENAPHON.

This should entreat your highness to rejoice,
Since fortune gives you opportunity
To gain the title of a conqueror   125
By curing of this maimed empery.
Afric and Europe bordering on your land
And continent to your dominions,
How easily may you with a mighty host
Pass into Graecia, as did Cyrus once,   130

106.1. *with . . . others*] *this edn.; not*   121. ships] *O1, O3–4;* shippe *O2.*
in O1–4.   130. Pass] *O1–2;* Haste *O3–4.*
118. resolve] *O1–2;* dissolue *O3–4.*

106.1. *Manent*] there remain.   107. *mated*] daunted.
109. *pass*] care.   117. *regiment*] rule, government.
118. *resolve*] dissolve, melt.   119. *equinoctial line*] equator.
123. *entreat*] induce.   126. *empery*] empire.
128. *continent to*] continuous with.
130. *Cyrus*] The founder of the Persian Empire, he subdued the Greek
cities of Asia Minor. He was killed in 529 B.C.

And cause them to withdraw their forces home,
Lest you subdue the pride of Christendom!

COSROE.

But, Menaphon, what means this trumpet's sound?

MENAPHON.

Behold, my lord, Ortygius and the rest
Bringing the crown to make you emperor!   135

Enter Ortygius *and* Ceneus *bearing a crown, with others.*

ORTYGIUS.

Magnificent and mighty prince Cosroe,
We, in the name of other Persian states
And commons of this mighty monarchy,
Present thee with th'imperial diadem.

CENEUS.

The warlike soldiers and the gentlemen,   140
That heretofore have fill'd Persepolis
With Afric captains taken in the field,
Whose ransom made them march in coats of gold,
With costly jewels hanging at their ears
And shining stones upon their lofty crests,   145
Now living idle in the walled towns,
Wanting both pay and martial discipline,
Begin in troops to threaten civil war
And openly exclaim against the king.
Therefore, to stay all sudden mutinies,   150
We will invest your highness emperor;
Whereat the soldiers will conceive more joy
Than did the Macedonians at the spoil
Of great Darius and his wealthy host.

COSROE.

Well, since I see the state of Persia droop   155
And languish in my brother's government,
I willingly receive th'imperial crown
And vow to wear it for my country's good

132. you] *O1–3*; they *O4*.   149. the] *O1, O3–4*; their *O2*.
135.1. Ceneus] *Rob.*; *Conerus O1–4*.

137. *states*] persons of rank.
153–154. *Than . . . host*] Alexander the Great, King of Macedon,
defeated Darius III, King of Persia, at the battle of Issus in 333 B.C.

In spite of them shall malice my estate.

ORTYGIUS.

And in assurance of desir'd success   160
We here do crown thee monarch of the East,
Emperor of Asia and of Persia,
Great lord of Media and Armenia,
Duke of Africa and Albania,
Mesopotamia and of Parthia,   165
East India and the late-discovered isles,
Chief lord of all the wide, vast Euxine sea,
And of the ever-raging Caspian lake.
Long live Cosroe, mighty emperor!

COSROE.

And Jove may never let me longer live   170
Than I may seek to gratify your love
And cause the soldiers that thus honor me
To triumph over many provinces;
By whose desires of discipline in arms
I doubt not shortly but to reign sole king,   175
And with the army of Theridamas,
Whither we presently will fly, my lords,
To rest secure against my brother's force.

ORTYGIUS.

We knew, my lord, before we brought the crown,
Intending your investion so near   180
The residence of your despised brother,
The lords would not be too exasperate

162. and of Persia] *O1, O3–4*; and   169. Long] *O1–2*; *All.* Long *O3–4*.
Persea O2.   179. knew] *O1–3*; knowe *O4*.
168. ever-raging] *O1–3*; riuer rag-   182. lords] *O3–4*; Lord *O1–2*.
ing *O4*.

---

159. *shall malice*] who will show ill will towards.
162–168. *Emperor . . . lake*] the first of several catalogues of resonant and
evocative proper names in *Tamburlaine*. For some account of where Ortelius
locates the various places Marlowe mentions in these lists and elsewhere,
see Seaton and Ellis-Fermor. In the present edition, such geographical
information is given only when it seems to be of special interest.
166. *the late-discovered isles*] possibly the West Indies.
167. *Euxine sea*] Black Sea.   170. *Jove may*] may Jove.
171. *gratify*] requite.   177. *presently*] immediately, at once.
180. *investion*] investiture.   182. *exasperate*] exasperated.

> To injure or suppress your worthy title.
> Or if they would, there are in readiness
> Ten thousand horse to carry you from hence   185
> In spite of all suspected enemies.

COSROE.

> I know it well, my lord, and thank you all.

ORTYGIUS.

> Sound up the trumpets, then. God save the king!   *Exeunt.*

[I.ii]

[*Enter*] Tamburlaine *leading* Zenocrate [*followed by* Magnetes *and* Agydas]; Techelles, Usumcasane, *other Lords and Soldiers loaden with treasure.*

TAMBURLAINE.

> Come, lady, let not this appall your thoughts;
> The jewels and the treasure we have ta'en
> Shall be reserv'd, and you in better state
> Than if you were arriv'd in Syria,
> Even in the circle of your father's arms,   5
> The mighty Soldan of Egyptia.

ZENOCRATE.

> Ah, shepherd, pity my distressed plight
> (If, as thou seem'st, thou art so mean a man)
> And seek not to enrich thy followers
> By lawless rapine from a silly maid,   10
> Who, traveling with these Median lords
> To Memphis, from my uncle's country of Media,
> Where all my youth I have been governed,
> Have pass'd the army of the mighty Turk,
> Bearing his privy signet and his hand   15

---

183. injure] *O1*; iniurie *O2–4.*   in *O1–4.*
188. God] *O1–2*; *All.* God *O3–4.*   0.2. Usumcasane, *other*] *O1–3*;
[I.ii]   *Vsumcasane, & other O4.*
0.1–2. *followed . . .* Agydas] *Rob.*; *not*   12. Media] *O1–2*; *Meda O3–4.*

---

3. *reserv'd*] kept safe.
3. *better state*] greater splendor.
10. *silly*] helpless, defenseless.
15. *his . . . hand*] a document validated by the sovereign's own seal and signature.

To safe conduct us thorough Africa.

MAGNETES.

And since we have arriv'd in Scythia,
Besides rich presents from the puissant Cham,
We have his highness' letters to command
Aid and assistance if we stand in need.   20

TAMBURLAINE.

But now you see these letters and commands
Are countermanded by a greater man,
And through my provinces you must expect
Letters of conduct from my mightiness,
If you intend to keep your treasure safe.   25
But, since I love to live at liberty,
As easily may you get the Soldan's crown
As any prizes out of my precinct:
For they are friends that help to wean my state
Till men and kingdoms help to strengthen it,   30
And must maintain my life exempt from servitude.
But tell me, madam, is your grace betroth'd?

ZENOCRATE.

I am, my lord—for so you do import.

TAMBURLAINE.

I am a lord, for so my deeds shall prove,
And yet a shepherd by my parentage.   35
But, lady, this fair face and heavenly hue
Must grace his bed that conquers Asia
And means to be a terror to the world,
Measuring the limits of his empery
By east and west, as Phoebus doth his course.   40
Lie here, ye weeds that I disdain to wear!
This complete armor and this curtle-axe

16. thorough] *O1–2*; throw *O3–4*.

---

16. *thorough*] through.
18. *Cham*] Tartar or Mongol emperor.
28. *my precinct*] the area which I control.
29. *For . . . state*] for these prizes are friends that help the growth of my power.
40. *Phoebus*] the sun.
41. *weeds*] garments.
42. *curtle-axe*] heavy slashing sword, cutlass.

Are adjuncts more beseeming Tamburlaine.
And, madam, whatsoever you esteem
Of this success and loss unvalued,   45
Both may invest you empress of the East;
And these that seem but silly country swains
May have the leading of so great an host
As with their weight shall make the mountains quake,
Even as when windy exhalations,   50
Fighting for passage, tilt within the earth.

TECHELLES.

As princely lions when they rouse themselves,
Stretching their paws and threat'ning herds of beasts,
So in his armor looketh Tamburlaine.
Methinks I see kings kneeling at his feet,   55
And he with frowning brows and fiery looks
Spurning their crowns from off their captive heads.

USUMCASANE.

And making thee and me, Techelles, kings,
That even to death will follow Tamburlaine.

TAMBURLAINE.

Nobly resolv'd, sweet friends and followers!   60
These lords, perhaps, do scorn our estimates
And think we prattle with distempered spirits.
But since they measure our deserts so mean,
That in conceit bear empires on our spears,
Affecting thoughts coequal with the clouds,   65
They shall be kept our forced followers

---

43. *more beseeming*] better suiting.
45. *success*] event, i.e., her capture.
45. *unvalued*] invaluable.   47. *silly*] simple, homely.
49–51. *the . . . earth*] It was held that the sun's heat acted upon the watery components of the earth's surface to produce "vapors" and upon its terrestrial components to produce "exhalations." Vapors had the central place in current explanations of clouds, rain, hail, snow, mist, dew, and frost, while exhalations had the central place in those of thunder and lightning, comets, shooting stars, the Milky Way, winds, and earthquakes. Earthquakes were thought to be the natural results of vapors and exhalations compressed within subterranean hollows and struggling to escape. See Heninger, pp. 128–134.
62. *distempered*] deranged, sick.
64. *conceit*] imagination.

Till with their eyes they view us emperors.

ZENOCRATE.

    The gods, defenders of the innocent,
    Will never prosper your intended drifts,
    That thus oppress poor friendless passengers.   70
    Therefore at least admit us liberty,
    Even as thou hop'st to be eternized
    By living Asia's mighty emperor.

AGYDAS.

    I hope our lady's treasure and our own
    May serve for ransom to our liberties.   75
    Return our mules and empty camels back,
    That we may travel into Syria,
    Where her betrothed lord, Alcidamus,
    Expects th'arrival of her highness' person.

MAGNETES.

    And wheresoever we repose ourselves   80
    We will report but well of Tamburlaine.

TAMBURLAINE.

    Disdains Zenocrate to live with me?
    Or you, my lords, to be my followers?
    Think you I weigh this treasure more than you?
    Not all the gold in India's wealthy arms   85
    Shall buy the meanest soldier in my train.
    Zenocrate, lovelier than the love of Jove,
    Brighter than is the silver Rhodope,
    Fairer than whitest snow on Scythian hills,
    Thy person is more worth to Tamburlaine   90
    Than the possession of the Persian crown,
    Which gracious stars have promis'd at my birth.
    A hundred Tartars shall attend on thee,
    Mounted on steeds swifter than Pegasus.

67. they] *O2–4*; thee *O1*.   88. Rhodope] *Rob.*; Rhodolfe *O1–4*.

---

69. *drifts*] purposes.
72–73. *eternized/ By living*] immortalized by living to become.
75. *to our liberties*] restoring us to liberty.
81. *but*] only.
88. *Rhodope*] snow-capped mountains of Thrace. Ellis-Fermor quotes evidence to show that they were famous for their silver mines.
94. *Pegasus*] the well-known winged horse of Greek mythology.

Thy garments shall be made of Median silk,   95
Enchas'd with precious jewels of mine own,
More rich and valurous than Zenocrate's.
With milk-white harts upon an ivory sled
Thou shalt be drawn amidst the frozen pools
And scale the icy mountains' lofty tops,   100
Which with thy beauty will be soon resolv'd.
My martial prizes with five hundred men,
Won on the fifty-headed Volga's waves,
Shall all we offer to Zenocrate,
And then myself to fair Zenocrate.   105

TECHELLES.

What now? In love?

TAMBURLAINE.

Techelles, women must be flattered.
But this is she with whom I am in love.

Enter a Soldier.

SOLDIER.

News, news!

TAMBURLAINE.

How now, what's the matter?   110

SOLDIER.

A thousand Persian horsemen are at hand,
Sent from the king to overcome us all.

TAMBURLAINE.

How now, my lords of Egypt and Zenocrate?
Now must your jewels be restor'd again,
And I that triumph'd so be overcome.   115
How say you, lordings, is not this your hope?

AGYDAS.

We hope yourself will willingly restore them.

---

99. pools] *O1–3*; Poles *O4*.   *O2*; We all shall *O4*.
101. resolv'd] *O1–3*; desolu'd *O4*.   115 triumph'd] *O1–3*; tryumph
104. Shall all we] *O1, O3*; Shall we   *O4*.

---

96. *Enchas'd*] adorned. Normally a metal-worker's term but here used
of the adorning of textiles.
97. *valurous*] valuable.
101. *resolv'd*] melted.
103. *fifty-headed*] i.e., with numerous sources and tributaries.

TAMBURLAINE.

    Such hope, such fortune, have the thousand horse.
    Soft ye, my lords and sweet Zenocrate;
    You must be forced from me ere you go.   120
    A thousand horsemen? We five hundred foot?
    An odds too great for us to stand against?
    But are they rich? And is their armor good?

SOLDIER.

    Their plumed helms are wrought with beaten gold,
    Their swords enamell'd, and about their necks   125
    Hangs massy chains of gold down to the waist:
    In every part exceeding brave and rich.

TAMBURLAINE.

    Then shall we fight courageously with them,
    Or look you I should play the orator?

TECHELLES.

    No, cowards and faint-hearted runaways   130
    Look for orations when the foe is near.
    Our swords shall play the orators for us.

USUMCASANE.

    Come, let us meet them at the mountain foot
    And with a sudden and an hot alarm
    Drive all their horses headlong down the hill.   135

TECHELLES.

    Come, let us march.

TAMBURLAINE.

    Stay, Techelles, ask a parley first.

              The Soldiers enter.

    Open the mails, yet guard the treasure sure.
    Lay out our golden wedges to the view,
    That their reflections may amaze the Persians;   140
    And look we friendly on them when they come.

---

133. foot] *O1–3*; top *O4*.   134. alarm] *O1, O3–4*; alarum *O2*.

119. *Soft ye*] wait! stop!
127. *brave*] splendid.
133. *at . . . foot*] presumably on one of the foothills, since he hopes that from there they will drive the foe *headlong down the hill* (l. 135).
134. *alarm*] surprise attack.
138. *mails*] trunks, baggage.   139. *wedges*] ingots.

But if they offer word or violence
We'll fight, five hundred men-at-arms to one,
Before we part with our possession.
And 'gainst the general we will lift our swords,   145
And either lanch his greedy thirsting throat,
Or take him prisoner, and his chain shall serve
For manacles till he be ransom'd home.

TECHELLES.

I hear them come. Shall we encounter them?

TAMBURLAINE.

Keep all your standings and not stir a foot;   150
Myself will bide the danger of the brunt.

Enter Theridamas *with others.*

THERIDAMAS.

Where is this Scythian, Tamburlaine?

TAMBURLAINE.

Whom seek'st thou, Persian? I am Tamburlaine.

THERIDAMAS.

Tamburlaine!
A Scythian shepherd so embellished   155
With nature's pride and richest furniture!
His looks do menace heaven and dare the gods;
His fiery eyes are fix'd upon the earth
As if he now devis'd some stratagem
Or meant to pierce Avernus' darksome vaults   160
To pull the triple-headed dog from hell.

TAMBURLAINE.

Noble and mild this Persian seems to be,
If outward habit judge the inward man.

TECHELLES.

His deep affections make him passionate.

152. this] *O1–3;* the *O4.*

---

146. *lanch*] pierce.   151. *bide*] face, encounter.
151. *brunt*] assault, onset.   156. *furniture*] equipment.
160. *Avernus*] a gloomy lake near Naples, filling the crater of an extinct
volcano. The ancients regarded it as the entrance to the underworld.
161. *the triple-headed dog*] Cerberus, who guarded the entrance of Hades.
Hercules dragged him to the upper world.
164. *affections*] feelings.

TAMBURLAINE.

 With what a majesty he rears his looks!—   165
 In thee, thou valiant man of Persia,
 I see the folly of thy emperor.
 Art thou but captain of a thousand horse,
 That by characters graven in thy brows,
 And by thy martial face and stout aspect,   170
 Deserv'st to have the leading of an host?
 Forsake thy king and do but join with me,
 And we will triumph over all the world.
 I hold the Fates bound fast in iron chains,
 And with my hand turn Fortune's wheel about,   175
 And sooner shall the sun fall from his sphere
 Than Tamburlaine be slain or overcome.
 Draw forth thy sword, thou mighty man-at-arms,
 Intending but to raze my charmed skin,
 And Jove himself will stretch his hand from heaven   180
 To ward the blow and shield me safe from harm.
 See how he rains down heaps of gold in showers
 As if he meant to give my soldiers pay;
 And, as a sure and grounded argument
 That I shall be the monarch of the East,   185
 He sends this Soldan's daughter rich and brave
 To be my queen and portly emperess.
 If thou wilt stay with me, renowned man,
 And lead thy thousand horse with my conduct,
 Besides thy share of this Egyptian prize,   190
 Those thousand horse shall sweat with martial spoil
 Of conquered kingdoms and of cities sack'd.
 Both we will walk upon the lofty clifts,

167. thy] *O1–2*; the *O3–4*.   193. clifts] *O1, O3–4*; cliffes *O2*.

---

 170. *stout*] bold.   172. *but*] only.
 174. *the Fates*] Clotho, Lachesis, and Atropos, sister-goddesses who presided over the birth and life of men.
 176. *his sphere*] the transparent hollow globe that was believed to carry the sun about the stationary earth.
 179. *raze*] graze.   186. *brave*] splendid.
 187. *portly*] stately.
 189. *with my conduct*] under my command.
 193. *clifts*] cliffs.

And Christian merchants, that with Russian stems
Plough up huge furrows in the Caspian Sea,   195
Shall vail to us as lords of all the lake.
Both we will reign as consuls of the earth,
And mighty kings shall be our senators.
Jove sometime masked in a shepherd's weed,
And by those steps that he hath scal'd the heavens   200
May we become immortal like the gods.
Join with me now in this my mean estate
(I call it mean because, being yet obscure,
The nations far remov'd admire me not)
And, when my name and honor shall be spread   205
As far as Boreas claps his brazen wings,
Or fair Boötes sends his cheerful light,
Then shalt thou be competitor with me
And sit with Tamburlaine in all his majesty.

THERIDAMAS.

Not Hermes, prolocutor to the gods,   210
Could use persuasions more pathetical.

TAMBURLAINE.

Nor are Apollo's oracles more true
Than thou shalt find my vaunts substantial.

TECHELLES.

We are his friends, and if the Persian king
Should offer present dukedoms to our state   215
We think it loss to make exchange for that

207. Boötes] *O3*; *Botëes* *O1–2*;
Boetes O4.

---

194. *stems*] prows, sterns (hence, by synecdoche, ships).
196. *vail*] lower their topsails in homage.
199. *masked*] disguised himself.   199. *weed*] clothing.
200. *that*] by which.   202. *estate*] condition.
206–207. *As . . . light*] to the farthest north. Boreas is the north wind;
Boötes, the Bear, is a northern constellation.
208. *competitor*] partner.
210. *prolocutor to*] spokesman for. Hermes, the herald of the gods, was
himself the god of eloquence.
211. *pathetical*] moving.
212. *Apollo's oracles*] the predictions inspired by the god of prophecy.
215. *offer . . . state*] offer to make us dukes immediately.
216. *that*] that which.

We are assured of by our friend's success.

USUMCASANE.

    And kingdoms at the least we all expect,

    Besides the honor in assured conquests,

    Where kings shall crouch unto our conquering swords   220

    And hosts of soldiers stand amaz'd at us,

    When with their fearful tongues they shall confess

    These are the men that all the world admires.

THERIDAMAS.

    What strong enchantments tice my yielding soul!

    Ah, these resolved noble Scythians!   225

    But shall I prove a traitor to my king?

TAMBURLAINE.

    No, but the trusty friend of Tamburlaine.

THERIDAMAS.

    Won with thy words and conquered with thy looks,

    I yield myself, my men and horse to thee,

    To be partaker of thy good or ill   230

    As long as life maintains Theridamas.

TAMBURLAINE.

    Theridamas, my friend, take here my hand,

    Which is as much as if I swore by heaven

    And call'd the gods to witness of my vow.

    Thus shall my heart be still combin'd with thine,   235

    Until our bodies turn to elements,

    And both our souls aspire celestial thrones.

    Techelles and Casane, welcome him.

TECHELLES.

    Welcome, renowned Persian, to us all.

USUMCASANE.

    Long may Theridamas remain with us.   240

TAMBURLAINE.

    These are my friends in whom I more rejoice

    Than doth the king of Persia in his crown;

225. Ah] *Brooke, conj. Brereton*; Are   228. with thy looks] *O1–2, O4*; with
O1–4.   looks *O3.*

---

222. *fearful*] timorous, full of fear.   224. *tice*] entice.
225. *resolved*] resolute.   235. *still*] always.
236. *elements*] i.e., earth, water, air, and fire.
237. *aspire*] mount up to.

And, by the love of Pylades and Orestes,
Whose statues we adore in Scythia,
Thyself and them shall never part from me   245
Before I crown you kings in Asia.
Make much of them, gentle Theridamas,
And they will never leave thee till the death.

THERIDAMAS.

Nor thee, nor them, thrice-noble Tamburlaine,
Shall want my heart to be with gladness pierc'd   250
To do you honor and security.

TAMBURLAINE.

A thousand thanks, worthy Theridamas.
And now, fair madam and my noble lords,
If you will willingly remain with me,
You shall have honors as your merits be: 255
Or else you shall be forc'd with slavery.

AGYDAS.

We yield unto thee, happy Tamburlaine.

TAMBURLAINE.

For you then, madam, I am out of doubt.

ZENOCRATE.

I must be pleas'd perforce. Wretched Zenocrate!   *Exeunt.*

[II.i]

     [*Enter*] Cosroe, Menaphon, Ortygius, Ceneus, *with other Soldiers.*

COSROE.

Thus far are we towards Theridamas,
And valiant Tamburlaine, the man of fame,
The man that in the forehead of his fortune

244. statues] *O3–4*; statutes *O1–2*.   [II.i]
246. kings] *O1–3*; King *O4*.   2. the] *O1–2*; that *O3–4*.
254. will] *O1–2*; *not in O3–4*.

---

243. *Pylades and Orestes*] Pylades was the faithful friend who helped Orestes to avenge his father's murder by assassinating his mother, Clytemnestra, and who supported him through the sufferings which followed.

249–250. *Nor . . . heart*] neither to you nor to them . . . shall my heart be found lacking.

251. *security*] protection.

259. *perforce*] forcibly, whether I like it nor not.

Bears figures of renown and miracle.
But tell me, that hast seen him, Menaphon,   5
What stature wields he, and what personage?

MENAPHON.

Of stature tall, and straightly fashioned,
Like his desire, lift upwards and divine;
So large of limbs, his joints so strongly knit,
Such breadth of shoulders as might mainly bear   10
Old Atlas' burden. 'Twixt his manly pitch
A pearl more worth than all the world is plac'd,
Wherein by curious sovereignty of art
Are fix'd his piercing instruments of sight,
Whose fiery circles bear encompassed   15
A heaven of heavenly bodies in their spheres,
That guides his steps and actions to the throne
Where honor sits invested royally.
Pale of complexion, wrought in him with passion,
Thirsting with sovereignty, with love of arms,   20
His lofty brows in folds do figure death,
And in their smoothness amity and life.
About them hangs a knot of amber hair,
Wrapped in curls, as fierce Achilles' was,
On which the breath of heaven delights to play,   25
Making it dance with wanton majesty.
His arms and fingers long and sinewy,
Betokening valor and excess of strength—
In every part proportioned like the man

20. with love] *O1–2*; and loue   and fingers long and snowy *O1–3*;
O3–4.   long, his fingers snowy-white *O4*.
27. and fingers . . . sinewy] *Dyce*;

4. *figures of*] facial characteristics expressive of. Compare I.ii.169,
above.
5. *that*] thou that.   8. *lift*] lifted.
10. *mainly*] with vigor.
11. *Atlas*] the Titan whom the ancients represented as supporting the
heavens and all the stars upon his shoulders.
11. *pitch*] width of shoulders.   12. *pearl*] i.e., his head.
14–17. *his . . . throne*] his eyes, of which the blazing orbs enclose a whole
universe of stars and planets in their various spheres, propitiously disposed
to cause him to gain the throne.
21. *in folds*] when furrowed.   26. *wanton*] unrestrained.

Should make the world subdued to Tamburlaine.   30
COSROE.

Well hast thou portray'd in thy terms of life
The face and personage of a wondrous man.
Nature doth strive with Fortune and his stars
To make him famous in accomplish'd worth,
And well his merits show him to be made   35
His fortune's master and the king of men,
That could persuade at such a sudden pinch,
With reasons of his valor and his life,
A thousand sworn and overmatching foes.
Then, when our powers in points of swords are join'd   40
And clos'd in compass of the killing bullet,
Though strait the passage and the port be made
That leads to palace of my brother's life,
Proud is his fortune if we pierce it not.
And when the princely Persian diadem   45
Shall overweigh his weary witless head
And fall like mellowed fruit, with shakes of death,
In fair Persia noble Tamburlaine
Shall be my regent and remain as king.
ORTYGIUS.

In happy hour we have set the crown   50
Upon your kingly head that seeks our honor
In joining with the man ordain'd by heaven
To further every action to the best.
CENEUS.

He that with shepherds and a little spoil
Durst in disdain of wrong and tyranny   55
Defend his freedom 'gainst a monarchy,
What will he do supported by a king,
Leading a troop of gentlemen and lords,
And stuff'd with treasure for his highest thoughts?
COSROE.

And such shall wait on worthy Tamburlaine.   60

30. subdued] *O1–3*; subdue *O4*.   44. is] *O1–3*; in *O4*.

31. *terms of life*] lively terms.
33. *Nature . . . stars*] physical causes, chance, and the occult influences
of the stars all compete.
41. *compass*] range.   42. *port*] gateway.   59. *stuff'd*] supplied.

Our army will be forty thousand strong
When Tamburlaine and brave Theridamas
Have met us by the river Araris;
And all conjoin'd to meet the witless king
That now is marching near to Parthia,   65
And with unwilling soldiers faintly arm'd,
To seek revenge on me and Tamburlaine;
To whom, sweet Menaphon, direct me straight.

MENAPHON.

I will, my lord.   *Exeunt.*

[II.ii]

     [*Enter*] Mycetes, Meander, *with other Lords and Soldiers.*

MYCETES.

Come, my Meander, let us to this gear.
I tell you true, my heart is swoll'n with wrath
On this same thievish villain, Tamburlaine,
And of that false Cosroe, my traitorous brother.
Would it not grieve a king to be so abus'd   5
And have a thousand horsemen ta'en away?
And, which is worst, to have his diadem
Sought for by such scald knaves as love him not?
I think it would. Well then, by heavens I swear,
Aurora shall not peep out of her doors   10
But I will have Cosroe by the head
And kill proud Tamburlaine with point of sword.
Tell you the rest, Meander; I have said.

MEANDER.

Then having pass'd Armenian deserts now
And pitch'd our tents under the Georgian hills   15

69. S.D. *Exeunt*] *O1–3*; *not in O4.*   7. worst] *O1, O3–4*; worse *O2.*
[II.ii]   15. pitch'd] *O2–4*; pitch *O1.*

63. *Araris*] presumably the Araxes (the modern Aras), which flows
through Armenia into the Caspian.
[II.ii]
1. *gear*] matter, business.
3, 4. *On, of*] here used interchangeably.
5. *abus'd*] deceived.
8. *scald*] mean, contemptible.
10. *Aurora*] the goddess of the dawn.

Whose tops are covered with Tartarian thieves
That lie in ambush, waiting for a prey,
What should we do but bid them battle straight
And rid the world of those detested troops,
Lest if we let them linger here a while   20
They gather strength by power of fresh supplies?
This country swarms with vile outrageous men
That live by rapine and by lawless spoil,
Fit soldiers for the wicked Tamburlaine;
And he that could with gifts and promises   25
Inveigle him that led a thousand horse,
And make him false his faith unto his king,
Will quickly win such as are like himself.
Therefore cheer up your minds, prepare to fight!
He that can take or slaughter Tamburlaine   30
Shall rule the province of Albania.
Who brings that traitor's head, Theridamas,
Shall have a government in Media,
Beside the spoil of him and all his train.
But if Cosroe (as our spials say,   35
And as we know) remains with Tamburlaine,
His highness' pleasure is that he should live
And be reclaim'd with princely lenity.

[*Enter a* Spy.]

SPY.

An hundred horsemen of my company,
Scouting abroad upon these champion plains,   40
Have view'd the army of the Scythians,
Which make reports it far exceeds the king's.

MEANDER.

Suppose they be in number infinite,

24. the] *O1–3*; that *O4*.
27. his king] *O1–2*; the King *O3–4*.
28. are] *O1, O3–4*; be *O2*.
34. Beside] *O1–3*; Besides *O4*.

38.1. *Enter a* Spy] *Dyce*; *not in O1–4*.
42. make reports] *O1, O3*; make report *O2*; makes reporte *O4*.

16. *Tartarian*] Tartar.   18. *straight*] immediately.
22. *outrageous*] fierce, violent.   27. *false*] betray.
34. *Beside*] besides.   35. *spials*] spies, scouts.
40. *champion plains*] stretches of level, open country.

Yet, being void of martial discipline,
All running headlong after greedy spoils   45
And more regarding gain than victory,
Like to the cruel brothers of the earth,
Sprung of the teeth of dragons venomous,
Their careless swords shall lanch their fellows' throats
And make us triumph in their overthrow.   50

MYCETES.
Was there such brethren, sweet Meander, say,
That sprung of teeth of dragons venomous?

MEANDER.
So poets say, my lord.

MYCETES.
And 'tis a pretty toy to be a poet.
Well, well, Meander, thou art deeply read,   55
And, having thee, I have a jewel sure.
Go on, my lord, and give your charge, I say.
Thy wit will make us conquerors today.

MEANDER.
Then, noble soldiers, to entrap these thieves
That live confounded in disordered troops,   60
If wealth or riches may prevail with them,
We have our camels laden all with gold,
Which you that be but common soldiers
Shall fling in every corner of the field,
And, while the base-born Tartars take it up,   65
You, fighting more for honor than for gold,
Shall massacre those greedy-minded slaves;
And, when their scattered army is subdu'd
And you march on their slaughtered carcasses,
Share equally the gold that bought their lives   70
And live like gentlemen in Persia.

46. than] *O1–3*; them *O4*.   48. teeth of] *O1–2*; *not in O3–4*.

47–49. *Like . . . throats*] Having killed a dragon, Cadmus sowed its teeth
in the earth. From them, armed men sprang up. They began fighting and
slaying one another. The five survivors helped Cadmus to found Thebes.
   49. *lanch*] pierce.
   54. *toy*] trifling pastime.
   58. *wit*] understanding, intelligence.
   60. *confounded*] confused.

Strike up the drum and march courageously.
Fortune herself doth sit upon our crests.

MYCETES.

He tells you true, my masters, so he does.
Drums, why sound ye not when Meander speaks?   75

Exeunt.

[II.iii]

[*Enter*] Cosroe, Tamburlaine, Theridamas, Techelles, *Usumcasane,
Ortygius, with others.*

COSROE.

Now, worthy Tamburlaine, have I repos'd
In thy approved fortunes all my hope.
What think'st thou, man, shall come of our attempts?
For even as from assured oracle
I take thy doom for satisfaction.   5

TAMBURLAINE.

And so mistake you not a whit, my lord.
For fates and oracles of heaven have sworn
To royalize the deeds of Tamburlaine,
And make them bless'd that share in his attempts.
And doubt you not but, if you favor me   10
And let my fortunes and my valor sway
To some direction in your martial deeds,
The world will strive with hosts of men-at-arms
To swarm unto the ensign I support.
The host of Xerxes, which by fame is said   15
To drink the mighty Parthian Araris,

72. the] *O1–2*; *not in O3–4.*   7. of] *Rob.*; *not in O1–4.*
75. ye] *O1–3*; you *O4.*   12. some] *O1, O3–4*; scorne *O2.*
[II.iii]   13. will] *O1–2*; shall *O3–4.*

2. *approved*] tried, tested.   5. *doom*] judgment, opinion.
5. *satisfaction*] certainty.   6. *whit*] bit.
8. *royalize*] celebrate.
11–12. *sway . . . direction*] "prevail so as to give me some degree of control"
(Ellis-Fermor).
14. *ensign*] banner.
15–16. *The . . . Araris*] Xerxes, King of Persia, invaded Greece with a
vast army, overcame a tiny Spartan force under Leonidas at Thermopylae,
and was defeated at Salamis (480 B.C.). The legend which Marlowe uses to
illustrate the size of the Persian army was fairly widely known. It may have
developed from a hint in Herodotus (vii.21).

Was but a handful to that we will have.
Our quivering lances shaking in the air
And bullets like Jove's dreadful thunderbolts
Enroll'd in flames and fiery smoldering mists   20
Shall threat the gods more than Cyclopian wars;
And with our sun-bright armor, as we march,
We'll chase the stars from heaven and dim their eyes
That stand and muse at our admired arms.

THERIDAMAS.

You see, my lord, what working words he hath.   25
But, when you see his actions top his speech,
Your speech will stay or so extol his worth
As I shall be commended and excus'd
For turning my poor charge to his direction.
And these his two renowned friends, my lord,   30
Would make one thrust and strive to be retain'd
In such a great degree of amity.

TECHELLES.

With duty and with amity we yield
Our utmost service to the fair Cosroe.

COSROE.

Which I esteem as portion of my crown.   35
Usumcasane and Techelles both,
When she that rules in Rhamnis' golden gates
And makes a passage for all prosperous arms
Shall make me solely emperor of Asia,
Then shall your meeds and valors be advanc'd   40
To rooms of honor and nobility.

26. top] *Dyce*; stop *O1–4*.   34. the] *O1–2*; thee *O3–4*.
33. and] *O4*; not *O1–3*.   40. meeds] *O1–3*; deeds *O4*.

---

17. *that*] that which.
21. *Cyclopian wars*] the struggle between Zeus and the Titans (with whom Marlowe identifies the one-eyed giants called Cyclopes).
25. *working*] effective, moving.
26. *top*] surpass.
27. *stay*] temporarily stop.
31. *make one*] cause a person to.
37. *she . . . gates*] Nemesis, the goddess of vengeance, who had a celebrated sanctuary at Rhamnus (Marlowe's Rhamnis) in Attica.
40. *meeds*] merits, worths.
41. *rooms*] places, appointments.

TAMBURLAINE.

Then haste, Cosroe, to be king alone,
That I with these my friends and all my men
May triumph in our long-expected fate.
The king your brother is now hard at hand.   45
Meet with the fool, and rid your royal shoulders
Of such a burden as outweighs the sands
And all the craggy rocks of Caspia.

[*Enter a* Messenger.]

MESSENGER.

My lord, we have discovered the enemy
Ready to charge you with a mighty army.   50

COSROE.

Come, Tamburlaine, now whet thy winged sword,
And lift thy lofty arm into the clouds
That it may reach the king of Persia's crown
And set it safe on my victorious head.

TAMBURLAINE.

See where it is, the keenest curtle-axe   55
That e'er made passage thorough Persian arms.
These are the wings shall make it fly as swift
As doth the lightning or the breath of heaven
And kill as sure as it swiftly flies.

COSROE.

Thy words assure me of kind success.   60
Go, valiant soldier, go before and charge
The fainting army of that foolish king.

TAMBURLAINE.

Usumcasane and Techelles, come.
We are enough to scare the enemy,
And more than needs to make an emperor.   [*Exeunt.*] 65

48.1. *Enter a* Messenger] *Rob.*; *not*   64. enough] *O1, O3–4*; enow *O2*.
in O1–4.   65. S.D. *Exeunt*] *Rob.*; *not in O1–4.*

---

48. *Caspia*] the Caspian Sea.
56. *thorough*] through.
57. *shall*] which shall.
60. *kind*] favorable, gracious.

[II.iv]

To the battle, and Mycetes *comes out alone with his crown in his hand, offering to hide it.*

MYCETES.

    Accurs'd be he that first invented war!
    They knew not, ah, they knew not, simple men,
    How those were hit by pelting cannon shot
    Stand staggering like a quivering aspen leaf
    Fearing the force of Boreas' boist'rous blasts.   5
    In what a lamentable case were I
    If nature had not given me wisdom's lore,
    For kings are clouts that every man shoots at,
    Our crown the pin that thousands seek to cleave.
    Therefore in policy I think it good   10
    To hide it close—a goodly stratagem,
    And far from any man that is a fool.
    So shall not I be known, or, if I be,
    They cannot take away my crown from me.
    Here will I hide it in this simple hole.   15

Enter Tamburlaine.

TAMBURLAINE.

    What, fearful coward, straggling from the camp
    When kings themselves are present in the field?

MYCETES.

    Thou liest.

TAMBURLAINE.   Base villain, dar'st thou give the lie?

MYCETES.

    Away, I am the king, go, touch me not.
    Thou break'st the law of arms unless thou kneel   20

4. Stand staggering] *O1–3*; Stand   18. give the] *O1–3*; giue me the *O4*.
those staggering *O4*.

0.2. *offering*] endeavoring.   3. *were*] who were.
5. *Boreas*] the north wind.
8–9. *kings . . . cleave*] a metaphor from archery. "The clout is the central
mark of the butts, to hit which is the aim of the archer; the pin is the nail
in its centre that fastens it in place. 'To cleave the pin' is, of course, a
triumph achieved only by the highest skill" (Ellis-Fermor).
11. *close*] secretly.   16. *fearful*] timorous, full of fear.
18. *give the lie*] accuse a person to his face of lying.

And cry me, "Mercy, noble king!"

TAMBURLAINE.

Are you the witty king of Persia?

MYCETES.

Ay, marry, am I. Have you any suit to me?

TAMBURLAINE.

I would entreat you to speak but three wise words.

MYCETES.

So I can, when I see my time.   25

TAMBURLAINE.

Is this your crown?

MYCETES.

Ay, didst thou ever see a fairer?

TAMBURLAINE.

You will not sell it, will ye?

MYCETES.

Such another word, and I will have thee executed.

Come, give it me.   30

TAMBURLAINE.

No, I took it prisoner.

MYCETES.

You lie, I gave it you.

TAMBURLAINE.

Then 'tis mine.

MYCETES.

No, I mean I let you keep it.

TAMBURLAINE.

Well, I mean you shall have it again.   35

Here, take it for a while; I lend it thee

Till I may see thee hemm'd with armed men.

Then shalt thou see me pull it from thy head.

Thou art no match for mighty Tamburlaine.   [*Exit.*]

MYCETES.

O gods, is this Tamburlaine the thief?   40

I marvel much he stole it not away.

       Sound trumpets to the battle, and he runs in.

39. S.D. *Exit*] *Rob.*; *not in O1–4.*

---

22. *witty*] wise (ironical).

23. *Ay, marry*] yes, to be sure. In the form "marry," the name of the Virgin Mary was much used as an ejaculation.

[II.v]

[Enter] Cosroe, Tamburlaine, Theridamas, Menaphon, Meander,
Ortygius, Techelles, Usumcasane, *with others.*

TAMBURLAINE.

    Hold thee, Cosroe; wear two imperial crowns.
    Think thee invested now as royally,
    Even by the mighty hand of Tamburlaine,
    As if as many kings as could encompass thee
    With greatest pomp had crown'd thee emperor.   5

COSROE.

    So do I, thrice renowned man-at-arms;
    And none shall keep the crown but Tamburlaine.
    Thee do I make my regent of Persia
    And general lieutenant of my armies.
    Meander, you that were our brother's guide   10
    And chiefest counselor in all his acts,
    Since he is yielded to the stroke of war,
    On your submission we with thanks excuse
    And give you equal place in our affairs.

MEANDER.

    Most happy emperor, in humblest terms   15
    I vow my service to your majesty
    With utmost virtue of my faith and duty.

COSROE.

    Thanks, good Meander. Then, Cosroe, reign
    And govern Persia in her former pomp.
    Now send embassage to thy neighbor kings,   20
    And let them know the Persian king is chang'd
    From one that knew not what a king should do
    To one that can command what 'longs thereto.
    And now we will to fair Persepolis
    With twenty thousand expert soldiers.   25
    The lords and captains of my brother's camp
    With little slaughter take Meander's course
    And gladly yield them to my gracious rule.

6. man-at-arms] *O1–3*; men at   11. chiefest] *O1, O3–4*; chiefe *O2.*
armes *O4.*   15. happy] *O1–2*; happiest *O3–4.*

23. *'longs*] belongs, pertains.
25. *expert*] proved.

Ortygius and Menaphon, my trusty friends,
Now will I gratify your former good   30
And grace your calling with a greater sway.

ORTYGIUS.

And as we ever aim'd at your behoof
And sought your state all honor it deserv'd,
So will we with our powers and our lives
Endeavor to preserve and prosper it.   35

COSROE.

I will not thank thee, sweet Ortygius;
Better replies shall prove my purposes.
And now, Lord Tamburlaine, my brother's camp
I leave to thee and to Theridamas,
To follow me to fair Persepolis.   40
Then will we march to all those Indian mines
My witless brother to the Christians lost,
And ransom them with fame and usury.
And till thou overtake me, Tamburlaine,
Staying to order all the scattered troops,   45
Farewell, lord regent and his happy friends.
I long to sit upon my brother's throne.

MENAPHON.

Your majesty shall shortly have your wish,
And ride in triumph through Persepolis.

Exeunt. Manent Tamburlaine, Techelles, Theridamas, Usumcasane.

TAMBURLAINE.

And ride in triumph through Persepolis!   50
Is it not brave to be a king, Techelles,
Usumcasane, and Theridamas?
Is it not passing brave to be a king,

32. aim'd] *O3–4*; and *O1–2*.   41. we] *O1–2*; I *O3–4*.
33. it] *O1, O3–4*; is *O2*.   48. S.P. MENAPHON] *O1, O3–4*;
34. and our lives] *O1, O3–4*; and   *Mean. O2*.
liues *O2*.

---

30. *gratify . . . good*] requite the good service you have already done me.
32. *behoof*] advantage.   33. *state*] power, position.
37. *Better replies*] i.e., deeds, not words.
43. *with . . . usury*] to our renown and profit.
49.1. *Manent*] there remain.
51, 53. *brave*] wonderful.   53. *passing*] exceedingly.

And ride in triumph through Persepolis?

TECHELLES.

O, my lord, 'tis sweet and full of pomp.   55

USUMCASANE.

To be a king is half to be a god.

THERIDAMAS.

A god is not so glorious as a king.
I think the pleasure they enjoy in heaven
Cannot compare with kingly joys in earth.
To wear a crown enchas'd with pearl and gold,   60
Whose virtues carry with it life and death;
To ask and have, command and be obeyed;
When looks breed love, with looks to gain the prize,
Such power attractive shines in princes' eyes.

TAMBURLAINE.

Why, say, Theridamas, wilt thou be a king?   65

THERIDAMAS.

Nay, though I praise it, I can live without it.

TAMBURLAINE.

What says my other friends, will you be kings?

TECHELLES.

Ay, if I could, with all my heart, my lord.

TAMBURLAINE.

Why, that's well said, Techelles; so would I.
And so would you, my masters, would you not?   70

USUMCASANE.

What then, my lord?

TAMBURLAINE.

Why then, Casane, shall we wish for aught
The world affords in greatest novelty
And rest attemptless, faint, and destitute?
Methinks we should not. I am strongly mov'd   75
That if I should desire the Persian crown
I could attain it with a wondrous ease;
And would not all our soldiers soon consent

---

60. *enchas'd*] adorned. See I.ii.96, note, above.
61. *virtues*] powers.
73. *in greatest novelty*] no matter how new and rare.
74. *faint*] cowardly.   75. *I . . . mov'd*] I feel deeply.

If we should aim at such a dignity?

THERIDAMAS.

I know they would with our persuasions.   80

TAMBURLAINE.

Why then, Theridamas, I'll first assay
To get the Persian kingdom to myself;
Then thou for Parthia; they for Scythia and Media;
And, if I prosper, all shall be as sure
As if the Turk, the Pope, Afric, and Greece   85
Came creeping to us with their crowns apace.

TECHELLES.

Then shall we send to this triumphing king
And bid him battle for his novel crown?

USUMCASANE.

Nay, quickly then, before his room be hot.

TAMBURLAINE.

'Twill prove a pretty jest, in faith, my friends.   90

THERIDAMAS.

A jest to charge on twenty thousand men?
I judge the purchase more important far.

TAMBURLAINE.

Judge by thyself, Theridamas, not me,
For presently Techelles here shall haste
To bid him battle ere he pass too far   95
And lose more labor than the gain will quite.
Then shalt thou see the Scythian Tamburlaine
Make but a jest to win the Persian crown.
Techelles, take a thousand horse with thee
And bid him turn him back to war with us   100
That only made him king to make us sport.
We will not steal upon him cowardly

86. apace] *O1–2*; apeece *O3–4*.   100. him back] *Rob.*; his back
97. the] *O1, O3–4*; this *O2*.   *O1–4*.

---

81. *assay*] try.
88. *novel*] newly acquired.
89. *before . . . hot*] before he has warmed this throne by occupying it.
92. *purchase*] undertaking.
94. *presently*] immediately.
96. *lose*] Presumably the subject is understood to be "we."
96. *quite*] requite, pay for.

But give him warning and more warriors.
Haste thee, Techelles, we will follow thee.
What saith Theridamas?

THERIDAMAS.   Go on, for me.   *Exeunt.* 105

[II.vi]

[*Enter*] Cosroe, Meander, Ortygius, *Menaphon, with other Soldiers.*

COSROE.

What means this devilish shepherd to aspire
With such a giantly presumption,
To cast up hills against the face of heaven,
And dare the force of angry Jupiter?
But, as he thrust them underneath the hills   5
And press'd out fire from their burning jaws,
So will I send this monstrous slave to hell,
Where flames shall ever feed upon his soul.

MEANDER.

Some powers divine, or else infernal, mix'd
Their angry seeds at his conception,   10
For he was never sprung of human race,
Since with the spirit of his fearful pride
He dares so doubtlessly resolve of rule
And by profession be ambitious.

ORTYGIUS.

What god, or fiend, or spirit of the earth,   15
Or monster turned to a manly shape,
Or of what mold or mettle he be made,
What star or state soever govern him,
Let us put on our meet encount'ring minds,

103. and] *O1–3*; with *O4*.   [II.vi]
                                        13. dares] *O1–2*; dare *O3–4*.

---

105. *for me*] as far as I am concerned.
[II.vi]
1–6. *What . . . jaws*] The Giants conspired to dethrone Zeus (Jupiter)
and heaped Pelion on Ossa in order to scale the walls of heaven. Zeus
routed them and buried many of them under Etna and other volcanoes.
13–14. *so . . . ambitious*] so unhesitatingly to set his mind upon political
power and so openly to announce his ambition.
17. *mold or mettle*] earth or substance.
19. *Let . . . minds*] let us put ourselves in a proper frame of mind for
facing the challenge.

And in detesting such a devilish thief,   20
In love of honor and defense of right,
Be arm'd against the hate of such a foe,
Whether from earth, or hell, or heaven he grow.

COSROE.

Nobly resolv'd, my good Ortygius,
And since we all have suck'd one wholesome air,   25
And with the same proportion of elements
Resolve, I hope we are resembled,
Vowing our loves to equal death and life.
Let's cheer our soldiers to encounter him,
That grievous image of ingratitude,   30
That fiery thirster after sovereignty,
And burn him in the fury of that flame
That none can quench but blood and empery.
Resolve, my lords and loving soldiers, now
To save your king and country from decay.   35
Then strike up, drum; and all the stars that make
The loathsome circle of my dated life
Direct my weapon to his barbarous heart
That thus opposeth him against the gods
And scorns the powers that govern Persia!   40
                                                     [Exeunt.]

[II.vii]
Enter to the battle; and after the battle enter Cosroe *wounded,* Theridamas,
Theridamas, Techelles, Usumcasane, *with others.*

COSROE.

Barbarous and bloody Tamburlaine,
Thus to deprive me of my crown and life!
Treacherous and false Theridamas,

---

25. one] *O1, O3–4;* on *O2.*   40.1. *Exeunt*] *Dyce; not in O1–4.*

25–28. *since . . . life*] since we, being men, have all breathed the same
wholesome air and are to decompose at death into the same proportions of
earth, water, air, and fire, I trust that we are alike also in our loving deter-
mination to live or die together.
29. *encounter him*] meet him in battle.
32. *that flame*] his own ambition.
37. *dated*] limited, transitory.

Even at the morning of my happy state,
Scarce being seated in my royal throne,   5
To work my downfall and untimely end!
An uncouth pain torments my grieved soul,
And Death arrests the organ of my voice,
Who, ent'ring at the breach thy sword hath made,
Sacks every vein and artier of my heart.   10
Bloody and insatiate Tamburlaine!

TAMBURLAINE.

The thirst of reign and sweetness of a crown,
That caus'd the eldest son of heavenly Ops
To thrust his doting father from his chair
And place himself in the empyreal heaven,   15
Mov'd me to manage arms against thy state.
What better precedent than mighty Jove?
Nature that fram'd us of four elements,
Warring within our breasts for regiment,
Doth teach us all to have aspiring minds.   20
Our souls, whose faculties can comprehend
The wondrous architecture of the world
And measure every wand'ring planet's course,
Still climbing after knowledge infinite,
And always moving as the restless spheres,   25
Wills us to wear ourselves and never rest
Until we reach the ripest fruit of all,
That perfect bliss and sole felicity,
The sweet fruition of an earthly crown.

THERIDAMAS.

And that made me to join with Tamburlaine,   30

27. fruit] *O1, O3–4*; fruites *O2*.

---

7. *uncouth*] strange, savage.
10. *artier*] artery.
13. *the . . . Ops*] Jupiter, the son of Saturn and Ops, who supplanted Saturn as lord of heaven.
15. *the empyreal heaven*] the empyrean, i.e., the immovable outermost sphere of the universe, the abode of God.
16. *manage arms*] wage war.   18. *fram'd*] made.
18. *elements*] i.e., earth, water, air, and fire.
19. *regiment*] rule.
25. *spheres*] the concentric transparent hollow globes that were believed to carry the planets and the stars about the stationary earth.

For he is gross and like the massy earth
That moves not upwards, nor by princely deeds
Doth mean to soar above the highest sort.

TECHELLES.

And that made us, the friends of Tamburlaine,
To lift our swords against the Persian king.   35

USUMCASANE.

For as, when Jove did thrust old Saturn down,
Neptune and Dis gain'd each of them a crown,
So do we hope to reign in Asia,
If Tamburlaine be plac'd in Persia.

COSROE.

The strangest men that ever nature made!   40
I know not how to take their tyrannies.
My bloodless body waxeth chill and cold,
And with my blood my life slides through my wound.
My soul begins to take her flight to hell
And summons all my senses to depart.   45
The heat and moisture which did feed each other,
For want of nourishment to feed them both,
Is dry and cold, and now doth ghastly death
With greedy talents gripe my bleeding heart
And like a harpy tires on my life.   50
Theridamas and Tamburlaine, I die:
And fearful vengeance light upon you both!

                [*Dies.* Tamburlaine] *takes the crown and puts it on.*

42. chill] *O1–2, O4*; child *O3.*   52.1. *Dies*] *Rob.*; *not in O1–4.*
50. harpy] *O2*; Harpyr *O1, O3*;   52.1. Tamburlaine] *Rob.*; *He O1–4.*
Harper *O4.*

36–37. *when . . . crown*] When Jupiter supplanted Saturn, he gave the
empire of the sea to his brother Neptune, and of the infernal regions to his
brother Pluto (Dis).

    41. *tyrannies*] merciless deeds.

    46–50. *The . . . life*] Loss of the warm and moist humor, blood, the
counterpart in the human physique of the element, air, has unbalanced
Cosroe's constitution. The cold and dry humor, melancholy, the counterpart in the human physique of the element, earth, increasingly prepon-
derates. Death is overpowering him.

    49. *talents*] talons.

    50. *harpy*] The harpies were hideous bird-like monsters with the faces
of women who were supposed to carry off persons or things.

    50. *tires*] preys, feeds ravenously.

TAMBURLAINE.

Not all the curses which the Furies breathe
Shall make me leave so rich a prize as this.
Theridamas, Techelles, and the rest,   55
Who think you now is king of Persia?

ALL.

Tamburlaine! Tamburlaine!

TAMBURLAINE.

Though Mars himself, the angry god of arms,
And all the earthly potentates conspire
To dispossess me of this diadem,   60
Yet will I wear it in despite of them
As great commander of this eastern world,
If you but say that Tamburlaine shall reign.

ALL.

Long live Tamburlaine and reign in Asia!

TAMBURLAINE.

So; now it is more surer on my head   65
Than if the gods had held a parliament
And all pronounc'd me king of Persia.   [*Exeunt.*]

Finis Actus 2.

[III.i]
[*Enter*] Bajazeth, *the* Kings of Fez, Morocco, *and* Argier, [Basso,] *with
others, in great pomp.*

BAJAZETH.

Great kings of Barbary and my portly bassoes,
We hear the Tartars and the eastern thieves,
Under the conduct of one Tamburlaine,
Presume a bickering with your emperor,

53. the Furies] *O1, O3–4;*   [III.i]
furies *O2.*   0.1. Basso] *Kirsch.; not in O1–4.*
67. S.D. *Exeunt*] *Rob.; not in O1–4.*

53. *the Furies*] the avenging deities of Greek and Roman mythology.
[III.i]
    0.1. *Basso*] high-ranking Turkish officer, pasha.
    1. *Barbary*] the region along the north coast of Africa comprising the
kingdoms of Fez, Morocco, and Argier (Algeria).
    3. *conduct*] leadership.
    4. *bickering*] skirmishing.

And thinks to rouse us from our dreadful siege   5
Of the famous Grecian Constantinople.
You know our army is invincible;
As many circumcised Turks we have
And warlike bands of Christians renied
As hath the Ocean or the Terrene sea   10
Small drops of water when the moon begins
To join in one her semicircled horns.
Yet would we not be brav'd with foreign power,
Nor raise our siege before the Grecians yield
Or breathless lie before the city walls.   15

KING OF FEZ.

Renowned emperor and mighty general,
What if you sent the bassoes of your guard
To charge him to remain in Asia,
Or else to threaten death and deadly arms
As from the mouth of mighty Bajazeth?   20

BAJAZETH.

Hie thee, my basso, fast to Persia.
Tell him thy·lord, the Turkish emperor,
Dread lord of Afric, Europe, and Asia,
Great king and conqueror of Graecia,
The Ocean, Terrene, and the coal-black sea,   25
The high and highest monarch of the world,
Wills and commands (for say not I entreat)
Not once to set his foot in Africa
Or spread his colors in Graecia,
Lest he incur the fury of my wrath.   30
Tell him I am content to take a truce,
Because I hear he bears a valiant mind;

21. basso] *O1–3*; Brother *O4*.   28. in] *O1–3*; on *O4*.
28. Not] *O1–3*; Nor *O4*.

---

9. *renied*] apostate, renegade.

10. *Terrene*] Mediterranean. So also in l. 25.

11–12. *when . . . horns*] i.e., when the moon becomes full. The tides are
then high.

13. *brav'd with*] challenged by.

21. *Hie thee*] hasten.

29. *colors*] military ensigns, flags. In this sense, the word occurs frequently
in *Tamburlaine*.

But if, presuming on his silly power,
He be so mad to manage arms with me,
Then stay thou with him (say I bid thee so)   35
And if, before the sun have measured heaven
With triple circuit, thou regreet us not,
We mean to take his morning's next arise
For messenger he will not be reclaim'd
And mean to fetch thee in despite of him.   40

BASSO.

Most great and puissant monarch of the earth,
Your basso will accomplish your behest
And show your pleasure to the Persian,
As fits the legate of the stately Turk.   *Exit* Basso.

KING OF ARGIER.

They say he is the king of Persia;   45
But if he dare attempt to stir your siege
'Twere requisite he should be ten times more,
For all flesh quakes at your magnificence.

BAJAZETH.

True, Argier, and tremble at my looks.

KING OF MOROCCO.

The spring is hinder'd by your smothering host,   50
For neither rain can fall upon the earth
Nor sun reflex his virtuous beams thereon,
The ground is mantled with such multitudes.

BAJAZETH.

All this is true as holy Mahomet,
And all the trees are blasted with our breaths.   55

KING OF FEZ.

What thinks your greatness best to be achiev'd
In pursuit of the city's overthrow?

BAJAZETH.

I will the captive pioners of Argier
Cut off the water that by leaden pipes

36. measured   heaven]   *O1–2*;
measured the heauen *O3–4*.

---

33. *silly*] feeble.
39. *reclaim'd*] restrained.   42. *behest*] command.
43. *pleasure*] will.   52. *reflex*] cast.
53. *mantled*] covered.   58. *pioners*] trench-diggers.

Runs to the city from the mountain Carnor
Two thousand horse shall forage up and do
That no relief or succor come by land,
And all the sea my galleys countermand.
Then shall our footmen lie within the trenc
And with their cannons mouth'd like Orcus
Batter the walls, and we will enter in;
And thus the Grecians shall be conquered.

[III.ii]   [*Enter*] Agydas, Zenocrate, *Anippe, wit*

AGYDAS.

Madam Zenocrate, may I presume
To know the cause of these unquiet fits
That work such trouble to your wonted rest?
'Tis more than pity such a heavenly face
Should by heart's sorrow wax so wan and pale,   5
When your offensive rape by Tamburlaine,
Which of your whole displeasures should be most,
Hath seem'd to be digested long ago.

ZENOCRATE.

Although it be digested long ago,
As his exceeding favors have deserv'd,   10
And might content the queen of heaven as well
As it hath chang'd my first conceiv'd disdain,
Yet, since, a farther passion feeds my thoughts
With ceaseless and disconsolate conceits,
Which dyes my looks so lifeless as they are   15
And might, if my extremes had full events,
Make me the ghastly counterfeit of death.

67. S.D. *Exeunt*] *O1–2*; *not in O3–4*.   [III.ii]
14. ceaseless] *O1–3*; carelesse *O4*.

63. *countermand*] control.
65. *Orcus' gulf*] the entrance to hell. Orcus was a Roman name for
Hades.
[III.ii]
3. *wonted*] accustomed.   6. *rape*] seizure.
11. *the queen of heaven*] Juno.   13. *since*] since that time.
14. *conceits*] ideas, notions.
16. *if . . . events*] if my violent feelings were to produce their full con-
sequences.
17. *counterfeit*] portrait, likeness.

AGYDAS.

    Eternal heaven sooner be dissolv'd,
    And all that pierceth Phoebe's silver eye,
    Before such hap fall to Zenocrate!   20

ZENOCRATE.

    Ah, life and soul, still hover in his breast
    And leave my body senseless as the earth,
    Or else unite you to his life and soul,
    That I may live and die with Tamburlaine!

    Enter[, behind,] Tamburlaine with Techelles and others.

AGYDAS.

    With Tamburlaine? Ah, fair Zenocrate,   25
    Let not a man so vile and barbarous,
    That holds you from your father in despite
    And keeps you from the honors of a queen,
    Being suppos'd his worthless concubine,
    Be honored with your love but for necessity.   30
    So now the mighty Soldan hears of you,
    Your highness needs not doubt but in short time
    He will with Tamburlaine's destruction
    Redeem you from this deadly servitude.

ZENOCRATE.

    Leave to wound me with these words,   35
    And speak of Tamburlaine as he deserves.
    The entertainment we have had of him
    Is far from villainy or servitude,
    And might in noble minds be counted princely.

AGYDAS.

    How can you fancy one that looks so fierce,   40
    Only disposed to martial stratagems?

19. Phoebe's] *O1–3*; *Phœbus O4*.   23. you] *O1–2*; me *O3–4*.
21. his] *O1–3*; the *O4*.   24.1. *behind*] *Rob.*; *not in O1–4*.

---

    19. *all . . . eye*] all that the moon beholds.
    20. *hap*] chance.
    23. *you*] She is still addressing her *life and soul* (l. 21).
    27. *in despite*] in defiance.
    31. *So*] provided that.
    37. *entertainment*] treatment.
    38. *villainy*] boorishness.   40. *fancy*] fall in love with.

Who, when he shall embrace you in his arms,
Will tell how many thousand men he slew,
And, when you look for amorous discourse,
Will rattle forth his facts of war and blood,   45
Too harsh a subject for your dainty ears.

ZENOCRATE.

As looks the sun through Nilus' flowing stream,
Or when the morning holds him in her arms,
So looks my lordly love, fair Tamburlaine;
His talk much sweeter than the Muses' song   50
They sung for honor 'gainst Pierides,
Or when Minerva did with Neptune strive;
And higher would I rear my estimate
Than Juno, sister to the highest god,
If I were match'd with mighty Tamburlaine.   55

AGYDAS.

Yet be not so inconstant in your love,
But let the young Arabian live in hope
After your rescue to enjoy his choice.
You see, though first the king of Persia,
Being a shepherd, seem'd to love you much,   60
Now, in his majesty, he leaves those looks,
Those words of favor, and those comfortings,
And gives no more than common courtesies.

ZENOCRATE.

Thence rise the tears that so distain my cheeks,
Fearing his love through my unworthiness.   65

Tamburlaine *goes to her and takes her away lovingly by the hand, looking wrathfully on* Agydas, *and says nothing.* [*Exeunt all except* Agydas.]

50. much] *O1–3;* more *O4.*   65.2. *Exeunt . . .* Agydas]   *Rob.;*
                                                not in *O1–4.*

---

45. *facts*] deeds.
47. *Nilus*] the river Nile.
51. *Pierides*] the nine daughters of Pierus, who entered into a contest with the nine Muses, the goddesses of the various kinds of poetry, arts, and sciences. After their defeat, the Pierides were metamorphosed into birds.
52. *Minerva . . . strive*] Minerva (Athena) contended with Neptune (Poseidon) for the possession of Athens.
54. *Juno*] sister and wife of Jupiter.
64. *distain*] stain, discolor.   65. *Fearing*] fearing to lose.

AGYDAS.

    Betray'd by fortune and suspicious love,
    Threaten'd with frowning wrath and jealousy,
    Surpris'd with fear of hideous revenge,
    I stand aghast; but most astonied
    To see his choler shut in secret thoughts,   70
    And wrapp'd in silence of his angry soul.
    Upon his brows was portray'd ugly death,
    And in his eyes the fury of his heart,
    That shine as comets, menacing revenge,
    And casts a pale complexion on his cheeks.   75
    As when the seaman sees the Hyades
    Gather an army of Cimmerian clouds
    (Auster and Aquilon with winged steeds,
    All sweating, tilt about the watery heavens,
    With shivering spears enforcing thunderclaps,   80
    And from their shields strike flames of lightning),
    All fearful folds his sails and sounds the main,
    Lifting his prayers to the heavens for aid
    Against the terror of the winds and waves,
    So fares Agydas for the late-felt frowns   85
    That sent a tempest to my daunted thoughts
    And makes my soul divine her overthrow.

    Enter Techelles *with a naked dagger*[, *and* Usumcasane].

TECHELLES.

    See you, Agydas, how the king salutes you.

68. of] *O1, O3–4*; and *O2*.   87.1. *and* Usumcasane] *Rob.*; *not in*
73. fury] *O1, O3–4*; furies *O2*.   *O1–4.*

   69. *astonied*] dismayed.
   74. *comets*] generally considered to be tokens of disaster. See Part II,
V.i.89, note.
   76. *Hyades*] a group of seven stars. Its rising simultaneously with the sun
was supposed to bring rain.
   77. *Cimmerian*] black. The ancients believed that the Cimmerii lived in
perpetual darkness.
   78. *Auster and Aquilon*] the south and north winds. The former was
commonly imagined as wrapped in clouds, the latter as strong and harsh.
See Heninger, pp. 121–124.
   79. *tilt*] fight. The winds were believed to be naturally contentious
among themselves.
   82. *sounds the main*] ascertains the depth of the sea.

He bids you prophesy what it imports.

AGYDAS.

I prophesied before, and now I prove   90
The killing frowns of jealousy and love.
He needed not with words confirm my fear,
For words are vain where working tools present
The naked action of my threaten'd end.
It says, "Agydas, thou shalt surely die,   95
And of extremities elect the least:
More honor and less pain it may procure
To die by this resolved hand of thine
Than stay the torments he and heaven have sworn."
Then haste, Agydas, and prevent the plagues   100
Which thy prolonged fates may draw on thee.
Go wander free from fear of tyrant's rage,
Removed from the torments and the hell
Wherewith he may excruciate thy soul,
And let Agydas by Agydas die,   105
And with this stab slumber eternally.   [*Stabs himself.*]

TECHELLES.

Usumcasane, see how right the man
Hath hit the meaning of my lord the king.

USUMCASANE.

Faith and, Techelles, it was manly done;
And, since he was so wise and honorable,   110
Let us afford him now the bearing hence
And crave his triple-worthy burial.

TECHELLES.

Agreed, Casane; we will honor him.

[*Exeunt, bearing out the body.*]

89. imports.] *O3–4*; imports. *Exit.*   *O1–3.*
O1–2.   113.1. *Exeunt . . . body*] *Rob.*; *not in*
106. S.D. *Stabs himself*] *O4*; *not in*   *O1–4.*

90. *prove*] find out by experience.
98. *resolved*] resolute.
99. *stay*] await.

[III.iii]

[*Enter*] Tamburlaine, Techelles, Usumcasane, Theridamas, Basso, Zenocrate, [Anippe,] *with others.*

TAMBURLAINE.

    Basso, by this thy lord and master knows
    I mean to meet him in Bithynia.
    See how he comes! Tush, Turks are full of brags
    And menace more than they can well perform.
    He meet me in the field and fetch thee hence!   5
    Alas, poor Turk, his fortune is too weak
    T'encounter with the strength of Tamburlaine.
    View well my camp and speak indifferently:
    Do not my captains and my soldiers look
    As if they meant to conquer Africa?   10

BASSO.

    Your men are valiant, but their number few,
    And cannot terrify his mighty host.
    My lord, the great commander of the world,
    Besides fifteen contributory kings,
    Hath now in arms ten thousand janissaries,   15
    Mounted on lusty Mauritanian steeds,
    Brought to the war by men of Tripoli;
    Two hundred thousand footmen that have serv'd
    In two set battles fought in Graecia;
    And for the expedition of this war,   20
    If he think good, can from his garrisons
    Withdraw as many more to follow him.

TECHELLES.

    The more he brings, the greater is the spoil,
    For, when they perish by our warlike hands,

0.2. Anippe] *Dyce; not in O1–4.*   5. fetch] *O1–3;* fetcht *O4.*
4. menace] *O1–3;* meane *O4.*

---

  1. *by this*] by this time.
  2. *Bithynia*] a district in northern Asia Minor.
  8. *indifferently*] impartially.
  14. *contributory*] tributary.
  15. *janissaries*] Turkish guardsmen.
  16. *Mauritanian*] Mauritania, in northwest Africa, was famous for its horses.
  20. *expedition*] speedy waging.

We mean to seat our footmen on their steeds   25
And rifle all those stately janissars.

TAMBURLAINE.

But will those kings accompany your lord?

BASSO.

Such as his highness please; but some must stay
To rule the provinces he late subdu'd.

TAMBURLAINE.

Then fight courageously! Their crowns are yours!   30
This hand shall set them on your conquering heads
That made me emperor of Asia.

USUMCASANE.

Let him bring millions infinite of men,
Unpeopling Western Africa and Greece,
Yet we assure us of the victory.   35

THERIDAMAS.

Even he that in a trice vanquish'd two kings
More mighty than the Turkish emperor
Shall rouse him out of Europe and pursue
His scattered army till they yield or die.

TAMBURLAINE.

Well said, Theridamas! Speak in that mood,   40
For "will" and "shall" best fitteth Tamburlaine,
Whose smiling stars gives him assured hope
Of martial triumph ere he meet his foes.
I that am term'd the scourge and wrath of God,
The only fear and terror of the world,   45
Will first subdue the Turk, and then enlarge
Those Christian captives which you keep as slaves,
Burdening their bodies with your heavy chains
And feeding them with thin and slender fare,
That naked row about the Terrene sea,   50
And, when they chance to breathe and rest a space,

---

25. seat] *O1, O3–4*; set *O2*.   51. breathe and rest] *O1, O3–4*;
42. gives] *O1, O3–4*; giue *O2*.   rest or breath *O2*.

---

26. *janissars*] janissaries, Turkish guardsmen.
29. *late*] recently, lately.
38. *rouse him*] drive him like a beast from its lair.
45. *fear*] object of dread.
46. *enlarge*] set free.

Are punish'd with bastones so grievously
That they lie panting on the galley's side
And strive for life at every stroke they give.
These are the cruel pirates of Argier,   55
That damned train, the scum of Africa,
Inhabited with straggling runagates,
That make quick havoc of the Christian blood.
But as I live that town shall curse the time
That Tamburlaine set foot in Africa.   60

Enter Bajazeth *with his Bassoes and contributory* Kings [of Fez, Morocco, *and* Argier; Zabina *and* Ebea].

BAJAZETH.

Bassoes and janissaries of my guard,
Attend upon the person of your lord,
The greatest potentate of Africa.

TAMBURLAINE.

Techelles and the rest, prepare your swords.
I mean t'encounter with that Bajazeth.   65

BAJAZETH.

Kings of Fez, Moroccus, and Argier,
He calls me Bajazeth, whom you call lord!
Note the presumption of this Scythian slave!
I tell thee, villain, those that lead my horse
Have to their names titles of dignity;   70
And dar'st thou bluntly call me Bajazeth?

TAMBURLAINE.

And know thou, Turk, that those which lead my horse
Shall lead thee captive thorough Africa;
And dar'st thou bluntly call me Tamburlaine?

BAJAZETH.

By Mahomet my kinsman's sepulcher   75
And by the holy Alcoran I swear

53. they] *O1–3; not in O4.*   60.2. Zabina *and* Ebea] *Dyce; not in*
60.1. *and contributory*] *O1–2; and his*   *O1–4.*
contributory O3–4.   70. titles] *O1–2; title O3–4.*

---

52. *bastones*] cudgels.   56. *train*] troop.
57. *runagates*] deserters.   70. *to*] in addition to.
73. *thorough*] through.
76. *Alcoran*] the Koran, the sacred book of the Mohammedans.

He shall be made a chaste and lustless eunuch
And in my sarell tend my concubines,
And all his captains that thus stoutly stand
Shall draw the chariot of my emperess,   80
Whom I have brought to see their overthrow.

TAMBURLAINE.

By this my sword that conquer'd Persia,
Thy fall shall make me famous through the world.
I will not tell thee how I'll handle thee,
But every common soldier of my camp   85
Shall smile to see thy miserable state.

KING OF FEZ.

What means the mighty Turkish emperor
To talk with one so base as Tamburlaine?

KING OF MOROCCO.

Ye Moors and valiant men of Barbary,
How can ye suffer these indignities?   90

KING OF ARGIER.

Leave words, and let them feel your lances' points,
Which glided through the bowels of the Greeks.

BAJAZETH.

Well said, my stout contributory kings.
Your threefold army and my hugy host
Shall swallow up these base-born Persians.   95

TECHELLES.

Puissant, renowned, and mighty Tamburlaine,
Why stay we thus prolonging all their lives?

THERIDAMAS.

I long to see those crowns won by our swords,
That we may reign as kings of Africa.

USUMCASANE.

What coward would not fight for such a prize?   100

TAMBURLAINE.

Fight all courageously, and be you kings.

84. I'll] *O1–2*; I wil *O3–4*.   97. all] *O1, O3–4*; of *O2*.
87. the] *O1–3*; this *O4*.   99. reign] *O1, O3–4*; rule *O2*.
90. ye] *O1–3*; you *O4*.

78. *sarell*] women's quarters, seraglio.
79. *stoutly*] haughtily.
90. *suffer*] put up with.   94. *hugy*] huge.

I speak it, and my words are oracles.

BAJAZETH.

Zabina, mother of three braver boys
Than Hercules, that in his infancy
Did pash the jaws of serpents venomous,   105
Whose hands are made to gripe a warlike lance,
Their shoulders broad, for complete armor fit,
Their limbs more large and of a bigger size
Than all the brats ysprung from Typhon's loins,
Who, when they come unto their father's age,   110
Will batter turrets with their manly fists—
Sit here upon this royal chair of state
And on thy head wear my imperial crown
Until I bring this sturdy Tamburlaine
And all his captains bound in captive chains.   115

ZABINA.

Such good success happen to Bajazeth!

TAMBURLAINE.

Zenocrate, the loveliest maid alive,
Fairer than rocks of pearl and precious stone,
The only paragon of Tamburlaine,
Whose eyes are brighter than the lamps of heaven   120
And speech more pleasant than sweet harmony,
That with thy looks canst clear the darkened sky
And calm the rage of thund'ring Jupiter—
Sit down by her, adorned with my crown,
As if thou wert the empress of the world.   125
Stir not, Zenocrate, until thou see
Me march victoriously with all my men,
Triumphing over him and these his kings,

103. braver] *O1–3*; braue *O4*.

104–105. *Hercules . . . venomous*] While still in his cradle, Hercules killed
with his own hands two serpents that had been sent to destroy him.

105. *pash*] smash.

109. *ysprung*] sprung. The same archaic prefix occurs in Part II,
IV.iii.119.

109. *Typhon*] in Greek mythology, a hundred-headed giant, the father of
various monsters.

116. *success*] result.

119. *paragon*] match, consort in marriage.

Which I will bring as vassals to thy feet.
Till then, take thou my crown, vaunt of my worth,   130
And manage words with her as we will arms.

ZENOCRATE.

And may my love, the king of Persia,
Return with victory and free from wound!

BAJAZETH.

Now shalt thou feel the force of Turkish arms,
Which lately made all Europe quake for fear.   135
I have of Turks, Arabians, Moors, and Jews
Enough to cover all Bithynia.
Let thousands die! Their slaughtered carcasses
Shall serve for walls and bulwarks to the rest;
And, as the heads of Hydra, so my power,   140
Subdued, shall stand as mighty as before.
If they should yield their necks unto the sword,
Thy soldiers' arms could not endure to strike
So many blows as I have heads for thee.
Thou knowest not, foolish-hardy Tamburlaine,   145
What 'tis to meet me in the open field,
That leave no ground for thee to march upon.

TAMBURLAINE.

Our conquering swords shall marshal us the way
We use to march upon the slaughtered foe,
Trampling their bowels with our horses' hoofs,   150
Brave horses bred on the white Tartarian hills.
My camp is like to Julius Caesar's host,
That never fought but had the victory;
Nor in Pharsalia was there such hot war
As these my followers willingly would have.   155
Legions of spirits fleeting in the air

---

130. *vaunt*] boast, brag.

131. *manage . . . arms*] fight her with words as we shall fight with weapons.

140. *Hydra*] a many-headed monster, one of Typhon's *brats* (l. 109). As Hercules struck off each of its heads, two new ones grew in the place. This difficulty was overcome by the application of a hot iron to the wound as each head fell. Eventually, Hercules was the victor.

148. *marshal*] guide, lead.   151. *Tartarian*] Tartar.

154. *Pharsalia*] Julius Caesar defeated Pompey there in 48 B.C.

156. *fleeting*] gliding.

Direct our bullets and our weapons' points
And make your strokes to wound the senseless air;
And when she sees our bloody colors spread,
Then Victory begins to take her flight,   160
Resting herself upon my milk-white tent.
But come, my lords, to weapons let us fall;
The field is ours, the Turk, his wife, and all.

Exit with his followers.

BAJAZETH.

Come, kings and bassoes, let us glut our swords,
That thirst to drink the feeble Persians' blood.   165

Exit with his followers.

ZABINA.

Base concubine, must thou be plac'd by me
That am the empress of the mighty Turk?

ZENOCRATE.

Disdainful Turkess and unreverend boss,
Call'st thou me concubine that am betroth'd
Unto the great and mighty Tamburlaine?   170

ZABINA.

To Tamburlaine, the great Tartarian thief!

ZENOCRATE.

Thou wilt repent these lavish words of thine
When thy great basso-master and thyself
Must plead for mercy at his kingly feet
And sue to me to be your advocates.   175

ZABINA.

And sue to thee? I tell thee, shameless girl,
Thou shalt be laundress to my waiting-maid.
How lik'st thou her, Ebea, will she serve?

EBEA.

Madam, she thinks perhaps she is too fine,
But I shall turn her into other weeds   180

158. your] *Dyce*; our *O1–4*.   175. advocates] *O1–2*; Aduocate
158. air] *Brooke, conj. Dyce 2*; lure   *O3–4*.
O1, O3–4; lute *O2*.   180. weeds] *O1–2, O4*; weed *O3*.

168. *unreverend boss*] irreverent gross woman.
172. *lavish*] unrestrained.
175. *your advocates*] an advocate for the two of you.
180. *weeds*] clothing.

And make her dainty fingers fall to work.

ZENOCRATE.

Hear'st thou, Anippe, how thy drudge doth talk,
And how my slave, her mistress, menaceth?
Both for their sauciness shall be employed
To dress the common soldiers' meat and drink,   185
For we will scorn they should come near ourselves.

ANIPPE.

Yet sometimes let your highness send for them
To do the work my chambermaid disdains.

They sound the battle within and stay.

ZENOCRATE.

Ye gods and powers that govern Persia
And made my lordly love her worthy king,   190
Now strengthen him against the Turkish Bajazeth,
And let his foes, like flocks of fearful roes
Pursu'd by hunters, fly his angry looks,
That I may see him issue conqueror.

ZABINA.

Now, Mahomet, solicit God himself,   195
And make him rain down murdering shot from heaven
To dash the Scythians' brains, and strike them dead
That dare to manage arms with him
That offered jewels to thy sacred shrine
When first he warr'd against the Christians.   200

To the battle again.

ZENOCRATE.

By this the Turks lie welt'ring in their blood,
And Tamburlaine is lord of Africa.

ZABINA.

Thou art deceiv'd. I heard the trumpets sound
As when my emperor overthrew the Greeks
And led them captive into Africa.   205
Straight will I use thee as thy pride deserves;
Prepare thyself to live and die my slave.

181–182.] *O1–3; printed twice in O4.*   201. lie] *O1–3;* lies *O4.*
188.1. *sound the] O1–2; sound to the*   202. And] *O1–3;* as *O4.*
O3–4.   204. As] *O1–3;* and *O4.*

185. *dress*] prepare.

–58–

ZENOCRATE.

    If Mahomet should come from heaven and swear
    My royal lord is slain or conquered,
    Yet should he not persuade me otherwise   210
    But that he lives and will be conqueror.

Bajazeth *flies, and he* [Tamburlaine] *pursues him. The battle short, and*
they enter. Bajazeth *is overcome.*

TAMBURLAINE.

    Now, king of bassoes, who is conqueror?

BAJAZETH.

    Thou, by the fortune of this damned foil.

TAMBURLAINE.

    Where are your stout contributory kings?

        Enter Techelles, Theridamas, Usumcasane.

TECHELLES.

    We have their crowns; their bodies strow the field.   215

TAMBURLAINE.

    Each man a crown? Why, kingly fought, i'faith.
    Deliver them into my treasury.

ZENOCRATE.

    Now let me offer to my gracious lord
    His royal crown again so highly won.

TAMBURLAINE.

    Nay, take the Turkish crown from her, Zenocrate,   220
    And crown me emperor of Africa.

ZABINA.

    No, Tamburlaine! Though now thou gat the best,
    Thou shalt not yet be lord of Africa.

THERIDAMAS.

    Give her the crown, Turkess, you were best.

        He takes it from her and gives it Zenocrate.

211.1. *battle short*] *O1–2; Battel is*   213. foil] *Dyce 2*; soile *O1–4.*
short O3–4.

---

    211. *he*] i.e., Tamburlaine.
    213. *foil*] defeat.
    214. *stout*] bold.   222. *gat*] got.

ZABINA.

    Injurious villains, thieves, runagates,   225

    How dare you thus abuse my majesty?

THERIDAMAS.

    Here, madam, you are empress. She is none.

TAMBURLAINE.

    Not now, Theridamas, her time is past.

    The pillars that have bolstered up those terms

    Are fall'n in clusters at my conquering feet.   230

ZABINA.

    Though he be prisoner, he may be ransomed.

TAMBURLAINE.

    Not all the world shall ransom Bajazeth.

BAJAZETH.

    Ah, fair Zabina, we have lost the field,

    And never had the Turkish emperor

    So great a foil by any foreign foe.   235

    Now will the Christian miscreants be glad,

    Ringing with joy their superstitious bells,

    And making bonfires for my overthrow.

    But, ere I die, those foul idolaters

    Shall make me bonfires with their filthy bones,   240

    For, though the glory of this day be lost,

    Afric and Greece have garrisons enough

    To make me sovereign of the earth again.

TAMBURLAINE.

    Those walled garrisons will I subdue,

    And write myself great lord of Africa.   245

    So from the East unto the furthest West

    Shall Tamburlaine extend his puissant arm.

    The galleys and those pilling brigandines

    That yearly sail to the Venetian gulf

233–234.] *O1–3*; *l. 234 precedes l.*   *O4.*
233, and is given to Tamburlaine, in   246. furthest] *O1–3*; farthest *O4.*

---

    225. *Injurious*] insulting.   225. *runagates*] vagabonds.

    229. *terms*] A term is a statuary bust supported by a pillar out of which it seems to spring.

    236. *miscreants*] infidels.

    248. *pilling*] plundering, pillaging.

    248. *brigandines*] small skirmishing vessels, often used for piracy.

And hover in the straits for Christians' wrack,   250
Shall lie at anchor in the Isle Asant
Until the Persian fleet and men-of-war,
Sailing along the oriental sea,
Have fetch'd about the Indian continent
Even from Persepolis to Mexico   255
And thence unto the Straits of Jubalter,
Where they shall meet and join their force in one,
Keeping in awe the Bay of Portingale
And all the ocean by the British shore;
And by this means I'll win the world at last.   260

BAJAZETH.

Yet set a ransom on me, Tamburlaine.

TAMBURLAINE.

What, think'st thou Tamburlaine esteems thy gold?
I'll make the kings of India ere I die
Offer their mines to sue for peace to me,
And dig for treasure to appease my wrath.   265
Come, bind them both, and one lead in the Turk;
The Turkess let my love's maid lead away.   *They bind them.*

BAJAZETH.

Ah, villains, dare ye touch my sacred arms?
O Mahomet! O sleepy Mahomet!

ZABINA.

O cursed Mahomet, that makest us thus   270
The slaves to Scythians rude and barbarous!

TAMBURLAINE.

Come, bring them in, and for this happy conquest
Triumph, and solemnize a martial feast.   *Exeunt.*

Finis Actus Tertii.

259. British] *O1, O3–4*; brightest   268. ye] *O1, O3–4*; you *O2.*
O2.   270. makest] *O1–3*; makes *O4.*
262. think'st] *O1–3*; thinks *O4.*   273. martial] *O1–3*; materiall *O4.*

250. *wrack*] destruction.
251. *Asant*] Zante, off the western coast of Greece.
254. *fetch'd about*] circumnavigated.
255. *from . . . Mexico*] i.e., across the Pacific.
256. *Jubalter*] Gibraltar.
258. *Portingale*] Portugal. The bay is the Bay of Biscay.

[IV.i]

[*Enter*] Soldan of Egypt *with three or four Lords*, Capolin[, Messenger].

SOLDAN OF EGYPT.

    Awake, ye men of Memphis! Hear the clang
    Of Scythian trumpets! Hear the basilisks
    That, roaring, shake Damascus' turrets down!
    The rogue of Volga holds Zenocrate,
    The Soldan's daughter, for his concubine,   5
    And with a troop of thieves and vagabonds
    Hath spread his colors to our high disgrace,
    While you faint-hearted base Egyptians
    Lie slumbering on the flow'ry banks of Nile,
    As crocodiles that unaffrighted rest   10
    While thund'ring cannons rattle on their skins.

MESSENGER.

    Nay, mighty Soldan, did your greatness see
    The frowning looks of fiery Tamburlaine
    That with his terror and imperious eyes
    Commands the hearts of his associates,   15
    It might amaze your royal majesty.

SOLDAN OF EGYPT.

    Villain, I tell thee, were that Tamburlaine
    As monstrous as Gorgon, prince of hell,
    The Soldan would not start a foot from him.
    But speak, what power hath he?

MESSENGER.   Mighty lord,   20

    Three hundred thousand men in armor clad
    Upon their prancing steeds, disdainfully
    With wanton paces trampling on the ground;
    Five hundred thousand footmen threat'ning shot,
    Shaking their swords, their spears, and iron bills,   25
    Environing their standard round, that stood

0.1. Messenger] *Rob.*; *not in O1–4.*

---

    2. *basilisks*] heavy cannons.
    18. *monstrous*] unnatural.
    18. *Gorgon*] Demogorgon, one of the potentates of hell whom Doctor Faustus invokes in Marlowe's play.
    23. *wanton*] sportive.
    25. *bills*] long-handled axes.

As bristle-pointed as a thorny wood;
Their warlike engines and munition
Exceed the forces of their martial men.

SOLDAN OF EGYPT.

Nay, could their numbers countervail the stars,   30
Or ever-drizzling drops of April showers,
Or withered leaves that Autumn shaketh down,
Yet would the Soldan by his conquering power
So scatter and consume them in his rage
That not a man should live to rue their fall.   35

CAPOLIN.

So might your highness, had you time to sort
Your fighting men and raise your royal host.
But Tamburlaine by expedition
Advantage takes of your unreadiness.

SOLDAN OF EGYPT.

Let him take all th'advantages he can.   40
Were all the world conspir'd to fight for him,
Nay, were he devil, as he is no man,
Yet in revenge of fair Zenocrate,
Whom he detaineth in despite of us,
This arm should send him down to Erebus   45
To shroud his shame in darkness of the night.

MESSENGER.

Pleaseth your mightiness to understand,
His resolution far exceedeth all.
The first day when he pitcheth down his tents,
White is their hue, and on his silver crest   50
A snowy feather spangled white he bears,
To signify the mildness of his mind,
That satiate with spoil refuseth blood.
But when Aurora mounts the second time

31. ever-drizzling] *O1, O3–4*; dris-   42. he devil] *O1–3*; he the deuill
ling *O2*.   *O4*.
35. should] *O1, O3–4*; shal *O2*.   50. White] *O1–3*; While *O4*.

---

30. *countervail*] equal.   38. *expedition*] speed.
45. *Erebus*] The name of this son of Chaos signifies darkness; it was
therefore applied to the gloomy region under the earth, through which
the shades pass into Hades.
54. *Aurora*] the goddess of the dawn.

As red as scarlet is his furniture;   55
Then must his kindled wrath be quench'd with blood,
Not sparing any that can manage arms.
But, if these threats move not submission,
Black are his colors, black pavilion;
His spear, his shield, his horse, his armor, plumes,   60
And jetty feathers menace death and hell;
Without respect of sex, degree, or age,
He razeth all his foes with fire and sword.

SOLDAN OF EGYPT.

Merciless villain, peasant ignorant
Of lawful arms or martial discipline!   65
Pillage and murder are his usual trades.
The slave usurps the glorious name of war.
See, Capolin, the fair Arabian king,
That hath been disappointed by this slave
Of my fair daughter and his princely love,   70
May have fresh warning to go war with us,
And be reveng'd for her disparagement.   [*Exeunt.*]

[IV.ii]

[*Enter*] Tamburlaine, Techelles, Theridamas, *Usumcasane*, Zenocrate,
Anippe, *two Moors drawing* Bajazeth *in his cage, and his wife* [Zabina]
following him.

TAMBURLAINE.

Bring out my footstool.   *They take him out of the cage.*

BAJAZETH.

Ye holy priests of heavenly Mahomet,
That, sacrificing, slice and cut your flesh,
Staining his altars with your purple blood,
Make heaven to frown and every fixed star   5

72. S.D. *Exeunt*] *Rob.; not in O1–4.*

---

55. *furniture*] personal equipment (dress, accouterments, tent, etc.).
57. *manage*] wield.   62. *degree*] rank.
63. *razeth*] destroys.   71. *with*] in alliance with.
[IV.ii]
5–7. *every . . . throat*] Marlowe here exploits the current meteorological
notion that the sun and stars drew up "vapors" and "exhalations" from
the earth. See I.ii.49–51, note, above.

To suck up poison from the moorish fens
And pour it in this glorious tyrant's throat!

TAMBURLAINE.

The chiefest God, first mover of that sphere
Enchas'd with thousands ever-shining lamps,
Will sooner burn the glorious frame of heaven   10
Than it should so conspire my overthrow.
But, villain, thou that wishest this to me,
Fall prostrate on the low disdainful earth
And be the footstool of great Tamburlaine
That I may rise into my royal throne.   15

BAJAZETH.

First shalt thou rip my bowels with thy sword
And sacrifice my heart to death and hell
Before I yield to such a slavery.

TAMBURLAINE.

Base villain, vassal, slave to Tamburlaine,
Unworthy to embrace or touch the ground   20
That bears the honor of my royal weight,
Stoop, villain, stoop! Stoop, for so he bids
That may command thee piecemeal to be torn
Or scattered like the lofty cedar trees
Struck with the voice of thund'ring Jupiter.   25

BAJAZETH.

Then, as I look down to the damned fiends,
Fiends, look on me; and thou, dread god of hell,
With ebon scepter strike this hateful earth
And make it swallow both of us at once!

He gets up upon him to his chair.

---

7. it] *O1, O3–4; not in O2.*
8. sphere] *O1–3;* speare *O4.*
11. it should] *O1, O3–4;* should it *O2.*

12. this] *O1–3;* it *O4.*
15. into] *O1, O3–4;* vnto *O2.*
17. heart] *O1, O3–4;* soule *O2.*

---

7. *glorious*] swaggering.
8–9. *that . . . lamps*] the transparent hollow globe that was believed to carry the fixed stars about the stationary earth.
9. *Enchas'd*] adorned. See I.ii.96, note, above.
27. *god of hell*] Pluto.

TAMBURLAINE.

Now clear the triple region of the air,   30
And let the majesty of heaven behold
Their scourge and terror tread on emperors.
Smile, stars that reign'd at my nativity,
And dim the brightness of their neighbor lamps;
Disdain to borrow light of Cynthia,   35
For I, the chiefest lamp of all the earth,
First rising in the east with mild aspect,
But fixed now in the meridian line,
Will send up fire to your turning spheres
And cause the sun to borrow light of you.   40
My sword struck fire from his coat of steel,
Even in Bithynia, when I took this Turk,
As when a fiery exhalation,
Wrapp'd in the bowels of a freezing cloud,
Fighting for passage, makes the welkin crack 45
And casts a flash of lightning to the earth.
But, ere I march to wealthy Persia
Or leave Damascus and th'Egyptian fields,
As was the fame of Clymene's brainsick son

45. makes] *Rob.*; make *O1–4.*   49. Clymene's] *O2*; *Clymeus O1,*
46. to] *O1–3*; on *O4.*   *O3–4.*

30. *triple . . . air*] "The highest region was heated by proximity to the sphere of Fire and by the friction of the rotating spheres of heaven. The lowest region was warmed by reflection of the Sun's radiation from the earth's surface . . . . The middle region of the Air, having no direct source of heat, was consequently Cold" (Heninger, p. 41).

35. *Cynthia*] the moon.

36–38. *I . . . line*] "Tamburlaine, likening himself to a sun, says that he has now reached the meridian line, or noon of his fortunes. He further implies that he, unlike other suns, is 'fixed' in the meridian and will not decline" (Ellis-Fermor).

39. *spheres*] See II.vii.25, note, above.

43–46. *a . . . earth*] It was believed that a "vapor," drawn by the sun's heat from the watery components of the earth's surface, might enclose and compress an "exhalation," drawn from the terrestrial components. The compacted exhalation's rolling about inside the cloud accounted for thunder. If the exhalation broke out by force, having ignited itself in its struggles, the result was thunder and lightning. See Heninger, pp. 72–87.

45. *welkin*] sky.

49. *Clymene's brainsick son*] Phaëton. He presumed to drive the chariot of the sun; but his incapacity was such that he would have set the earth on fire if Zeus had not killed him with a flash of lightning.

That almost brent the axletree of heaven,   50
So shall our swords, our lances, and our shot
Fill all the air with fiery meteors;
Then, when the sky shall wax as red as blood,
It shall be said I made it red myself,
To make me think of nought but blood and war.   55

ZABINA.

Unworthy king, that by thy cruelty
Unlawfully usurpest the Persian seat,
Dar'st thou that never saw an emperor
Before thou met my husband in the field,
Being thy captive, thus abuse his state,   60
Keeping his kingly body in a cage,
That roofs of gold and sun-bright palaces
Should have prepar'd to entertain his grace?
And treading him beneath thy loathsome feet,
Whose feet the kings of Africa have kiss'd?   65

TECHELLES.

You must devise some torment worse, my lord,
To make these captives rein their lavish tongues.

TAMBURLAINE.

Zenocrate, look better to your slave.

ZENOCRATE.

She is my handmaid's slave, and she shall look
That these abuses flow not from her tongue.   70
Chide her, Anippe.

ANIPPE.

Let these be warnings for you then, my slave,
How you abuse the person of the king;
Or else I swear to have you whipp'd stark nak'd.

BAJAZETH.

Great Tamburlaine, great in my overthrow,   75

50. brent] *O1–2*; burnt *O3–4*.   72. for you then] *O1–2*; then for
65. kings] *O1–3*; King *O4*.   you *O3–4*.
70. from] *O1, O3–4*; in *O2*.

---

50. *brent*] burnt.
50. *axletree of heaven*] on which all the spheres were believed to revolve.
52. *meteors*] This word was used for atmospheric phenomena of every kind.
60. *abuse his state*] do violence to his high rank.
67. *lavish tongues*] free-speaking mouths.

Ambitious pride shall make thee fall as low.
For treading on the back of Bajazeth
That should be horsed on four mighty kings.

TAMBURLAINE.

Thy names and titles and thy dignities
Are fled from Bajazeth and remain with me,   80
That will maintain it against a world of kings.
Put him in again.   *[They put him into the cage.]*

BAJAZETH.

Is this a place for mighty Bajazeth?
Confusion light on him that helps thee thus.

TAMBURLAINE.

There, whiles he lives, shall Bajazeth be kept,   85
And where I go be thus in triumph drawn;
And thou, his wife, shalt feed him with the scraps
My servitors shall bring thee from my board,
For he that gives him other food than this
Shall sit by him and starve to death himself.   90
This is my mind and I will have it so.
Not all the kings and emperors of the earth,
If they would lay their crowns before my feet,
Shall ransom him or take him from his cage.
The ages that shall talk of Tamburlaine,   95
Even from this day to Plato's wondrous year,
Shall talk how I have handled Bajazeth.
These Moors, that drew him from Bithynia
To fair Damascus, where we now remain,
Shall lead him with us wheresoe'er we go.   100
Techelles, and my loving followers,
Now may we see Damascus' lofty towers,

79. dignities] *O1–2*; dignitis *O3*;   *O1–4*.
dignitie *O4*.   85. whiles] *O1–3*; while *O4*.
82. S.D. *They . . . cage*] *Rob.*; *not in*   87. shalt] *O1, O3–4*; shal *O2*.

76. *pride . . . low*] a variant of the proverb, "Pride will have a fall" (Tilley, P 581).

85. *whiles*] while.

96. *Plato's wondrous year*] the period of time which is completed when the seven so-called planets (the moon, Mercury, Venus, the sun, Mars, Jupiter, and Saturn) return simultaneously to their original starting-points. See Plato, *Timaeus*, 39D. The idea was well-known to medieval and Renaissance thinkers, and the length of the Great World-Year was variously computed. Plato had apparently put it at 36,000 years.

Like to the shadows of Pyramides
That with their beauties grac'd the Memphian fields.
The golden stature of their feathered bird   105
That spreads her wings upon the city walls
Shall not defend it from our battering shot.
The townsmen mask in silk and cloth of gold,
And every house is as a treasury;
The men, the treasure, and the town is ours.   110

THERIDAMAS.

Your tents of white now pitch'd before the gates,
And gentle flags of amity display'd,
I doubt not but the governor will yield,
Offering Damascus to your majesty.

TAMBURLAINE.

So shall he have his life, and all the rest.   115
But, if he stay until the bloody flag
Be once advanc'd on my vermilion tent,
He dies, and those that kept us out so long.
And when they see me march in black array,
With mournful streamers hanging down their heads,   120
Were in that city all the world contain'd,
Not one should scape, but perish by our swords.

ZENOCRATE.

Yet would you have some pity for my sake,
Because it is my country's and my father's.

TAMBURLAINE.

Not for the world, Zenocrate, if I have sworn.   125
Come, bring in the Turk.   *Exeunt.*

105. stature] *O1–2*; statue *O3–4*.

---

103. *Pyramides*] This word could be applied to obelisks and spires as well as to what are now normally called pyramids. So there is no absurdity in Tamburlaine's likening the towers of Damascus to the *shadows*, or faint semblances, of the Pyramids.

105. *stature*] statue.

105. *bird*] eagle. See E. Seaton, "Marlowe's Light Reading," *Elizabethan and Jacobean Studies* (ed. H. Davis and H. Gardner, Oxford, 1959), pp. 17–35.

108. *mask*] attire themselves.

115. *all the rest*] all the rest will have theirs.

116. *stay*] delay.

120. *streamers*] pennons.

124. *my country's . . . father's*] i.e., their city.

[IV.iii]

[*Enter*] Soldan, Arabia, Capolin, *with streaming colors, and Soldiers.*

SOLDAN OF EGYPT.

Methinks we march as Meleager did,
Environed with brave Argolian knights,
To chase the savage Calydonian boar;
Or Cephalus with lusty Theban youths
Against the wolf that angry Themis sent   5
To waste and spoil the sweet Aonian fields.
A monster of five hundred thousand heads,
Compact of rapine, piracy, and spoil,
The scum of men, the hate and scourge of God,
Raves in Egyptia and annoyeth us.   10
My lord, it is the bloody Tamburlaine,
A sturdy felon and a base-bred thief
By murder raised to the Persian crown,
That dares control us in our territories.
To tame the pride of this presumptuous beast,   15
Join your Arabians with the Soldan's power;
Let us unite our royal bands in one
And hasten to remove Damascus' siege.
It is a blemish to the majesty
And high estate of mighty emperors   20

0.1. *streaming*] *O3–4*; *steaming O1–2.*   12. and] *O1, O3–4; not in O2.*
3. Calydonian] *O2*; Caldonian *O1*;   14. dares] *O1*; dare *O2–4.*
Calcedonian *O3–4.*   17. bands] *O1–3*; handes *O4.*
4. lusty] *O1–3; not in O4.*

---

1. *Meleager*] He led the heroes who killed the monstrous boar that was laying waste the fields of his native Calydon.

2. *Argolian*] Argolis was a district of the Peloponnesus, the southern part of Greece.

4. *Cephalus*] a hunter who possessed a dog and a spear that never missed their object. He destroyed a wild beast (Marlowe calls it a wolf) that was doing great damage in the Theban territories.

4. *lusty*] vigorous, strong.

5. *Themis*] a Greek deity, standing for order and equity.

6. *Aonian*] Boeotian. Boeotia was a country in central Greece; Thebes was its capital.

7. *of . . . heads*] i.e., with an army of 500,000 men.

10. *annoyeth*] molests.

14. *control*] overpower.   20. *estate*] condition.

That such a base usurping vagabond
Should brave a king or wear a princely crown.

KING OF ARABIA.

Renowned Soldan, have ye lately heard
The overthrow of mighty Bajazeth
About the confines of Bithynia?   25
The slavery wherewith he persecutes
The noble Turk and his great emperess?

SOLDAN OF EGYPT.

I have, and sorrow for his bad success.
But, noble lord of great Arabia,
Be so persuaded that the Soldan is   30
No more dismay'd with tidings of his fall
Than in the haven when the pilot stands
And views a stranger's ship rent in the winds
And shivered against a craggy rock.
Yet in compassion of his wretched state   35
A sacred vow to heaven and him I make,
Confirming it with Ibis' holy name,
That Tamburlaine shall rue the day, the hour,
Wherein he wrought such ignominious wrong
Unto the hallowed person of a prince,   40
Or kept the fair Zenocrate so long
As concubine, I fear, to feed his lust.

KING OF ARABIA.

Let grief and fury hasten on revenge.
Let Tamburlaine for his offenses feel
Such plagues as heaven and we can pour on him.   45
I long to break my spear upon his crest
And prove the weight of his victorious arm;
For Fame, I fear, hath been too prodigal
In sounding through the world his partial praise.

SOLDAN OF EGYPT.

Capolin, hast thou survey'd our powers?   50

38. the hour] *O1–3*; and houre *O4*.

---

25. *confines*] borders.
28. *bad success*] ill fortune.
37. *Ibis*] a sacred bird of the Egyptians.
47. *prove*] find out by experience.
49. *partial*] biased, prejudiced.

CAPOLIN.

    Great emperors of Egypt and Arabia,
    The number of your hosts united is
    A hundred and fifty thousand horse,
    Two hundred thousand foot, brave men-at-arms,
    Courageous and full of hardiness,   55
    As frolic as the hunters in the chase
    Of savage beasts amid the desert woods.

KING OF ARABIA.

    My mind presageth fortunate success,
    And, Tamburlaine, my spirit doth foresee
    The utter ruin of thy men and thee.   60

SOLDAN OF EGYPT.

    Then rear your standards, let your sounding drums
    Direct our soldiers to Damascus' walls.
    Now, Tamburlaine, the mighty Soldan comes
    And leads with him the great Arabian king
    To dim thy baseness and obscurity,   65
    Famous for nothing but for theft and spoil;
    To raze and scatter thy inglorious crew
    Of Scythians and slavish Persians.   *Exeunt.*

[IV.iv]

The banquet, and to it cometh Tamburlaine *all in scarlet,* Theridamas,
Techelles, Usumcasane, *the* Turk [Bajazeth *in his cage,* Zenocrate,
Zabina], *with others.*

TAMBURLAINE.

    Now hang our bloody colors by Damascus,
    Reflexing hues of blood upon their heads,
    While they walk quivering on their city walls,
    Half dead for fear before they feel my wrath.
    Then let us freely banquet and carouse   5
    Full bowls of wine unto the god of war,

55. and] *O1–3; not in O4.*
65. thy] *O1–3;* the *O4.*
65. and] *O1–3;* of *O4.*

[IV.iv]
0.2–3. *in* . . . Zabina] *Dyce; not in*
O1–4.

   56. *frolic*] merry.   67. *raze*] destroy.
[IV.iv]
   2. *Reflexing*] casting.

That means to fill your helmets full of gold
And make Damascus' spoils as rich to you
As was to Jason Colchos' golden fleece.
And now, Bajazeth, hast thou any stomach?   10

BAJAZETH.

Ay, such a stomach, cruel Tamburlaine, as I could
Willingly feed upon thy blood-raw heart.

TAMBURLAINE.

Nay, thine own is easier to come by. Pluck out that
And 'twill serve thee and thy wife. Well, Zenocrate,
Techelles, and the rest, fall to your victuals.   15

BAJAZETH.

Fall to, and never may your meat digest!
Ye Furies that can mask invisible,
Dive to the bottom of Avernus' pool
And in your hands bring hellish poison up
And squeeze it in the cup of Tamburlaine.   20
Or, winged snakes of Lerna, cast your stings,
And leave your venoms in this tyrant's dish.

ZABINA.

And may this banquet prove as ominous
As Progne's to th'adulterous Thracian king
That fed upon the substance of his child.   25

ZENOCRATE.

My lord, how can you suffer these
Outrageous curses by these slaves of yours?

17. mask] *O1–2*; walke *O3–4*.

---

9. *Jason*] He led the Argonauts to Colchos (Colchis) to obtain the Golden
Fleece.

10. *stomach*] (1) hunger, (2) anger.

15. *fall to*] make a start on (used especially of eating).

17. *Furies*] See II.vii.53, note, above.

17. *mask invisible*] assume invisibility.

18. *Avernus' pool*] See I.ii.160, note, above.

21. *Lerna*] a district in Argolis, celebrated as the place where Hercules
killed the Hydra (see III.iii.140, note, above). After his victory, Hercules
poisoned his arrows with the monster's bile; as a result, the wounds they
inflicted became incurable.

24. *Progne*] Tereus, King of Thrace, raped and mutilated Philomela, the
sister of his wife Progne (Procne). Progne accordingly murdered her son
Itys and served up his flesh to Tereus.

27. *Outrageous*] violent.

TAMBURLAINE.

    To let them see, divine Zenocrate,
    I glory in the curses of my foes,
    Having the power from the empyreal heaven   30
    To turn them all upon their proper heads.

TECHELLES.

    I pray you give them leave, madam. This speech is a goodly
    refreshing to them.

THERIDAMAS.

    But, if his highness would let them be fed, it would do them
    more good.   35

TAMBURLAINE.

    Sirrah, why fall you not to? Are you so daintily brought up,
    you cannot eat your own flesh?

BAJAZETH.

    First, legions of devils shall tear thee in pieces.

USUMCASANE.

    Villain, knowest thou to whom thou speakest?

TAMBURLAINE.

    O, let him alone. Here, eat, sir! Take it from my sword's   40
    point, or I'll thrust it to thy heart.

                          He takes it and stamps upon it.

THERIDAMAS.

    He stamps it under his feet, my lord.

TAMBURLAINE.

    Take it up, villain, and eat it, or I will make thee slice the
    brawns of thy arms into carbonadoes and eat them.

USUMCASANE.

    Nay, 'twere better he kill'd his wife, and then she shall be   45
    sure not to be starv'd, and he be provided for a month's
    victual beforehand.

---

32. goodly] *O1–2*; good *O3–4*.   40. Here] *O1–2*; there *O3–4*.
33. to] *O1, O3–4*; for *O2*.   40. it from] *O1–3*; it vp from *O4*.
36. you not] *O1–2*; ye not *O3–4*.   43. slice] *O1–2*; flice *O3*; fleece *O4*.

---

    30. *the empyreal heaven*] See II.vii.15, note, above.
    31. *proper*] own.   32. *leave*] i.e., permission to speak.
    36. *why . . . to?*] why don't you start eating?
    36. *daintily*] over-nicely.
    44. *brawns*] muscles, fleshy parts.
    44. *carbonadoes*] steaks for broiling.

TAMBURLAINE.

Here is my dagger. Dispatch her while she is fat, for if she
live but a while longer she will fall into a consumption
with fretting, and then she will not be worth the eating.   50

THERIDAMAS.

Dost thou think that Mahomet will suffer this?

TECHELLES.

'Tis like he will, when he cannot let it.

TAMBURLAINE.

Go to, fall to your meat. What, not a bit? Belike he hath not
been watered today. Give him some drink.

They give him water to drink, and he flings it on the ground.

Fast, and welcome, sir, while hunger make you eat. How   55
now, Zenocrate, doth not the Turk and his wife make a
goodly show at a banquet?

ZENOCRATE.

Yes, my lord.

THERIDAMAS.

Methinks 'tis a great deal better than a consort of music.

TAMBURLAINE.

Yet music would do well to cheer up Zenocrate. Pray thee   60
tell, why art thou so sad? If thou wilt have a song, the Turk
shall strain his voice. But why is it?

ZENOCRATE.

My lord, to see my father's town besieg'd,
The country wasted where myself was born,
How can it but afflict my very soul?   65
If any love remain in you, my lord,
Or if my love unto your majesty
May merit favor at your highness' hands,
Then raise your siege from fair Damascus' walls
And with my father take a friendly truce.   70

49. will fall] *O1–3*; wil not fall *O4.*

---

51. *suffer*] allow.   52. *let*] hinder.
53. *Go to*] an exclamation used to express remonstrance, protest, etc.
53. *Belike*] perhaps.
54. *watered*] Tamburlaine speaks as if he were ordering drink for his
horses or cattle.
55. *while*] until.
59. *consort of music*] group of musicians.

TAMBURLAINE.

    Zenocrate, were Egypt Jove's own land,
    Yet would I with my sword make Jove to stoop.
    I will confute those blind geographers
    That make a triple region in the world,
    Excluding regions which I mean to trace   75
    And with this pen reduce them to a map,
    Calling the provinces, cities, and towns
    After my name and thine, Zenocrate.
    Here at Damascus will I make the point
    That shall begin the perpendicular.   80
    And wouldst thou have me buy thy father's love
    With such a loss? Tell me, Zenocrate.

ZENOCRATE.

    Honor still wait on happy Tamburlaine.
    Yet give me leave to plead for him, my lord.

TAMBURLAINE.

    Content thyself; his person shall be safe   85
    And all the friends of fair Zenocrate,
    If with their lives they will be pleas'd to yield
    Or may be forc'd to make me emperor;
    For Egypt and Arabia must be mine.
    —Feed, you slave! Thou may'st think thyself happy to be 90
    fed from my trencher.

BAJAZETH.

    My empty stomach, full of idle heat,
    Draws bloody humors from my feeble parts,
    Preserving life by hasting cruel death.
    My veins are pale, my sinews hard and dry,   95
    My joints benumb'd; unless I eat, I die.

81. thy] *O1–3*; my *O4*.   96. benumb'd] *O1–2*; be numb'd
94. hasting] *O1–2*; hastening *O3–4*.   *O3–4*.

---

    74. *triple region*] i.e., Europe, Asia, and Africa.
    76. *this pen*] i.e., his sword.
    76. *reduce them to*] put them down in.
    79–80. *Here . . . perpendicular*] The meridian-line of Tamburlaine's new map will pass through the city of Damascus. "Marlowe knew that the cartographer of his time had a wide choice for his initial meridian of longitude, his perpendicular" (Seaton, p. 14).
    91. *trencher*] wooden platter.
    93. *humors*] vital internal fluids.

ZABINA.

Eat, Bajazeth. Let us live in spite of them,
Looking some happy power will pity and enlarge us.

TAMBURLAINE.

Here, Turk, wilt thou have a clean trencher?

BAJAZETH.

Ay, tyrant, and more meat.   100

TAMBURLAINE.

Soft, sir, you must be dieted; too much eating will make
you surfeit.

THERIDAMAS.

So it would, my lord, specially having so small a walk and so
little exercise.

Enter a second course of crowns.

TAMBURLAINE.

Theridamas, Techelles, and Casane, here are the cates you 105
desire to finger, are they not?

THERIDAMAS.

Ay, my lord, but none save kings must feed with these.

TECHELLES.

'Tis enough for us to see them, and for Tamburlaine only
to enjoy them.

TAMBURLAINE.

Well, here is now to the Soldan of Egypt, the King of Arabia, 110
and the Governor of Damascus. Now take these three
crowns, and pledge me, my contributory kings.
I crown you here, Theridamas, King of Argier; Techelles,
King of Fez; and Usumcasane, King of Moroccus. How
say you to this, Turk? These are not your contributory 115
kings.

BAJAZETH.

Nor shall they long be thine, I warrant them.

TAMBURLAINE.

Kings of Argier, Moroccus, and of Fez,

103. specially] *O1–2;* especially
O3–4.

---

98. *Looking*] expecting.
98. *happy*] favorable.   98. *enlarge*] release.
101. *Soft*] wait! stop!   105. *cates*] delicacies.

-77-

You that have march'd with happy Tamburlaine
As far as from the frozen place of heaven   120
Unto the wat'ry morning's ruddy bower,
And thence by land unto the torrid zone,
Deserve these titles I endow you with,
By valor and by magnanimity.
Your births shall be no blemish to your fame,   125
For virtue is the fount whence honor springs,
And they are worthy she investeth kings.

THERIDAMAS.

And since your highness hath so well vouchsaf'd,
If we deserve them not with higher meeds
Than erst our states and actions have retain'd,   130
Take them away again and make us slaves.

TAMBURLAINE.

Well said, Theridamas. When holy fates
Shall 'stablish me in strong Egyptia,
We mean to travel to th'antarctic pole,
Conquering the people underneath our feet,   135
And be renown'd as never emperors were.
Zenocrate, I will not crown thee yet,
Until with greater honors I be grac'd.   [*Exeunt.*]

Finis Actus Quarti.

[V.i]

[*Enter*] *the* Governor of Damasco, *with three or four Citizens, and four*
Virgins *with branches of laurel in their hands.*

GOVERNOR OF DAMASCUS.

Still doth this man, or rather god of war,
Batter our walls and beat our turrets down;
And to resist with longer stubbornness

121. bower]. *O3–4*; hower *O1–2.*   131. again] *O1–2*; *not in O3–4.*
124. valor] *Rob.*; value *O1–4.*   138. S.D. *Exeunt*] *Rob.*; *not in O1–4.*
126. whence] *O1–3*; where *O4.*

125. *births*] lowly origins.
126. *virtue*] power and ability.   127. *they*] those who.
128. *vouchsaf'd*] deigned to grant them.
129. *meeds*] merits.   130. *erst*] formerly.
135. *underneath our feet*] in the southern hemisphere.

Or hope of rescue from the Soldan's power
Were but to bring our wilful overthrow   5
And make us desperate of our threaten'd lives.
We see his tents have now been altered
With terrors to the last and cruell'st hue.
His coal-black colors everywhere advanc'd
Threaten our city with a general spoil;   10
And, if we should with common rites of arms
Offer our safeties to his clemency,
I fear the custom proper to his sword,
Which he observes as parcel of his fame,
Intending so to terrify the world,   15
By any innovation or remorse
Will never be dispens'd with till our deaths.
Therefore, for these our harmless virgins' sakes,
Whose honors and whose lives rely on him,
Let us have hope that their unspotted prayers,   20
Their blubbered cheeks, and hearty humble moans
Will melt his fury into some remorse,
And use us like a loving conqueror.

FIRST VIRGIN.

If humble suits or imprecations
(Uttered with tears of wretchedness and blood   25
Shed from the heads and hearts of all our sex,
Some made your wives, and some your children)
Might have entreated your obdurate breasts
To entertain some care of our securities
Whiles only danger beat upon our walls,   30
These more than dangerous warrants of our death
Had never been erected as they be,

18. sakes] *O1–2*; sake *O3–4*.   29. care] *O1, O3–4*; cares *O2*.

---

13. *proper*] peculiar.   14. *parcel*] an essential part.
16–17. *By . . . with*] (his custom) will never be given up as a result of any change of policy or feeling of pity.
21. *blubbered*] flooded with tears. The word could still be used seriously when Marlowe wrote.
21. *hearty*] heartfelt.   22. *remorse*] pity.
24. *imprecations*] prayers, entreaties.
29. *securities*] safeties.
31. *These . . . death*] i.e., the black banners, etc.

Nor you depend on such weak helps as we.

GOVERNOR OF DAMASCUS.

Well, lovely virgins, think our country's care,
Our love of honor, loath to be enthrall'd   35
To foreign powers and rough imperious yokes,
Would not with too much cowardice or fear,
Before all hope of rescue were denied,
Submit yourselves and us to servitude.
Therefore, in that your safeties and our own,   40
Your honors, liberties, and lives were weigh'd
In equal care and balance with our own,
Endure as we the malice of our stars,
The wrath of Tamburlaine and power of wars,
Or be the means the overweighing heavens   45
Have kept to qualify these hot extremes,
And bring us pardon in your cheerful looks.

SECOND VIRGIN.

Then here, before the majesty of heaven
And holy patrons of Egyptia,
With knees and hearts submissive we entreat   50
Grace to our words and pity to our looks
That this device may prove propitious,
And through the eyes and ears of Tamburlaine
Convey events of mercy to his heart.
Grant that these signs of victory we yield   55
May bind the temples of his conquering head
To hide the folded furrows of his brows
And shadow his displeased countenance
With happy looks of ruth and lenity.
Leave us, my lord, and loving countrymen.   60
What simple virgins may persuade, we will.

GOVERNOR OF DAMASCUS.

Farewell, sweet virgins, on whose safe return

---

33. helps] *01–3*; help *04*.   41. weigh'd] *01, 03–4*; weigh *02*.
37. or] *01–3*; for *04*.   44. power] *01–3*; powers *04*.

---

45. *overweighing*] overruling.
46. *qualify . . . extremes*] moderate these violent extremes.
54. *Convey . . . mercy*] suggest merciful results.
55. *these . . . victory*] i.e., the *branches of laurel* (l. 0.2).

Depends our city, liberty, and lives.

Exeunt [all except the Virgins].

[*Enter*] Tamburlaine, Techelles, Theridamas, Usumcasane, *with others;* Tamburlaine *all in black and very melancholy.*

TAMBURLAINE.

What, are the turtles fray'd out of their nests?
Alas, poor fools, must you be first shall feel   65
The sworn destruction of Damascus?
They know my custom. Could they not as well
Have sent ye out when first my milk-white flags,
Through which sweet mercy threw her gentle beams,
Reflexing them on your disdainful eyes,   70
As now when fury and incensed hate
Flings slaughtering terror from my coal-black tents
And tells for truth submissions comes too late?

FIRST VIRGIN.

Most happy king and emperor of the earth,
Image of honor and nobility,   75
For whom the powers divine have made the world
And on whose throne the holy Graces sit,
In whose sweet person is compris'd the sum
Of nature's skill and heavenly majesty,
Pity our plights! O, pity poor Damascus!   80
Pity old age, within whose silver hairs
Honor and reverence evermore have reign'd.
Pity the marriage-bed, where many a lord
In prime and glory of his loving joy
Embraceth now with tears of ruth and blood   85
The jealous body of his fearful wife,

63.1. *all . . .* Virgins] *Dyce; not in O1–4.*
67. know] *O1, O3–4;* knew *O2.*
71. As] *O1–3;* and *O4.*
72. tents] *O1–2;* tent *O3–4.*
73. comes] *O1–2, O4;* come *O3.*
85. of ruth and] *O1–3;* and ruth of *O4.*

64. *turtles fray'd*] turtle-doves frightened.
65. *poor fools*] a form of address expressing pity.
65. *first shall*] the first that will.
77. *Graces*] Euphrosyne, Aglaia, and Thalia, three daughters of Zeus, who were regarded as the bestowers of beauty and charm.
86. *jealous*] apprehensive.

Whose cheeks and hearts, so punish'd with conceit
To think thy puissant never-stayed arm
Will part their bodies and prevent their souls
From heavens of comfort yet their age might bear,   90
Now wax all pale and withered to the death,
As well for grief our ruthless governor
Have thus refus'd the mercy of thy hand,
Whose scepter angels kiss and Furies dread,
As for their liberties, their loves, or lives.   95
O, then, for these and such as we ourselves,
For us, for infants, and for all our bloods,
That never nourish'd thought against thy rule,
Pity, O pity, sacred emperor,
The prostrate service of this wretched town,   100
And take in sign thereof this gilded wreath,
Whereto each man of rule hath given his hand
And wish'd, as worthy subjects, happy means
To be investers of thy royal brows
Even with the true Egyptian diadem.   105

TAMBURLAINE.

Virgins, in vain ye labor to prevent
That which mine honor swears shall be perform'd.
Behold my sword; what see you at the point?

FIRST VIRGIN.

Nothing but fear and fatal steel, my lord.

TAMBURLAINE.

Your fearful minds are thick and misty then,   110
For there sits Death, there sits imperious Death,
Keeping his circuit by the slicing edge.
But I am pleas'd you shall not see him there.
He now is seated on my horsemen's spears,

93. Have] *O1–2*; Hath *O3–4*.   106. ye] *O1, O3–4*; you *O2*.
98. nourish'd] *O1–2*; nourish *O3–4*.   111. imperious] *O1–3*; imprecious
103. wish'd] *O1–2*; wish *O3–4*.   *O4*.

87. *punish'd with conceit*] racked with the notion.
88. *never-stayed*] never-halted.
94. *Furies*] See II.vii.53, note, above.   97. *bloods*] lives.
111–112. *For . . . edge*] i.e., Death holds his court as a judge on Tamburlaine's sharp sword; when Tamburlaine wields the weapon, Death makes his circuit.

And on their points his fleshless body feeds.   115
Techelles, straight go charge a few of them
To charge these dames and show my servant, Death,
Sitting in scarlet on their armed spears.

VIRGINS.

O, pity us!

TAMBURLAINE.

Away with them, I say, and show them Death.   120
                    [Techelles *and others*] *take them away.*
I will not spare these proud Egyptians,
Nor change my martial observations
For all the wealth of Gihon's golden waves,
Or for the love of Venus, would she leave
The angry god of arms and lie with me.   125
They have refus'd the offer of their lives,
And know my customs are as peremptory
As wrathful planets, death, or destiny.

Enter Techelles.

What, have your horsemen shown the virgins Death?
TECHELLES.

They have, my lord, and on Damascus' walls   130
Have hoisted up their slaughtered carcasses.

TAMBURLAINE.

A sight as baneful to their souls, I think,
As are Thessalian drugs or mithridate.
But go, my lords, put the rest to the sword.
                    Exeunt [*all except* Tamburlaine].
Ah, fair Zenocrate, divine Zenocrate!   135
Fair is too foul an epithet for thee,

120.1. Techelles *and others*] *Dyce*;   134.1. *all* . . . Tamburlaine] *Dyce*;
They O1–4.   not in O1–4.

---

115. *fleshless body*] Death is imagined as a skeleton; but he is still robed
in a judge's *scarlet* (l. 118).
122. *observations*] customs.
123. *Gihon*] one of the rivers of Eden (Genesis 2:13).
125. *god of arms*] Mars was the lover of Venus.
133. *Thessalian*] Thessaly was reputed to be the land of witchcraft.
133. *mithridate*] used as an antidote against poison and infection; but
Tamburlaine refers to it as itself a poison.

That in thy passion for thy country's love
And fear to see thy kingly father's harm
With hair dishevell'd wip'st thy watery cheeks;
And like to Flora in her morning's pride,   140
Shaking her silver tresses in the air,
Rain'st on the earth resolved pearl in showers
And sprinklest sapphires on thy shining face,
Where Beauty, mother to the Muses, sits
And comments volumes with her ivory pen,   145
Taking instructions from thy flowing eyes,
Eyes, when that Ebena steps to heaven,
In silence of thy solemn evening's walk,
Making the mantle of the richest night,
The moon, the planets, and the meteors, light.   150
There angels in their crystal armors fight
A doubtful battle with my tempted thoughts
For Egypt's freedom and the Soldan's life,
His life that so consumes Zenocrate,
Whose sorrows lay more siege unto my soul   155
Than all my army to Damascus' walls;
And neither Persians' sovereign nor the Turk
Troubled my senses with conceit of foil
So much by much as doth Zenocrate.
What is beauty, saith my sufferings, then?   160
If all the pens that ever poets held
Had fed the feeling of their masters' thoughts,

151. fight] *O1–2*; fights *O3–4*.

---

137. *passion*] sorrow.

140. *Flora*] the Roman goddess of flowers and spring.

142. *resolved pearl*] melted pearl, i.e., tears.

144. *Beauty . . . Muses*] This genealogy has been substituted by Marlowe for the more usual one that makes Mnemosyne, i.e., Memory, the mother of the Musés.

147–150. *Eyes . . . light*] Tamburlaine declares that Zenocrate's eyes at evening give light to the moon, the planets, and the atmospheric phenomena of every kind.

147. *Ebena*] a deity unknown to classical mythology.

151–159. *There . . . Zenocrate*] Tamburlaine acknowledges that Zenocrate's eyes can come nearer than anything else to making him pause in his career of unremitting conquest.

158. *conceit of foil*] the idea of defeat.

And every sweetness that inspir'd their hearts,
Their minds, and muses on admired themes;
If all the heavenly quintessence they still   165
From their immortal flowers of poesy,
Wherein as in a mirror we perceive
The highest reaches of a human wit;
If these had made one poem's period,
And all combin'd in beauty's worthiness,   170
Yet should there hover in their restless heads
One thought, one grace, one wonder at the least,
Which into words no virtue can digest.
But how unseemly is it for my sex,
My discipline of arms and chivalry,   175
My nature, and the terror of my name,
To harbor thoughts effeminate and faint!
Save only that in beauty's just applause,
With whose instinct the soul of man is touch'd,
And every warrior that is rapt with love   180
Of fame, of valor, and of victory,
Must needs have beauty beat on his conceits.
I thus conceiving and subduing both
That which hath stopp'd the tempest of the gods,

---

165. *quintessence*] According to ancient and medieval philosophy, the heavenly bodies were composed of a "fifth essence," that was actually latent in all things. Alchemists sought to extract this "quintessence" by distillation and other methods.

165. *still*] distill.

168. *wit*] imagination.

169. *made . . . period*] united to form a single poetic whole.

173. *Which . . . digest*] which no power can express in words.

177. *faint*] feeble.

178–190. *Save . . . nobility*] a difficult passage, possibly corrupt. The following paraphrase borrows from that of Ellis-Fermor: "Excepting only that in a just reverence for beauty, with the prompting of which the soul of man is stirred, [lies one of the main sources of valor—] and every soldier . . . needs the stimulus of beauty to urge his thought to its highest achievement. I, who can both apprehend beauty and hold it to its due function, even that beauty which has calmed the rage of the gods themselves so that they have descended from the very height of heaven to feel the humble joys of human emotions and move in spheres no higher than weed-strown cottages—I shall reveal to the world, despite my birth, that manly prowess is alone the highest glory and alone confers true nobility."

Even from the fiery-spangled veil of heaven   185
To feel the lovely warmth of shepherds' flames
And march in cottages of strowed weeds,
Shall give the world to note, for all my birth,
That virtue solely is the sum of glory
And fashions men with true nobility.   190
Who's within there?

Enter two or three.

Hath Bajazeth been fed today?

ATTENDANT.

Ay, my lord.

TAMBURLAINE.

Bring him forth; and let us know if the town be ransack'd.

[*Exeunt* Attendants.]

Enter Techelles, Theridamas, Usumcasane, *and others.*

TECHELLES.

The town is ours, my lord, and fresh supply   195
Of conquest and of spoil is offered us.

TAMBURLAINE.

That's well, Techelles. What's the news?

TECHELLES.

The Soldan and the Arabian king together
March on us with such eager violence
As if there were no way but one with us.   200

TAMBURLAINE.

No more there is not, I warrant thee, Techelles.

They bring in the Turk [Bajazeth *in his cage and* Zabina].

THERIDAMAS.

We know the victory is ours, my lord,

185. fiery-spangled] *O1–2*; spangled
firie *O3–4*.
187. cottages] *O1–2*; cottges *O3*;
coatches *O4*.
194.1 *Exeunt* Attendants] *Dyce*; *not
in O1–4.*

194.2. and] *O1–2*; *with O3–4.*
199. March on us] *O1, O3–4*;
Martcht on with vs *O2*.
201.1. *in* . . . Zabina] *Rob.*; *not in
O1–4.*

189–190. *virtue . . . nobility*] an expansion of the proverb, "Virtue is the
true nobility" (Tilley, V 85).
200. *no . . . one*] "There is no way but one" was a proverbial expression
(Tilley, W 148).

But let us save the reverend Soldan's life
For fair Zenocrate that so laments his state.

TAMBURLAINE.

That will we chiefly see unto, Theridamas,   205
For sweet Zenocrate, whose worthiness
Deserves a conquest over every heart.
And now, my footstool, if I lose the field,
You hope of liberty and restitution.
Here let him stay, my masters, from the tents,   210
Till we have made us ready for the field.
Pray for us, Bajazeth; we are going.

                    Exeunt [all except Bajazeth *and* Zabina].

BAJAZETH.

Go, never to return with victory.
Millions of men encompass thee about
And gore thy body with as many wounds!   215
Sharp, forked arrows light upon thy horse!
Furies from the black Cocytus lake
Break up the earth and with their firebrands
Enforce thee run upon the baneful pikes!
Volleys of shot pierce through thy charmed skin,   220
And every bullet dipp'd in poisoned drugs!
Or roaring cannons sever all thy joints,
Making thee mount as high as eagles soar!

ZABINA.

Let all the swords and lances in the field
Stick in his breast as in their proper rooms!   225
At every pore let blood come dropping forth,
That ling'ring pains may massacre his heart
And madness send his damned soul to hell!

203. reverend] *O1–2*; reuerent *O3–4*.   *O1–4*.
212.1. *all . . .* Zabina] *Dyce*; *not in*   226. pore] *O1–3*; dore *O4*.

---

209. *of*] for.
217. *Furies*] See II.vii.53, note, above.
217. *Cocytus*] A Greek river of this name was supposed to be connected
with Hades. Hence it came to be described as a river in Hades. Marlowe
converts it into a lake.
219. *baneful*] deadly.
225. *in their . . . rooms*] in their own particular places, "where they
belong."

BAJAZETH.

Ah, fair Zabina, we may curse his power,
The heavens may frown, the earth for anger quake,   230
But such a star hath influence in his sword
As rules the skies and countermands the gods
More than Cimmerian Styx or destiny.
And then shall we in this detested guise,
With shame, with hunger, and with horror aye   235
Griping our bowels with retorqued thoughts—
And have no hope to end our ecstasies.

ZABINA.

Then is there left no Mahomet, no god,
No fiend, no fortune, nor no hope of end
To our infamous, monstrous slaveries?   240
Gape earth, and let the fiends infernal view
A hell as hopeless and as full of fear
As are the blasted banks of Erebus,
Where shaking ghosts with ever-howling groans
Hover about the ugly ferryman   245
To get a passage to Elysium.
Why should we live? O, wretches, beggars, slaves!
Why live we, Bajazeth, and build up nests
So high within the region of the air,
By living long in this oppression,   250
That all the world will see and laugh to scorn
The former triumphs of our mightiness
In this obscure infernal servitude?

236. retorqued] *O1–3*; retortued   242. A] *Rob.*; As *O1–4*.
O4.   246. Elysium] *Rob.*; *Elisiã O1–4*.

---

233. *Cimmerian*] See III.ii.77, note, above.
233. *Styx*] the principal river in Hades, by the waters of which the gods themselves swore their most solemn oaths.
236. *retorqued thoughts*] thoughts twisted back upon themselves. After these words, Bajazeth abandons his sentence and quickly brings his speech to a conclusion.
237. *ecstasies*] frenzies.
243. *Erebus*] See IV.i.45, note, above.
245. *ferryman*] Charon, who conveyed the souls of the dead across the rivers of Hades.
246. *Elysium*] The Roman poets, unlike Homer, place the Elysian fields in Hades; Marlowe apparently identifies them with it.

BAJAZETH.

O life more loathsome to my vexed thoughts
Than noisome parbreak of the Stygian snakes,   255
Which fills the nooks of hell with standing air,
Infecting all the ghosts with cureless griefs!
O dreary engines of my loathed sight,
That sees my crown, my honor, and my name
Thrust under yoke and thraldom of a thief,   260
Why feed ye still on day's accursed beams
And sink not quite into my tortur'd soul?
You see my wife, my queen and emperess,
Brought up and propped by the hand of fame,
Queen of fifteen contributory queens,   265
Now thrown to rooms of black abjection,
Smear'd with blots of basest drudgery,
And villainess to shame, disdain, and misery.
Accursed Bajazeth, whose words of ruth,
That would with pity cheer Zabina's heart   270
And make our souls resolve in ceaseless tears,
Sharp hunger bites upon and gripes the root
From whence the issues of my thoughts do break.
O poor Zabina! O my queen, my queen,
Fetch me some water for my burning breast   275
To cool and comfort me with longer date,
That in the shorten'd sequel of my life
I may pour forth my soul into thine arms
With words of love, whose moaning intercourse
Hath hitherto been stay'd with wrath and hate   280
Of our expressless bann'd inflictions.

---

254. thoughts] *O1-2*; thought   266. abjection] *O1, O3*; obiection
O3-4.   *O2, O4*.
261. ye] *O1-3*; you *O4*.   269. ruth] *O1-3*; truth *O4*.

---

255. *noisome . . . snakes*] stinking vomit of the snakes of Styx. See note on
l. 233.
256. *standing*] stagnant.
257. *griefs*] sicknesses, diseases.
258. *engines*] instruments.   266. *abjection*] degradation.
268. *villainess*] bondwoman.   271. *resolve*] dissolve, melt.
276. *date*] term of existence.   280. *stay'd*] stopped, checked.
281. *expressless*] inexpressible.   281. *bann'd*] cursed.

ZABINA.

Sweet Bajazeth, I will prolong thy life
As long as any blood or spark of breath
Can quench or cool the torments of my grief.

She goes out.

BAJAZETH.

Now, Bajazeth, abridge thy baneful days,   285
And beat thy brains out of thy conquer'd head,
Since other means are all forbidden me
That may be ministers of my decay.
O highest lamp of ever-living Jove,
Accursed day, infected with my griefs,   290
Hide now thy stained face in endless night
And shut the windows of the lightsome heavens.
Let ugly Darkness with her rusty coach
Engirt with tempests, wrapp'd in pitchy clouds,
Smother the earth with never-fading mists,   295
And let her horses from their nostrils breathe
Rebellious winds and dreadful thunder-claps
That in this terror Tamburlaine may live,
And my pin'd soul, resolv'd in liquid air,
May still excruciate his tormented thoughts.   300
Then let the stony dart of senseless cold
Pierce through the center of my withered heart
And make a passage for my loathed life!

He brains himself against the cage.

Enter Zabina.

ZABINA.

What do mine eyes behold? My husband dead!
His skull all riven in twain, his brains dash'd out!   305
The brains of Bajazeth, my lord and sovereign!
O Bajazeth, my husband and my lord!
O Bajazeth! O Turk! O emperor! Give him his liquor?

286. thy brains] *O1–2*; the braines   289. ever-living] *O1–3*; euerlasting
O3–4.   *O4*.
                                              299. air] *O3–4*; ay *O1–2*.

---

285. *baneful*] hateful.
288. *decay*] death.   299. *pin'd*] tormented.
299. *resolv'd*] dissolved.   305. *riven*] split.

Not I. Bring milk and fire, and my blood I bring him
again. Tear me in pieces. Give me the sword with a ball of 310
wild-fire upon it. Down with him, down with him! Go
to my child! Away, away, away! Ah, save that infant, save
him, save him! I, even I, speak to her. The sun was down—
streamers white, red, black. Here, here, here! Fling the
meat in his face! Tamburlaine, Tamburlaine! Let the 315
soldiers be buried. Hell, death, Tamburlaine, hell! Make
ready my coach, my chair, my jewels. I come, I come, I
come!   *She runs against the cage and brains herself.*

                    [*Enter*] Zenocrate *with* Anippe.

ZENOCRATE.
          Wretched Zenocrate, that livest to see
          Damascus' walls dy'd with Egyptian blood,   320
          Thy father's subjects and thy countrymen;
          Thy streets strowed with dissevered joints of men
          And wounded bodies gasping yet for life;
          But most accurs'd, to see the sun-bright troop
          Of heavenly virgins and unspotted maids,   325
          Whose looks might make the angry god of arms
          To break his sword and mildly treat of love,
          On horsemen's lances to be hoisted up
          And guiltlessly endure a cruel death.
          For every fell and stout Tartarian steed,   330
          That stamp'd on others with their thund'ring hoofs,
          When all their riders charg'd their quivering spears,
          Began to check the ground and rein themselves,
          Gazing upon the beauty of their looks.
          Ah, Tamburlaine, wert thou the cause of this   335
          That term'st Zenocrate thy dearest love,
          Whose lives were dearer to Zenocrate

310. pieces. Give] *O1, O3–4*; peeces,   317–318. I come, I come, I come]
& giue *O2*.   *O1–2*; I come, I come *O3–4*.
315–316. Let . . . Tamburlaine]   318.1. *Enter*] *O4*; *not in O1–3*.
O1–2; *not in O3–4*.

---

  314. *streamers*] pennons.
  326. *god of arms*] Mars.
  330. *fell and stout*] fierce and proud.
  332. *charg'd*] leveled.   333. *check*] stamp on.

Than her own life, or aught save thine own love?
But see, another bloody spectacle!
Ah, wretched eyes, the enemies of my heart,   340
How are ye glutted with these grievous objects,
And tell my soul more tales of bleeding ruth!
See, see, Anippe, if they breathe or no.

ANIPPE.

No breath, nor sense, nor motion in them both.
Ah, madam, this their slavery hath enforc'd,   345
And ruthless cruelty of Tamburlaine.

ZENOCRATE.

Earth, cast up fountains from thy entrails,
And wet thy cheeks for their untimely deaths;
Shake with their weight in sign of fear and grief.
Blush, heaven, that gave them honor at their birth   350
And let them die a death so barbarous.
Those that are proud of fickle empery
And place their chiefest good in earthly pomp.
Behold the Turk and his great emperess!
Ah, Tamburlaine, my love, sweet Tamburlaine,   355
That fights for scepters and for slippery crowns,
Behold the Turk and his great emperess!
Thou that in conduct of thy happy stars
Sleep'st every night with conquest on thy brows,
And yet wouldst shun the wavering turns of war.   360
In fear and feeling of the like distress,
Behold the Turk and his great emperess!
Ah, mighty Jove and holy Mahomet,
Pardon my love! O, pardon his contempt
Of earthly fortune and respect of pity,   365
And let not conquest, ruthlessly pursu'd,
Be equally against his life incens'd
In this great Turk and hapless emperess!
And pardon me that was not mov'd with ruth
To see them live so long in misery.   370
Ah, what may chance to thee, Zenocrate?

347. thy] *O1–2*; thine *O3–4*.   360. war] *O1–2*; warres *O3–4*.
356. fights] *O1–2*; fightst *O3–4*.

---

358. *in conduct*] under the guidance.
365. *and respect*] and of consideration.   368. *In*] as in.

ANIPPE.

Madam, content yourself, and be resolv'd
Your love hath Fortune so at his command
That she shall stay and turn her wheel no more
As long as life maintains his mighty arm   375
That fights for honor to adorn your head.

Enter [Philemus,] *a Messenger.*

ZENOCRATE.

What other heavy news now brings Philemus?

PHILEMUS.

Madam, your father and th'Arabian king,
The first affecter of your excellence,
Comes now, as Turnus 'gainst Aeneas did,   380
Armed with lance into the Egyptian fields,
Ready for battle 'gainst my lord the king.

ZENOCRATE.

Now shame and duty, love and fear presents
A thousand sorrows to my martyred soul.
Whom should I wish the fatal victory,   385
When my poor pleasures are divided thus
And rack'd by duty from my cursed heart?
My father and my first betrothed love
Must fight against my life and present love,
Wherein the change I use condemns my faith   390
And makes my deeds infamous through the world.
But as the gods, to end the Trojans' toil,
Prevented Turnus of Lavinia
And fatally enrich'd Aeneas' love,
So, for a final issue to my griefs,   395
To pacify my country and my love,
Must Tamburlaine by their resistless powers
With virtue of a gentle victory
Conclude a league of honor to my hope;

395. final] *O1, O3–4*; small *O2.*

---

379. *affecter*] lover.
380. *Turnus 'gainst Aeneas*] rivals for the hand of Lavinia in Virgil's
Aeneid. Aeneas wins her despite her previous betrothal to Turnus.
390. *use*] have carried into effect, have made.
392–394. *as . . . love*] See note on l. 380.
399. *to*] in accordance with.

Then, as the powers divine have preordain'd,   400
With happy safety of my father's life
Send like defense of fair Arabia.

They sound to the battle. And Tamburlaine *enjoys the victory. After,*
Arabia *enters, wounded.*

KING OF ARABIA.
        What cursed power guides the murdering hands
        Of this infamous tyrant's soldiers
        That no escape may save their enemies   405
        Nor fortune keep themselves from victory?
        Lie down, Arabia, wounded to the death,
        And let Zenocrate's fair eyes behold
        That, as for her thou bear'st these wretched arms,
        Even so for her thou diest in these arms,   410
        Leaving thy blood for witness of thy love.
ZENOCRATE.
        Too dear a witness for such love, my lord.
        Behold Zenocrate, the cursed object
        Whose fortunes never mastered her griefs.
        Behold her wounded in conceit for thee,   415
        As much as thy fair body is for me.
KING OF ARABIA.
        Then shall I die with full contented heart,
        Having beheld divine Zenocrate,
        Whose sight with joy would take away my life
        As now it bringeth sweetness to my wound,   420
        If I had not been wounded as I am.
        Ah, that the deadly pangs I suffer now
        Would lend an hour's license to my tongue
        To make discourse of some sweet accidents
        Have chanc'd thy merits in this worthless bondage,   425
        And that I might be privy to the state

411. thy blood]   *O1, O3–4*; my
blood *O2.*

---

415. *conceit*] imagination.
424. *sweet accidents*] favorable occurrences.
425. *Have*] that have.
426. *privy to*] in the secret regarding.

Of thy deserv'd contentment and thy love.
But, making now a virtue of thy sight
To drive all sorrow from my fainting soul,
Since death denies me further cause of joy, 430
Depriv'd of care, my heart with comfort dies
Since thy desired hand shall close mine eyes. [*Dies.*]

Enter Tamburlaine *leading the* Soldan, Techelles, Theridamas,
Usumcasane, *with others.*

TAMBURLAINE.
    Come, happy father of Zenocrate,
    A title higher than thy Soldan's name.
    Though my right hand have thus enthralled thee, 435
    Thy princely daughter here shall set thee free,
    She that hath calm'd the fury of my sword,
    Which had ere this been bath'd in streams of blood
    As vast and deep as Euphrates or Nile.
ZENOCRATE.
    O sight thrice welcome to my joyful soul, 440
    To see the king my father issue safe
    From dangerous battle of my conquering love!
SOLDAN OF EGYPT.
    Well met, my only dear Zenocrate,
    Though with the loss of Egypt and my crown.
TAMBURLAINE.
    'Twas I, my lord, that gat the victory, 445
    And therefore grieve not at your overthrow,
    Since I shall render all into your hands,
    And add more strength to your dominions
    Than ever yet confirm'd th'Egyptian crown.
    The god of war resigns his room to me, 450
    Meaning to make me general of the world;
    Jove, viewing me in arms, looks pale and wan,

432. S.D. *Dies*] *Rob.; not in O1–4. in O2.*
432.2. Usumcasane] *O1, O3–4; not* 435. have] *O1–2;* hath *O3–4.*

442. *of*] with.
445. *gat*] got.
449. *confirm'd*] established firmly.
450. *The . . . room*] Mars resigns his function.

Fearing my power should pull him from his throne;
Where'er I come the Fatal Sisters sweat,
And grisly Death, by running to and fro   455
To do their ceaseless homage to my sword;
And here in Afric, where it seldom rains,
Since I arriv'd with my triumphant host,
Have swelling clouds drawn from wide-gasping wounds
Been oft resolv'd in bloody purple showers,   460
A meteor that might terrify the earth
And make it quake at every drop it drinks.
Millions of souls sit on the banks of Styx,
Waiting the back return of Charon's boat;
Hell and Elysium swarm with ghosts of men   465
That I have sent from sundry foughten fields
To spread my fame through hell and up to heaven.
And see, my lord, a sight of strange import,
Emperors and kings lie breathless at my feet.
The Turk and his great empress, as it seems,   470
Left to themselves while we were at the fight,
Have desperately dispatch'd their slavish lives;
With them Arabia too hath left his life;
All sights of power to grace my victory.
And such are objects fit for Tamburlaine,   475
Wherein, as in a mirror, may be seen
His honor, that consists in shedding blood
When men presume to manage arms with him.

SOLDAN OF EGYPT.

Mighty hath God and Mahomet made thy hand,
Renowned Tamburlaine, to whom all kings   480
Of force must yield their crowns and emperies;
And I am pleas'd with this my overthrow
If as beseems a person of thy state
Thou hast with honor us'd Zenocrate.

453. should] *O1–2*; shall *O3–4*.   463. Millions] *O1–3*; Million *O4*.
454. sweat] *O1–2*; sweare *O3–4*.   465. Elysium] *Rob.*; *Elisian O1–4*.

453. *pull . . . throne*] as he had pulled Saturn. See II.vii.13, note, above.
454. *Fatal Sisters*] See I.ii.174, note, above.
461. *meteor*] atmospheric phenomenon. See I.i.11, note, above.
463–465. *Millions . . . ghosts*] For Styx, Charon, and Elysium, see notes on
ll. 233, 245, and 246.

TAMBURLAINE.

    Her state and person wants no pomp, you see,   485
    And for all blot of foul inchastity,
    I record heaven, her heavenly self is clear.
    Then let me find no further time to grace
    Her princely temples with the Persian crown;
    But here these kings that on my fortunes wait,   490
    And have been crown'd for proved worthiness
    Even by this hand that shall establish them,
    Shall now, adjoining all their hands with mine,
    Invest her here my Queen of Persia.
    What saith the noble Soldan and Zenocrate?   495

SOLDAN OF EGYPT.

    I yield with thanks and protestations
    Of endless honor to thee for her love.

TAMBURLAINE.

    Then doubt I not but fair Zenocrate
    Will soon consent to satisfy us both.

ZENOCRATE.

    Else should I much forget myself, my lord.   500

THERIDAMAS.

    Then let us set the crown upon her head,
    That long hath linger'd for so high a seat.

TECHELLES.

    My hand is ready to perform the deed,
    For now her marriage-time shall work us rest.

USUMCASANE.

    And here's the crown, my lord; help set it on.   505

TAMBURLAINE.

    Then sit thou down, divine Zenocrate,
    And here we crown thee Queen of Persia
    And all the kingdoms and dominions
    That late the power of Tamburlaine subdued.

494. my] *O1, O3–4*; the *O2*.   500. Else] *O1, O3–4*; Then *O2*.
498. I not] *O1–2*; not I *O3–4*.   505. on] *O1, O3–4*; *not in O2*.

---

  485. *wants*] lacks.   486. *for*] from.
  487. *record heaven*] call heaven to witness.
  493. *adjoining*] uniting.
  497. *for her love*] for your love of her.
  504. *work us*] bring about for us.

As Juno, when the giants were suppress'd   510
That darted mountains at her brother Jove,
So looks my love, shadowing in her brows
Triumphs and trophies for my victories;
Or as Latona's daughter bent to arms,
Adding more courage to my conquering mind.   515
To gratify thee, sweet Zenocrate,
Egyptians, Moors, and men of Asia,
From Barbary unto the Western Indie,
Shall pay a yearly tribute to thy sire;
And from the bounds of Afric to the banks   520
Of Ganges shall his mighty arm extend.
And now, my lords and loving followers,
That purchas'd kingdoms by your martial deeds,
Cast off your armor, put on scarlet robes,
Mount up your royal places of estate,   525
Environed with troops of noblemen,
And there make laws to rule your provinces.
Hang up your weapons on Alcides' post,
For Tamburlaine takes truce with all the world.
Thy first-betrothed love, Arabia,   530
Shall we with honor, as beseems, entomb
With this great Turk and his fair emperess.
Then, after all these solemn exequies,
We will our celebrated rites of marriage solemnize.

                                                    [*Exeunt.*]

Finis Actus Quinti et Ultimi huius
Primae Partis.

516. thee, sweet] *Dyce 2*; the sweet   534.1. *Exeunt*] *Dyce 2*; *not in O1–4.*
O1–4.   534.2–3. *Actus . . . Partis*] *O1–3*; *not*
531. as beseems] *O1, O3–4*; as best   *in O4.*
beseemes *O2.*

510–511. *As . . . Jove*] See II.vi.1–6, note, above. Marlowe seems to have
had no classical authority for introducing Juno, the sister and wife of
Jupiter, into the story.
512. *shadowing*] harboring.
514. *Latona's daughter*] Diana (Artemis), the huntress.
523. *purchas'd*] won, obtained.   525. *estate*] authority.
528. *Alcides' post*] the doorpost of the temple of Alcides (Hercules).
534. 2–3. *Finis . . . Partis*] the end of the fifth and last act of this first part.

TAMBURLAINE THE GREAT

Part II

[CHARACTERS OF THE PLAY

TAMBURLAINE, KING OF PERSIA
CALYPHAS ⎫
AMYRAS   ⎬ *his sons*
CELEBINUS ⎭
THERIDAMAS, KING OF ARGIER   5
TECHELLES, KING OF FEZ
USUMCASANE, KING OF MOROCCO
ORCANES, KING OF NATOLIA
KING OF JERUSALEM
KING OF SORIA   10
KING OF TREBIZON
GAZELLUS, VICEROY OF BYRON
URIBASSA
SIGISMUND, KING OF HUNGARY
FREDERICK ⎫   15
BALDWIN   ⎬ *peers of Hungary*
CALLAPINE, *son of Bajazeth and prisoner of Tamburlaine*
ALMEDA, *his keeper*
KING OF AMASIA
GOVERNOR OF BABYLON   20
TWO CAPTAINS
The SON *of the Captain commanding Balsera*
MAXIMUS
PERDICAS
LORDS, CITIZENS, SOLDIERS, PIONERS, PHYSICIANS, MESSENGERS,   25
    and ATTENDANTS

ZENOCRATE, *wife of Tamburlaine*
OLYMPIA, *wife of the Captain commanding Balsera*
Turkish CONCUBINES]

---

5. *Argier*] Algeria.   8. *Natolia*] Asia Minor.
10. *Soria*] Syria.
12. *Byron*] a town near Babylon.
19. *Amasia*] a province in northern Asia Minor.
22. *Balsera*] This is the common Elizabethan form of the modern Basra.
Seaton suggests (p. 24) that Marlowe was thinking of Passera, a town on
the northern or Natolian frontier of Soria; written with its first "s" long,
"Passera" might well have been read from the map by him as "Balsera."
25. *Pioners*] trench-diggers.

Tamburlaine the Great

The Second Part of The Bloody Conquests of Mighty Tamburlaine. With his impassionate fury for the death of his lady and love, fair Zenocrate, his form of exhortation and discipline to his three sons, and the manner of his own death.

THE PROLOGUE

The general welcomes Tamburlaine receiv'd
When he arrived last upon our stage
Hath made our poet pen his second part,
Where death cuts off the progress of his pomp
And murd'rous fates throws all his triumphs down.   5
But what became of fair Zenocrate,
And with how many cities' sacrifice
He celebrated her sad funeral,
Himself in presence shall unfold at large.

[I.i]
[*Enter*] Orcanes, King of Natolia; Gazellus, Viceroy of Byron; Uribassa, *and their train, with drums and trumpets.*

ORCANES.

Egregious viceroys of these eastern parts,
Plac'd by the issue of great Bajazeth,

With . . . death] *O1–3; not in O4.*   5. triumphs] *O1–3; tryumph O4.*
[The Prologue]   8. sad] *Rob.; said O1–4.*
2. our] *O1–3; the O4.*

0.1. *Natolia*] Asia Minor.
0.1. *Byron*] a town near Babylon.
0.2. *train*] retinue.
1. *Egregious*] eminent, distinguished.   2. *issue*] offspring.

And sacred lord, the mighty Callapine,
Who lives in Egypt prisoner to that slave
Which kept his father in an iron cage,   5
Now have we march'd from fair Natolia
Two hundred leagues, and on Danubius' banks
Our warlike host in complete armor rest,
Where Sigismund, the king of Hungary,
Should meet our person to conclude a truce.   10
What, shall we parle with the Christian,
Or cross the stream and meet him in the field?

GAZELLUS.

King of Natolia, let us treat of peace.
We all are glutted with the Christians' blood,
And have a greater foe to fight against,   15
Proud Tamburlaine, that now in Asia
Near Guyron's head doth set his conquering feet
And means to fire Turkey as he goes.
'Gainst him, my lord, must you address your power.

URIBASSA.

Besides, King Sigismund hath brought from Christendom   20
More than his camp of stout Hungarians:
Slavonians, Almains, Rutters, Muffs, and Danes,
That with the halberd, lance, and murdering axe
Will hazard that we might with surety hold.

ORCANES.

Though from the shortest northern parallel,   25
Vast Gruntland, compass'd with the frozen sea,
Inhabited with tall and sturdy men,

19. must you] *O1, O3–4*; you must
O2.

---

11. *parle*] hold a parley.
17. *Guyron*] a town near the upper Euphrates, not far from the Natolian border.
19. *address*] direct.   22. *Slavonians*] Slavs.
22. *Almains*] Germans.   22. *Rutters*] cavalrymen.
22. *Muffs*] a derogatory name for Germans or Swiss.
23. *halberd*] long-handled military weapon combining the features of a spear and a battle-axe.
24. *hazard that*] endanger that which.
25. *from . . . parallel*] from beyond the most northerly line of latitude.
26. *Gruntland*] Greenland.

Giants as big as hugy Polypheme,
Millions of soldiers cut the arctic line,
Bringing the strength of Europe to these arms,   30
Our Turkey blades shall glide through all their throats
And make this champion mead a bloody fen.
Danubius' stream, that runs to Trebizon,
Shall carry wrapp'd within his scarlet waves
As martial presents to our friends at home   35
The slaughtered bodies of these Christians.
The Terrene main, wherein Danubius falls,
Shall by this battle be the Bloody Sea.
The wand'ring sailors of proud Italy
Shall meet those Christians fleeting with the tide,   40
Beating in heaps against their argosies,
And make fair Europe, mounted on her bull,

29. cut the] *O1–2*; out the *O3*; out
of *O4*.

---

28. *Giants*] It was "a commonplace that in early times northern Scandinavia was peopled by giants. To take a single example, Olaus Magnus
entitled the fifth book of his *Historia* [*de Gentibvs Septentrionalibvs* (Rome,
1555)] 'De Gigantibvs,' and in several places refers to the *Gigantes septen-
trionales*. As evidence of their former existence in the extreme north . . . he
cites, quoting from Saxo Grammaticus, the colossal stone monuments of
those areas, which could not have been made by men of human size"
(R. I. Page, "Lapland Sorcerers," *Saga-Book*, XVI (1963–1964), 215–232).
Marlowe refers to "Lapland giants" in the opening scene of *Doctor Faustus*;
the present passage shows that he imagined such creatures as occupying
other arctic regions as well as northern Scandinavia.

28. *hugy*] huge.

28. *Polypheme*] a one-eyed, man-eating giant whom Ulysses blinded in
order to save himself from destruction.

29. *cut . . . line*] cross the arctic circle from the north.

32. *champion mead*] level, open meadow-land.

33–41. *Danubius' . . . argosies*] Marlowe "sees the waters of the Danube
sweeping from the river-mouths in two strong currents, the one racing
across the Black Sea to Trebizond, the other swirling southwards to the
Bosporus, and so onward to the Hellespont and the Aegean. Both currents
bear the slaughtered bodies of Christian soldiers" (Seaton, p. 33).

37. *Terrene*] Mediterranean.   40. *fleeting*] floating.

41. *argosies*] large merchant-vessels.

42. *Europe*] When Europa's beauty charmed Zeus, he assumed the
shape of a bull and mingled with her father's herds. She caressed him and
sat upon his back. He thereupon plunged into the sea and swam with her
to Crete.

Trapp'd with the wealth and riches of the world,
Alight and wear a woeful mourning weed.

GAZELLUS.

Yet, stout Orcanes, prorex of the world,   45
Since Tamburlaine hath muster'd all his men,
Marching from Cairo northward with his camp
To Alexandria and the frontier towns,
Meaning to make a conquest of our land,
'Tis requisite to parle for a peace   50
With Sigismund, the king of Hungary,
And save our forces for the hot assaults
Proud Tamburlaine intends Natolia.

ORCANES.

Viceroy of Byron, wisely hast thou said.
My realm, the center of our empery,   55
Once lost, all Turkey would be overthrown;
And for that cause the Christians shall have peace.
Slavonians, Almains, Rutters, Muffs, and Danes
Fear nor Orcanes, but great Tamburlaine,
Nor he, but Fortune that hath made him great.   60
We have revolted Grecians, Albanese,
Sicilians, Jews, Arabians, Turks, and Moors,
Natolians, Sorians, black Egyptians,
Illyrians, Thracians, and Bithynians,
Enough to swallow forceless Sigismund,   65
Yet scarce enough t'encounter Tamburlaine.
He brings a world of people to the field.
From Scythia to the oriental plage
Of India, where raging Lantchidol
Beats on the regions with his boisterous blows,   70
That never seaman yet discovered,

63. Sorians, black] *O1*; Syrians, black *O2*; Sorians, and black *O3–4*. 63–64.] *O1–2*; *separated by the inter-* *vention of l. 118 in O3–4.* 64. Illyrians] *O3–4*; Illicians *O1–2*. 68. plage] *O1–2*; Place *O3–4*.

43. *Trapp'd*] adorned.   44. *weed*] garment.
45. *prorex*] viceroy.   55. *empery*] empire.
58. *Slavonians . . . Muffs*] See notes on l. 22.
59. *Fear*] frighten.   63. *Sorians*] Syrians.
68. *oriental plage*] eastern shore.
69. *Lantchidol*] a stretch of the Indian Ocean.

All Asia is in arms with Tamburlaine.
Even from the midst of fiery Cancer's tropic
To Amazonia under Capricorn,
And thence as far as Archipelago,   75
All Afric is in arms with Tamburlaine.
Therefore, viceroys, the Christians must have peace.

[*Enter*] Sigismund, Frederick, *Baldwin, and their train, with drums and trumpets.*

SIGISMUND.

    Orcanes, as our legates promis'd thee,
    We with our peers have cross'd Danubius' stream
    To treat of friendly peace or deadly war.   80
    Take which thou wilt, for, as the Romans us'd,
    I here present thee with a naked sword.
    Wilt thou have war, then shake this blade at me;
    If peace, restore it to my hands again,
    And I will sheathe it to confirm the same.   85

ORCANES.

    Stay, Sigismund. Forgett'st thou I am he
    That with the cannon shook Vienna walls
    And made it dance upon the continent,
    As when the massy substance of the earth
    Quiver about the axletree of heaven?   90
    Forgett'st thou that I sent a shower of darts,
    Mingled with powdered shot and feathered steel,
    So thick upon the blink-ey'd burghers' heads
    That thou thyself, then County Palatine,
    The King of Boheme, and the Austric Duke   95
    Sent heralds out which basely on their knees
    In all your names desir'd a truce of me?

72. in] *O1–2, O4; not in O3.*   77. viceroys] *O1, O3–4;* Viceroie
                                  O2.

   73–75. *from . . . Archipelago*] from the Canaries, where the meridian line intersects the tropic of Cancer, southward to Amazonia (near to the supposed source of the Nile) and the land under Capricorn, and thence northward again to the Aegean islands.
   90. *axletree of heaven*] See Part I, IV. ii.50, note.
   93. *blink-ey'd*] i.e., unable, in their fear, to look steadily upon the missiles.
   95. *Austric*] Austrian.

Forgett'st thou that to have me raise my siege
Wagons of gold were set before my tent,
Stamp'd with the princely fowl that in her wings   100
Carries the fearful thunderbolts of Jove?
How canst thou think of this and offer war?

SIGISMUND.

Vienna was besieg'd, and I was there,
Then County Palatine, but now a king,
And what we did was in extremity.   105
But now, Orcanes, view my royal host
That hides these plains and seems as vast and wide
As doth the desert of Arabia
To those that stand on Bagdet's lofty tower,
Or as the ocean to the traveler   110
That rests upon the snowy Apennines,
And tell me whether I should stoop so low,
Or treat of peace with the Natolian king?

GAZELLUS.

Kings of Natolia and of Hungary,
We came from Turkey to confirm a league,   115
And not to dare each other to the field.
A friendly parle might become ye both.

FREDERICK.

And we from Europe to the same intent,
Which if your general refuse or scorn
Our tents are pitch'd, our men stand in array,   120
Ready to charge you ere you stir your feet.

ORCANES.

So prest are we. But yet, if Sigismund
Speak as a friend and stand not upon terms,
Here is his sword. Let peace be ratified
On these conditions specified before,   125
Drawn with advice of our ambassadors.

117. ye] *O1, O3–4*; you *O2*.   *and 64 in O3–4.*
118.] *O1–2; inserted between ll. 63*   120. stand] *O1–2*; are *O3–4.*

100–101. *the . . . Jove*] the eagle. Supposedly invulnerable to lightning,
it was reputed to be Jove's armor-bearer.
109. *Bagdet*] Baghdad.
117. *parle*] discussion, parley.   122. *prest*] ready.
123. *stand . . . terms*] does not insist upon conditions.

SIGISMUND.

    Then here I sheathe it and give thee my hand,
    Never to draw it out or manage arms
    Against thyself or thy confederates,
    But whilst I live will be at truce with thee.   130

ORCANES.

    But, Sigismund, confirm it with an oath
    And swear in sight of heaven and by thy Christ.

SIGISMUND.

    By Him that made the world and sav'd my soul,
    The Son of God and issue of a maid,
    Sweet Jesus Christ, I solemnly protest   135
    And vow to keep this peace inviolable.

ORCANES.

    By sacred Mahomet, the friend of God,
    Whose holy Alcoran remains with us,
    Whose glorious body, when he left the world,
    Clos'd in a coffin mounted up the air   140
    And hung on stately Mecca's temple roof,
    I swear to keep this truce inviolable.
    Of whose conditions and our solemn oaths,
    Sign'd with our hands, each shall retain a scroll
    As memorable witness of our league.   145
    Now, Sigismund, if any Christian king
    Encroach upon the confines of thy realm,
    Send word Orcanes of Natolia
    Confirm'd this league beyond Danubius' stream,
    And they will, trembling, sound a quick retreat;   150
    So am I fear'd among all nations.

SIGISMUND.

    If any heathen potentate or king
    Invade Natolia, Sigismund will send
    A hundred thousand horse train'd to the war
    And back'd by stout lancers of Germany,   155

---

128. or] *O1–2*; and *O3–4*.
143. conditions] *O1, O3–4*; condition *O2*.
149. Confirm'd] *O1, O3–4*; Confirme *O2*.
155. by] *O1–2*; with *O3–4*.

---

128. *manage arms*] wage war.
138. *Alcoran*] See Part I, III.iii.76, note.
147. *confines*] borders.

The strength and sinews of the imperial seat.

ORCANES.

I thank thee, Sigismund; but, when I war,
All Asia Minor, Africa, and Greece
Follow my standard and my thund'ring drums.
Come, let us go and banquet in our tents.   160
I will dispatch chief of my army hence
To fair Natolia and to Trebizon
To stay my coming 'gainst proud Tamburlaine.
Friend Sigismund and peers of Hungary,
Come, banquet and carouse with us a while,   165
And then depart we to our territories.   *Exeunt.*

[I.ii]   [*Enter*] Callapine *with* Almeda, *his keeper.*

CALLAPINE.

Sweet Almeda, pity the ruthful plight
Of Callapine, the son of Bajazeth,
Born to be monarch of the western world,
Yet here detain'd by cruel Tamburlaine.

ALMEDA.

My lord, I pity it, and with my heart   5
Wish your release; but he whose wrath is death,
My sovereign lord, renowned Tamburlaine,
Forbids you further liberty than this.

CALLAPINE.

Ah, were I now but half so eloquent
To paint in words what I'll perform in deeds,   10
I know thou wouldst depart from hence with me.

ALMEDA.

Not for all Afric; therefore move me not.

CALLAPINE.

Yet hear me speak, my gentle Almeda.

ALMEDA.

No speech to that end, by your favor, sir.

---

161. *chief*] the best part, most.
163. *stay*] await.
[I.ii]
3. *western world*] Turkish empire (as seen from Asia).
12. *move*] urge.

CALLAPINE.

By Cairo runs—   15

ALMEDA.

No talk of running, I tell you, sir.

CALLAPINE.

A little further, gentle Almeda.

ALMEDA.

Well, sir, what of this?

CALLAPINE.

By Cairo runs to Alexandria bay

Darote's streams, wherein at anchor lies   20

A Turkish galley of my royal fleet,

Waiting my coming to the river side,

Hoping by some means I shall be releas'd,

Which when I come aboard will hoist up sail

And soon put forth into the Terrene sea,   25

Where 'twixt the isles of Cyprus and of Crete

We quickly may in Turkish seas arrive.

Then shalt thou see a hundred kings and more,

Upon their knees, all bid me welcome home.

Amongst so many crowns of burnish'd gold,   30

Choose which thou wilt, all are at thy command.

A thousand galleys mann'd with Christian slaves

I freely give thee, which shall cut the Straits

And bring armadoes from the coasts of Spain,

Fraughted with gold of rich America.   35

The Grecian virgins shall attend on thee,

Skilful in music and in amorous lays,

As fair as was Pygmalion's ivory girl

Or lovely Io metamorphosed.

20. at] *O1, O3–4*; an *O2*.   34. from] *O1, O3–4*; to *O2*.
28. a] *O1–2*; an *O3–4*.

---

20. *Darote*] a town "on the river-way from Cairo to Alexandria" (Seaton, p. 28).

31. *at thy command*] at your disposal, available to you.

34. *armadoes*] fleets of warships.

35. *Fraughted*] laden.

38. *Pygmalion's ivory girl*] When Pygmalion fell in love with a statue that he had made of a woman, the goddess Aphrodite gave the statue life.

39. *Io*] Loved by Zeus, she was transformed into a heifer through fear of Hera, his wife.

With naked negroes shall thy coach be drawn,   40
And, as thou rid'st in triumph through the streets,
The pavement underneath thy chariot wheels
With Turkey carpets shall be covered,
And cloth of Arras hung about the walls,
Fit objects for thy princely eye to pierce.   45
A hundred bassoes cloth'd in crimson silk
Shall ride before thee on Barbarian steeds;
And, when thou goest, a golden canopy
Enchas'd with precious stones, which shine as bright
As that fair veil that covers all the world   50
When Phoebus, leaping from his hemisphere,
Descendeth downward to th'Antipodes—
And more than this, for all I cannot tell.

ALMEDA.

How far hence lies the galley, say you?

CALLAPINE.

Sweet Almeda, scarce half a league from hence.   55

ALMEDA.

But need we not be spied going aboard?

CALLAPINE.

Betwixt the hollow hanging of a hill
And crooked bending of a craggy rock,
The sails wrapp'd up, the mast and tacklings down,
She lies so close that none can find her out.   60

ALMEDA.

I like that well. But tell me, my lord, if I should let you go,
would you be as good as your word? Shall I be made a
king for my labor?

CALLAPINE.

As I am Callapine the emperor,

---

44. *cloth of Arras*] rich tapestry fabric.
46. *bassoes*] high-ranking Turkish officers, pashas.
47. *Barbarian steeds*] Barbary steeds. Compare Part I, III.i.1 and III.iii.16
and notes.
48. *thou goest*] you walk.
49. *Enchas'd*] adorned. See Part I, I.ii.96, note.
51. *Phoebus*] the sun, here described as setting.
56. *need we not*] shall we not inevitably.
60. *close*] concealed.

And by the hand of Mahomet I swear,   65
Thou shalt be crown'd a king and be my mate.

ALMEDA.

Then here I swear, as I am Almeda,
Your keeper under Tamburlaine the Great,
For that's the style and title I have yet,
Although he sent a thousand armed men   70
To intercept this haughty enterprise,
Yet would I venture to conduct your grace
And die before I brought you back again.

CALLAPINE.

Thanks, gentle Almeda. Then let us haste,
Lest time be past and ling'ring let us both.   75

ALMEDA.

When you will, my lord. I am ready.

CALLAPINE.

Even straight. And farewell, cursed Tamburlaine.
Now go I to revenge my father's death.   *Exeunt.*

[I.iii]

[*Enter*] Tamburlaine, *with* Zenocrate, *and his three sons,* Calyphas,
Amyras, *and* Celebinus, *with drums and trumpets.*

TAMBURLAINE.

Now, bright Zenocrate, the world's fair eye,
Whose beams illuminate the lamps of heaven,
Whose cheerful looks do clear the cloudy air
And clothe it in a crystal livery,
Now rest thee here on fair Larissa plains,   5
Where Egypt and the Turkish empire parts,
Between thy sons that shall be emperors
And every one commander of a world.

ZENOCRATE.

Sweet Tamburlaine, when wilt thou leave these arms
And save thy sacred person free from scathe   10

---

66. *mate*] equal.   69. *style*] designation, title.
71. *haughty*] high-spirited.   75. *let*] hinder.
77. *straight*] immediately, straightway.
[I.iii]
5. *Larissa*] a town on the coast south of Gaza.

And dangerous chances of the wrathful war?

TAMBURLAINE.

When heaven shall cease to move on both the poles,
And when the ground whereon my soldiers march
Shall rise aloft and touch the horned moon,
And not before, my sweet Zenocrate.   15
Sit up and rest thee like a lovely queen.
So, now she sits in pomp and majesty,
When these my sons, more precious in mine eyes
Than all the wealthy kingdoms I subdued,
Plac'd by her side, look on their mother's face.   20
But yet methinks their looks are amorous,
Not martial as the sons of Tamburlaine.
Water and air, being symboliz'd in one,
Argue their want of courage and of wit;
Their hair as white as milk and soft as down,   25
Which should be like the quills of porcupines,
As black as jet and hard as iron or steel,
Bewrays they are too dainty for the wars;
Their fingers made to quaver on a lute,
Their arms to hang about a lady's neck,   30
Their legs to dance and caper in the air
Would make me think them bastards, not my sons,
But that I know they issued from thy womb
That never look'd on man but Tamburlaine.

ZENOCRATE.

My gracious lord, they have their mother's looks,   35
But, when they list, their conquering father's heart.
This lovely boy, the youngest of the three,
Not long ago bestrid a Scythian steed,

---

25. and] O1–2; as O3–4.

---

21. amorous] loving, gentle.
23–24. Water . . . wit] "The moist and cold qualities of water (corresponding to the phlegmatic humor) and the moist and hot qualities of air (corresponding to the sanguine humor) argue ill for the temperament which is overbalanced in these directions and lacks the firmness and fierceness due to a just admixture of the bile and choler (earth and fire)" (Ellis-Fermor).
28. Bewrays] reveals.
36. list] wish, choose.

Trotting the ring, and tilting at a glove,
Which when he tainted with his slender rod,   40
He rein'd him straight and made him so curvet
As I cried out for fear he should have fall'n.

TAMBURLAINE.

Well done, my boy! Thou shalt have shield and lance,
Armor of proof, horse, helm, and curtle-axe,
And I will teach thee how to charge thy foe   45
And harmless run among the deadly pikes.
If thou wilt love the wars and follow me,
Thou shalt be made a king and reign with me,
Keeping in iron cages emperors.
If thou exceed thy elder brothers' worth   50
And shine in complete virtue more than they,
Thou shalt be king before them, and thy seed
Shall issue crowned from their mother's womb.

CELEBINUS.

Yes, father, you shall see me if I live
Have under me as many kings as you,   55
And march with such a multitude of men
As all the world shall tremble at their view.

TAMBURLAINE.

These words assure me, boy, thou art my son.
When I am old and cannot manage arms,
Be thou the scourge and terror of the world.   60

AMYRAS.

Why may not I, my lord, as well as he,
Be term'd the scourge and terror of the world?

TAMBURLAINE.

Be all a scourge and terror to the world,
Or else you are not sons of Tamburlaine.

57. shall] *O1–3*; should *O4*.   62. of] *O1–3*; to *O4*.
58. words] *O1–2, O4*; word *O3*.   63. to] *O1–3*; of *O4*.

---

39. *tilting*] riding with a lance at a mark (here a glove).
40. *tainted*] touched, hit.
41. *curvet*] execute a leap which involved raising the forelegs and then springing off the hind legs while the forelegs were still in the air.
44. *proof*] tested strength.
44. *curtle-axe*] heavy slashing sword, cutlass.
51. *virtue*] valor, bravery.

CALYPHAS.

But while my brothers follow arms, my lord,   65
Let me accompany my gracious mother.
They are enough to conquer all the world,
And you have won enough for me to keep.

TAMBURLAINE.

Bastardly boy, sprung from some coward's loins,
And not the issue of great Tamburlaine!   70
Of all the provinces I have subdued
Thou shalt not have a foot, unless thou bear
A mind courageous and invincible;
For he shall wear the crown of Persia
Whose head hath deepest scars, whose breast most wounds, 75
Which being wroth sends lightning from his eyes,
And in the furrows of his frowning brows
Harbors revenge, war, death, and cruelty;
For in a field, whose superficies
Is covered with a liquid purple veil   80
And sprinkled with the brains of slaughtered men,
My royal chair of state shall be advanc'd;
And he that means to place himself therein
Must armed wade up to the chin in blood.

ZENOCRATE.

My lord, such speeches to our princely sons   85
Dismays their minds before they come to prove
The wounding troubles angry war affords.

CELEBINUS.

No, madam, these are speeches fit for us,
For if his chair were in a sea of blood
I would prepare a ship and sail to it,   90
Ere I would lose the title of a king.

AMYRAS.

And I would strive to swim through pools of blood
Or make a bridge of murdered carcasses,

79. superficies] *Rob.*; superfluities   92. through] *O1, O3–4*; thorow
O1–4.   *O2.*
                                        93. carcasses] *O1–3*; Carkasse *O4.*

---

76. *Which*] who.   76. *wroth*] angry, wrathful.
79. *superficies*] surface.
86. *prove*] find out by experience.

Whose arches should be fram'd with bones of Turks,
Ere I would lose the title of a king.   95
TAMBURLAINE.
    Well, lovely boys, you shall be emperors both,
Stretching your conquering arms from east to west.
And, sirrah, if you mean to wear a crown,
When we shall meet the Turkish deputy
And all his viceroys, snatch it from his head,   100
And cleave his pericranion with thy sword.
CALYPHAS.
    If any man will hold him, I will strike
And cleave him to the channel with my sword.
TAMBURLAINE.
    Hold him, and cleave him too, or I'll cleave thee;
For we will march against them presently.   105
Theridamas, Techelles, and Casane
Promis'd to meet me on Larissa plains
With hosts apiece against this Turkish crew;
For I have sworn by sacred Mahomet
To make it parcel of my empery.   110
The trumpets sound, Zenocrate. They come.

    Enter Theridamas *and his train, with drums and trumpets.*

Welcome, Theridamas, King of Argier.
THERIDAMAS.
    My lord, the great and mighty Tamburlaine,
Arch-monarch of the world, I offer here
My crown, myself, and all the power I have,   115
In all affection at thy kingly feet.
TAMBURLAINE.
    Thanks, good Theridamas.
THERIDAMAS.
    Under my colors march ten thousand Greeks,
And of Argier and Afric's frontier towns
Twice twenty thousand valiant men-at-arms,   120
All which have sworn to sack Natolia.

96. you] *O1, O3;* ye *O2, O4.*   99. we] *O1–3;* yon *O4.*

---

101. *pericranion*] skull (strictly, the membrane enveloping it).
103. *channel*] neck, throat.
110. *parcel of my empery*] part of my empire.

Five hundred brigandines are under sail,
Meet for your service on the sea, my lord,
That, launching from Argier to Tripoli,
Will quickly ride before Natolia   125
And batter down the castles on the shore.

TAMBURLAINE.

Well said, Argier. Receive thy crown again.

Enter Techelles *and* Usumcasane *together.*

Kings of Moroccus and of Fez, welcome.

USUMCASANE.

Magnificent and peerless Tamburlaine,
I and my neighbor King of Fez have brought   130
To aid thee in this Turkish expedition
A hundred thousand expert soldiers;
From Azamor to Tunis near the sea
Is Barbary unpeopled for thy sake,
And all the men in armor under me,   135
Which with my crown I gladly offer thee.

TAMBURLAINE.

Thanks, King of Moroccus; take your crown again.

TECHELLES.

And, mighty Tamburlaine, our earthly god,
Whose looks make this inferior world to quake,
I here present thee with the crown of Fez,   140
And with an host of Moors train'd to the war,
Whose coal-black faces make their foes retire
And quake for fear, as if infernal Jove,
Meaning to aid thee in these Turkish arms,
Should pierce the black circumference of hell   145
With ugly Furies bearing fiery flags
And millions of his strong tormenting spirits.

141. war] *O1–2*; warres *O3–4.*   144. thee] *Rob.*; them *O1–4.*
143. if infernal] *O1–3*; if the infer-   144. these] *O3–4*; this *O1–2.*
nall *O4.*

122. *brigandines*] small skirmishing vessels, often used for piracy.
123. *Meet*] suitable.
133. *Azamor*] a North African town.
143–147. *infernal . . . spirits*] The Furies, dwelling deep in the infernal
regions, were in the service of Pluto, the god of those parts. They are
often represented as carrying firebrands. See Part I, II.vii.53, note.

From strong Tesella unto Biledull
All Barbary is unpeopled for thy sake.

TAMBURLAINE.

Thanks, King of Fez; take here thy crown again.   150
Your presence, loving friends and fellow kings,
Makes me to surfeit in conceiving joy.
If all the crystal gates of Jove's high court
Were opened wide, and I might enter in
To see the state and majesty of heaven,   155
It could not more delight me than your sight.
Now will we banquet on these plains a while
And after march to Turkey with our camp,
In number more than are the drops that fall
When Boreas rents a thousand swelling clouds;   160
And proud Orcanes of Natolia
With all his viceroys shall be so afraid,
That, though the stones as at Deucalion's flood
Were turn'd to men, he should be overcome.
Such lavish will I make of Turkish blood   165
That Jove shall send his winged messenger
To bid me sheathe my sword and leave the field;
The sun, unable to sustain the sight,
Shall hide his head in Thetis' watery lap
And leave his steeds to fair Boötes' charge;   170
For half the world shall perish in this fight.
But now, my friends, let me examine ye.
How have ye spent your absent time from me?

USUMCASANE.

My lord, our men of Barbary have march'd

170. Boötes'] O3–4; Boetes O1–2.

---

148. *Tesella . . . Biledull*] a town and a province in North Africa.
160. *Boreas*] the north wind.
163. *Deucalion*] the Noah of Greek mythology. When his flood had subsided, he and his wife asked an oracle how they could repopulate the earth. They were told to throw stones behind them. Those thrown by Deucalion became men, and those thrown by his wife women.
165. *lavish*] spilling, squandering.
166. *his winged messenger*] Mercury.
169. *Thetis*] a sea goddess.
170. *steeds*] i.e., of his chariot.
170. *Boötes*] See Part I, I.ii.206–207, note.

Four hundred miles with armor on their backs,   175
And lain in leaguer fifteen months and more;
For, since we left you at the Soldan's court,
We have subdu'd the southern Guallatia
And all the land unto the coast of Spain;
We kept the narrow Strait of Gibraltar   180
And made Canaria call us kings and lords.
Yet never did they recreate themselves
Or cease one day from war and hot alarms;
And therefore let them rest a while, my lord.

TAMBURLAINE.

They shall, Casane, and 'tis time, i'faith.   185

TECHELLES.

And I have march'd along the river Nile
To Machda, where the mighty Christian priest,
Call'd John the Great, sits in a milk-white robe,
Whose triple mitre I did take by force,
And made him swear obedience to my crown.   190
From thence unto Cazates did I march,
Where Amazonians met me in the field,
With whom, being women, I vouchsaf'd a league,

---

176. *in leaguer*] in camp, especially in one engaged in a siege.

178. *Guallatia*] a region in the western Sahara.

181. *Canaria*] the Canary Islands.

186–205. *And . . . before*] Techelles marched up the Nile to Machda in Abyssinia, where he subdued the legendary Prester John. He then advanced to Cazates, which Ortelius locates at the side of the vast unnamed lake that he offers as the source of the Nile. (On a modern map, this lake, if it existed, would lie close to Angola's eastern border with the Congo.) After his negotiations with the Amazons, whose territory lay to the east of Cazates, Techelles pushed on to the great province of Zanzibar. (If Ortelius' indications were to be transferred to a modern map, this province would stretch from southern Angola to the Cape of Good Hope and so round to Mozambique. It is to be distinguished from the island of Zanzibar, which Ortelius shows correctly on the east coast of central Africa.) Techelles' return journey by way of Manico and Byather to Cubar took him, to use the names which are familiar today, across the River Congo and through Nigeria to a point well on the way towards Timbuktu. Turning east into Nubia, he then sacked Borno, its capital, which Ortelius sites near a "Borno lacus" that could be the modern Lake Chad. From there, he made his way back to Damascus.

189. *triple mitre*] papal tiara.

And with my power did march to Zanzibar,
The western part of Afric, where I view'd   195
The Ethiopian sea, rivers, and lakes,
But neither man nor child in all the land.
Therefore I took my course to Manico,
Where, unresisted, I remov'd my camp,
And, by the coast of Byather, at last   200
I came to Cubar, where the negroes dwell,
And, conquering that, made haste to Nubia.
There, having sack'd Borno the kingly seat,
I took the king and led him bound in chains
Unto Damasco, where I stay'd before.   205

TAMBURLAINE.

Well done, Techelles. What saith Theridamas?

THERIDAMAS.

I left the confines and the bounds of Afric
And made a voyage into Europe,
Where by the river Tyros I subdu'd
Stoka, Padalia, and Codemia;   210
Then cross'd the sea and came to Oblia
And Nigra Silva, where the devils dance,
Which in despite of them I set on fire.
From thence I cross'd the gulf call'd by the name
Mare Majore of th'inhabitants.   215
Yet shall my soldiers make no period
Until Natolia kneel before your feet.

TAMBURLAINE.

Then will we triumph, banquet, and carouse.
Cooks shall have pensions to provide us cates
And glut us with the dainties of the world.   220
Lachryma Christi and Calabrian wines

---

196. *The Ethiopian sea*] the name Ortelius gives to the ocean between his "Zanzibar" and South America.

207. *confines*] borders.

209–215. *by . . . th'inhabitants*] Padalia was a province to the northwest of the Mare Majore, or Black Sea; the Tyros, or Dniester, served as its southern boundary. Stoka and Codemia lay in the same region, and Nigra Silva (the Black Forest) partly separated the latter from Oblia. Ortelius gives slightly different forms to some of these names. See Seaton, p. 29.

216. *period*] pause.   219. *cates*] delicacies.

221. *Lachryma Christi*] a sweet Italian wine.

Shall common soldiers drink in quaffing bowls,
Ay, liquid gold, when we have conquer'd him,
Mingled with coral and with orient pearl.
Come, let us banquet and carouse the whiles.   225

Exeunt.

Finis Actus Primi.

[II.i] [*Enter*] Sigismund, Frederick, Baldwin, *with their train.*

SIGISMUND.

Now say, my lords of Buda and Bohemia,
What motion is it that inflames your thoughts
And stirs your valors to such sudden arms?

FREDERICK.

Your majesty remembers, I am sure,
What cruel slaughter of our Christian bloods   5
These heath'nish Turks and pagans lately made
Betwixt the city Zula and Danubius;
How through the midst of Varna and Bulgaria,
And almost to the very walls of Rome,
They have, not long since, massacred our camp.   10
It resteth now, then, that your majesty
Take all advantages of time and power
And work revenge upon these infidels.
Your highness knows, for Tamburlaine's repair,
That strikes a terror to all Turkish hearts,   15
Natolia hath dismiss'd the greatest part

224. orient] *Rob.*; orientall *O1–4.*

---

224. *orient*] lustrous (strictly, from the eastern seas).
[II.i]
 1. *Buda*] a Hungarian city, now part of Budapest.
 2. *motion*] desire, emotion.
 7. *Zula*] a city which Ortelius locates north of the Danube.
 8. *Varna*] a Bulgarian seaport.
 9. *Rome*] possibly Constantinople. See Seaton, p. 30.
 11. *resteth*] remains. 14. *repair*] arrival.
 16–21. *Natolia . . . Jerusalem*] Seaton (pp. 21–22) shows that these lines,
read with reference to Ortelius' maps, precisely describe the movement of
a Turkish army that was disengaging itself from the Christians and advancing through Asia Minor to meet Tamburlaine's threat from Egypt
through Syria (Soria).

Of all his army pitch'd against our power
Betwixt Cutheia and Orminius' mount,
And sent them marching up to Belgasar,
Acantha, Antioch, and Caesarea   20
To aid the Kings of Soria and Jerusalem.
Now, then, my lord, advantage take hereof
And issue suddenly upon the rest,
That in the fortune of their overthrow
We may discourage all the pagan troop   25
That dare attempt to war with Christians.
SIGISMUND.
    But calls not then your grace to memory
    The league we lately made with King Orcanes,
    Confirm'd by oath and articles of peace,
    And calling Christ for record of our truths?   30
    This should be treachery and violence
    Against the grace of our profession.
BALDWIN.
    No whit, my lord, for with such infidels,
    In whom no faith nor true religion rests,
    We are not bound to those accomplishments   35
    The holy laws of Christendom enjoin;
    But, as the faith which they profanely plight
    It not by necessary policy
    To be esteem'd assurance for ourselves,
    So what we vow to them should not infringe   40
    Our liberty of arms and victory.
SIGISMUND.
    Though I confess the oaths they undertake
    Breed little strength to our security,
    Yet those infirmities that thus defame
    Their faiths, their honors, and their religion   45
    Should not give us presumption to the like.

20. Acantha] *O1–2, O4*; *Acanthia*   40. what] *O1, O3–4*; that *O2*.
O3.   45. faiths] *O1–3*; fame *O4*.
22. hereof] *O1, O3–4*; thereof *O2*.

---

33. *No whit*] not in the least.
35. *accomplishments*] fulfillments of promises.
37. *plight*] pledge, engage.

Our faiths are sound and must be consummate,
Religious, righteous, and inviolate.

FREDERICK.

Assure your grace, 'tis superstition
To stand so strictly on dispensive faith,   50
And, should we lose the opportunity
That God hath given to venge our Christians' death
And scourge their foul blasphemous paganism,
As fell to Saul, to Balaam, and the rest
That would not kill and curse at God's command,   55
So surely will the vengeance of the Highest
And jealous anger of His fearful arm
Be pour'd with rigor on our sinful heads,
If we neglect this offered victory.

SIGISMUND.

Then arm, my lords, and issue suddenly,   60
Giving commandment to our general host
With expedition to assail the pagan,
And take the victory our God hath given.   *Exeunt.*

[II.ii]

     [*Enter*] Orcanes, Gazellus, Uribassa, *with their train.*

ORCANES.

Gazellus, Uribassa, and the rest,
Now will we march from proud Orminius' mount
To fair Natolia, where our neighbor kings
Expect our power and our royal presence,
T'encounter with the cruel Tamburlaine,   5

47. consummate] *Dyce 2*; con-   59. this] *O1–3*; the *O4*.
sinuate *O1–4*.

---

    47. *consummate*] fulfilled, perfect.
    50. *dispensive faith*] faith which is subject to dispensation, faith which may be set aside in a particular case.
    54. *Saul . . . Balaam*] Saul failed to kill Agag (I Samuel 15) and Balaam refused to curse the children of Israel (Numbers 22–24). But Frederick has forgotten that, whereas Saul was neglecting *God's command* (l. 55), Balaam was acting in accordance with it.
    62. *expedition*] speed.
[II.ii]
    4. *Expect*] wait for.

That nigh Larissa sways a mighty host
And with the thunder of his martial tools
Makes earthquakes in the hearts of men and heaven.

GAZELLUS.

And now come we to make his sinews shake
With greater power than erst his pride hath felt.   10
An hundred kings by scores will bid him arms,
And hundred thousands subjects to each score,
Which, if a shower of wounding thunderbolts
Should break out of the bowels of the clouds
And fall as thick as hail upon our heads   15
In partial aid of that proud Scythian,
Yet should our courages and steeled crests
And numbers more than infinite of men
Be able to withstand and conquer him.

URIBASSA.

Methinks I see how glad the Christian king   20
Is made for joy of your admitted truce,
That could not but before be terrified
With unacquainted power of our host.

Enter a Messenger.

MESSENGER.

Arm, dread sovereign and my noble lords!
The treacherous army of the Christians,   25
Taking advantage of your slender power,
Comes marching on us and determines straight
To bid us battle for our dearest lives.

ORCANES.

Traitors, villains, damned Christians!
Have I not here the articles of peace   30
And solemn covenants we have both confirm'd,
He by his Christ and I by Mahomet?

GAZELLUS.

Hell and confusion light upon their heads

7. martial] *O1, O3–4;* materiall   21. your] *O1–2;* our *O3–4.*
O2.

---

10. *erst*] hitherto.
11. *bid him arms*] challenge him to fight.
16. *partial*] biased, prejudiced.

That with such treason seek our overthrow
And cares so little for their prophet, Christ!   35

ORCANES.

Can there be such deceit in Christians,
Or treason in the fleshly heart of man,
Whose shape is figure of the highest God?
Then if there be a Christ, as Christians say,
But in their deeds deny him for their Christ,   40
If he be son to everliving Jove
And hath the power of his outstretched arm,
If he be jealous of his name and honor,
As is our holy prophet, Mahomet,
Take here these papers as our sacrifice   45
And witness of Thy servant's perjury.
Open, thou shining veil of Cynthia,
And make a passage from the empyreal heaven
That He that sits on high and never sleeps,
Nor in one place is circumscriptible,   50
But everywhere fills every continent
With strange infusion of His sacred vigor,
May in His endless power and purity
Behold and venge this traitor's perjury!
Thou, Christ, that art esteem'd omnipotent,   55
If thou wilt prove thyself a perfect God,
Worthy the worship of all faithful hearts,
Be now reveng'd upon this traitor's soul,
And make the power I have left behind
(Too little to defend our guiltless lives)   60
Sufficient to discomfort and confound
The trustless force of those false Christians.
To arms, my lords! On Christ still let us cry.
If there be Christ, we shall have victory.   [*Exeunt.*]

63. lords] *O1–3*; Lord *O4*.   64. S.D. *Exeunt*] *Rob.*; *not in O1–4.*

---

38. *figure*] image.
47. *Cynthia*] the moon.
48. *the empyreal heaven*] See Part I, II.vii.15, note.

[II.iii]

Sound to the battle, and Sigismund *comes out wounded.*

SIGISMUND.

Discomfited is all the Christian host,
And God hath thundered vengeance from on high
For my accurs'd and hateful perjury.
O just and dreadful punisher of sin,
Let the dishonor of the pains I feel   5
In this my mortal well-deserved wound
End all my penance in my sudden death;
And let this death, wherein to sin I die,
Conceive a second life in endless mercy.   [*Dies.*]

Enter Orcanes, Gazellus, Uribassa, *with others.*

ORCANES.

Now lie the Christians bathing in their bloods,   10
And Christ or Mahomet hath been my friend.

GAZELLUS.

See here the perjur'd traitor, Hungary,
Bloody and breathless for his villainy.

ORCANES.

Now shall his barbarous body be a prey
To beasts and fowls, and all the winds shall breathe   15
Through shady leaves of every senseless tree
Murmurs and hisses for his heinous sin.
Now scalds his soul in the Tartarean streams
And feeds upon the baneful tree of hell,
That Zoacum, that fruit of bitterness,   20
That in the midst of fire is engraff'd
Yet flourisheth as Flora in her pride,

1. Christian]   *O1–2*;   Christians   9. S.D. *Dies*] *Rob.*; *not in O1–4.*
O3–4.

---

1. *Discomfited*] routed.   16. *senseless*] unfeeling.
18. *Tartarean*] belonging to Tartarus. This was the region of Hades where
the most impious and guilty were supposed to be punished. According to
Virgil, it was surrounded by the flaming waters of the river Phlegethon.
19. *baneful*] poisonous, deadly.
20. *Zoacum*] a tree of hell described in the Koran xxxvii.60–64.
21. *engraff'd*] firmly rooted.
22. *Flora*] the Roman goddess of flowers and spring.

With apples like the heads of damned fiends.
The devils there, in chains of quenchless flame,
Shall lead his soul through Orcus' burning gulf   25
From pain to pain whose change shall never end.
What sayest thou yet, Gazellus, to his foil,
Which we referr'd to justice of his Christ
And to His power, which here appears as full
As rays of Cynthia to the clearest sight?   30

GAZELLUS.
'Tis but the fortune of the wars, my lord,
Whose power is often prov'd a miracle.

ORCANES.
Yet in my thoughts shall Christ be honored,
Not doing Mahomet an injury,
Whose power had share in this our victory;   35
And since this miscreant hath disgrac'd his faith,
And died a traitor both to heaven and earth,
We will both watch and ward shall keep his trunk
Amidst these plains for fowls to prey upon.
Go, Uribassa, give it straight in charge.   40

URIBASSA.
I will, my lord.   *Exit* Uribassa.

ORCANES.
And now, Gazellus, let us haste and meet
Our army, and our brother of Jerusalem,
Of Soria, Trebizon, and Amasia,
And happily, with full Natolian bowls   45
Of Greekish wine, now let us celebrate
Our happy conquest and his angry fate.   *Exeunt.*

34. an] *O1–3*; any *O4*.   40. Uribassa, give] *O1–3*; *Vribassa,*
38. shall] *O1, O3–4*; and *O2*.   and giue *O4*.

25. *Orcus*] See Part I, III.i.65, note.
27. *foil*] disgrace.
36. *miscreant*] vile wretch.
38. *We . . . ward*] we decree that a continued guard.
40. *give . . . charge*] command it immediately.
43. *Our army*] i.e., the main body of his army, which Orcanes had sent
ahead through Asia Minor to help to meet Tamburlaine's threat (Part II,
II.i.16–21), retaining only the rear guard with which, despite its smallness
(Part II, II.ii.59–60), he defeated the treacherous Christians.
44. *Amasia*] a province in northern Asia Minor.

[II.iv]

The arras is drawn, and Zenocrate *lies in her bed of state,* Tamburlaine
sitting by her; three Physicians *about her bed, tempering potions;* Theridamas, *Techelles, Usumcasane, and the three sons* [*Calyphas, Amyras, and
Celebinus*].

TAMBURLAINE.

Black is the beauty of the brightest day;
The golden ball of heaven's eternal fire,
That danc'd with glory on the silver waves,
Now wants the fuel that inflam'd his beams,
And, all with faintness and for foul disgrace,   5
He binds his temples with a frowning cloud,
Ready to darken earth with endless night.
Zenocrate, that gave him light and life,
Whose eyes shot fire from their ivory bowers
And tempered every soul with lively heat,   10
Now by the malice of the angry skies,
Whose jealousy admits no second mate,
Draws in the comfort of her latest breath,
All dazzled with the hellish mists of death.
Now walk the angels on the walls of heaven   15
As sentinels to warn th'immortal souls
To entertain divine Zenocrate.
Apollo, Cynthia, and the ceaseless lamps
That gently look'd upon this loathsome earth
Shine downwards now no more, but deck the heavens   20
To entertain divine Zenocrate.
The crystal springs, whose taste illuminates
Refined eyes with an eternal sight,
Like tried silver runs through Paradise

9. their] *O1, O3–4; not in O2.*   19. this] *O1–2;* the *O3–4.*

0.1. *The arras*] the curtain, of a rich tapestry fabric, enclosing the
discovery-space in the Elizabethan theater.
    0.2. *tempering*] concocting, compounding.
    4. *inflam'd*] added heat to.
    9. *bowers*] i.e., the places where they were set.
    10. *tempered*] disposed favorably.
    14. *dazzled*] overpowered, confounded.
    18. *Apollo, Cynthia*] the sun, the moon.
    24. *tried*] separated from the dross, purified.

To entertain divine Zenocrate.   25
The cherubins and holy seraphins,
That sing and play before the King of Kings,
Use all their voices and their instruments
To entertain divine Zenocrate.
And, in this sweet and curious harmony,   30
The god that tunes this music to our souls
Holds out his hand in highest majesty
To entertain divine Zenocrate.
Then let some holy trance convey my thoughts
Up to the palace of th'empyreal heaven,   35
That this my life may be as short to me
As are the days of sweet Zenocrate.
Physicians, will no physic do her good?

PHYSICIAN.

My lord, your majesty shall soon perceive;
And if she pass this fit, the worst is past.   40

TAMBURLAINE.

Tell me, how fares my fair Zenocrate?

ZENOCRATE.

I fare, my lord, as other empresses,
That, when this frail and transitory flesh
Hath suck'd the measure of that vital air
That feeds the body with his dated health,   45
Wanes with enforc'd and necessary change.

TAMBURLAINE.

May never such a change transform my love,
In whose sweet being I repose my life,
Whose heavenly presence, beautified with health,
Gives light to Phoebus and the fixed stars,   50
Whose absence makes the sun and moon as dark

38. no] *O1, O3–4*; not *O2*.   47. May] *O1, O3–4*; Nay *O2*.
43. and] *O1, O3–4*; a *O2*.   51. makes] *O3–4*; make *O1–2*.

30. *curious*] exquisite.
35. *th'empyreal heaven*] the empyrean. See Part I, II.vii.15, note.
45. *dated*] limited, transitory.   50. *Phoebus*] the sun.
51–54. *Whose . . . train*] By the head and tail (*train*) of the dragon (*serpent*),
Elizabethan astronomers meant the ascending and descending nodes of
the moon's path. Nodes are the points at which the orbit of a planet (here
the moon) cuts the ecliptic. Only when the moon is on or near the ecliptic
can eclipses occur, for only then are the sun and moon *oppos'd in one diameter*.

As when, oppos'd in one diameter,
Their spheres are mounted on the serpent's head,
Or else descended to his winding train.
Live still, my love, and so conserve my life,   55
Or, dying, be the author of my death.

ZENOCRATE.

Live still, my lord! O, let my sovereign live!
And sooner let the fiery element
Dissolve and make your kingdom in the sky
Than this base earth should shroud your majesty.   60
For, should I but suspect your death by mine,
The comfort of my future happiness
And hope to meet your highness in the heavens,
Turn'd to despair, would break my wretched breast,
And fury would confound my present rest.   65
But let me die, my love, yet let me die;
With love and patience let your true love die.
Your grief and fury hurts my second life.
Yet let me kiss my lord before I die,
And let me die with kissing of my lord.   70
But, since my life is lengthened yet a while,
Let me take leave of these my loving sons,
And of my lords, whose true nobility
Have merited my latest memory.
Sweet sons, farewell; in death resemble me,   75
And in your lives your father's excellency.
Some music, and my fit will cease, my lord.   *They call music.*

TAMBURLAINE.

Proud fury and intolerable fit
That dares torment the body of my love
And scourge the scourge of the immortal God!   80
Now are those spheres where Cupid us'd to sit,
Wounding the world with wonder and with love,

---

56. author] *O4*; anchor *O1–3*.   77. S.D. *call music*] *O1–2*; *call for*
76. excellency] *O1–2*; excellence   *musicke O3–4*.
O3–4.

58–59. *let . . . sky*] may the sphere of fire, which encloses the regions of
the air (see Part I, IV.ii.30, note), come to an end, and may you make
your kingdom among the heavenly spheres which lie beyond it.
    81. *those spheres*] i.e., her eyes.

Sadly supplied with pale and ghastly death,
Whose darts do pierce the center of my soul.
Her sacred beauty hath enchanted heaven,   85
And, had she liv'd before the siege of Troy,
Helen, whose beauty summon'd Greece to arms
And drew a thousand ships to Tenedos,
Had not been nam'd in Homer's Iliads;
Her name had been in every line he wrote.   90
Or had those wanton poets, for whose birth
Old Rome was proud, but gaz'd a while on her,
Nor Lesbia nor Corinna had been nam'd;
Zenocrate had been the argument
Of every epigram or elegy.   95

The music sounds, and she dies.

What, is she dead? Techelles, draw thy sword
And wound the earth, that it may cleave in twain
And we descend into th'infernal vaults
To hale the Fatal Sisters by the hair
And throw them in the triple moat of hell   100
For taking hence my fair Zenocrate.
Casane and Theridamas, to arms!
Raise cavalieros higher than the clouds,
And with the cannon break the frame of heaven.
Batter the shining palace of the sun   105
And shiver all the starry firmament,
For amorous Jove hath snatch'd my love from hence,
Meaning to make her stately queen of heaven.
What god soever holds thee in his arms,
Giving thee nectar and ambrosia,   110
Behold me here, divine Zenocrate,

---

88. *Tenedos*] a small island off the coast near Troy. See Part I, I.i.66, note.

90. *Her*] i.e., Zenocrate's.

93. *Lesbia . . . Corinna*] women celebrated in the Latin love poetry of the *wanton poets* (l. 91), Catullus and Ovid.

94. *argument*] subject, theme.

99. *Fatal Sisters*] See Part I, I.ii.174, note.

100. *triple . . . hell*] Perhaps Marlowe was thinking of the rivers of Hades. See Part II, III.ii.13.

103. *cavalieros*] mounds for heavy guns.

Raving, impatient, desperate, and mad,
Breaking my steeled lance, with which I burst
The rusty beams of Janus' temple doors,
Letting out death and tyrannizing war, 115
To march with me under this bloody flag.
And if thou pitiest Tamburlaine the Great,
Come down from heaven and live with me again!

THERIDAMAS.

Ah, good my lord, be patient. She is dead,
And all this raging cannot make her live. 120
If words might serve, our voice hath rent the air;
If tears, our eyes have watered all the earth;
If grief, our murdered hearts have strain'd forth blood.
Nothing prevails, for she is dead, my lord.

TAMBURLAINE.

"For she is dead!" Thy words do pierce my soul! 125
Ah, sweet Theridamas, say so no more.
Though she be dead, yet let me think she lives
And feed my mind that dies for want of her.
Where'er her soul be, thou [to the body] shalt stay with me,
Embalm'd with cassia, ambergris, and myrrh, 130
Not lapp'd in lead but in a sheet of gold,
And till I die thou shalt not be interr'd.
Then in as rich a tomb as Mausolus'
We both will rest and have one epitaph
Writ in as many several languages 135
As I have conquered kingdoms with my sword.
This cursed town will I consume with fire,
Because this place bereft me of my love;
The houses, burnt, will look as if they mourn'd;
And here will I set up her stature 140

129. S.D. *to the body*] *Rob.*; *not in O1–4.*   134. one] *O1, O3*; on *O2*; our *O4.*
132. shalt] *O1–3*; shall *O4.*   140. stature] *O1–2*; Statue *O3–4.*

---

114. *Janus' temple doors*] In Rome, these stood open in time of war and were closed in time of peace. Only three times in Roman history were they closed.
130. *cassia*] a fragrant shrub.
133. *Mausolus*] King of Caria, whose widow erected to his memory the costly monument called the Mausoleum.
140. *stature*] statue.

And march about it with my mourning camp,
Drooping and pining for Zenocrate.

The arras is drawn. [Exeunt.]

[III.i]

Enter the Kings of Trebizon *and* Soria, *one bringing a sword and another a scepter. Next,* Natolia *and* Jerusalem *with the imperial crown. After,* Callapine; *and, after him, other Lords [and* Almeda]. Orcanes *and* Jerusalem *crown him, and the other give him the scepter.*

ORCANES.

Callapinus Cyricelibes, otherwise Cybelius, son and
successive heir to the late mighty emperor, Bajazeth, by the
aid of God and his friend Mahomet, Emperor of Natolia,
Jerusalem, Trebizon, Soria, Amasia, Thracia, Illyria,
Carmonia, and all the hundred and thirty kingdoms late   5
contributory to his mighty father. Long live Callapinus,
Emperor of Turkey!

CALLAPINE.

Thrice worthy kings, of Natolia and the rest,
I will requite your royal gratitudes
With all the benefits my empire yields;
And were the sinews of th'imperial seat
So knit and strengthen'd as when Bajazeth
My royal lord and father fill'd the throne,
Whose cursed fate hath so dismember'd it,
Then should you see this thief of Scythia,   15
This proud usurping King of Persia,
Do us such honor and supremacy,
Bearing the vengeance of our father's wrongs,
As all the world should blot our dignities

142.1. *Exeunt*] *this edn.; not in* O1–4.   0.3. *and* Almeda] *Dyce; not in* O1–4.
[III.i]   14. fate] O1–3; Fates O4.

142.1. *The . . . Exeunt*] The curtain is closed in front of the discovery-
space, where Zenocrate lies dead, and Tamburlaine and the rest leave by
the doors of the stage.
[III.i]
    0.4. *other*] others.
    19–20. *As . . . infamies*] that men would unanimously efface our noble
names from the record of vile infamies, where Bajazeth's fall has caused
them to be placed.

Out of the book of base-born infamies.   20
And now I doubt not but your royal cares
Hath so provided for this cursed foe
That, since the heir of mighty Bajazeth
(An emperor so honored for his virtues)
Revives the spirits of true Turkish hearts,   25
In grievous memory of his father's shame,
We shall not need to nourish any doubt
But that proud Fortune, who hath followed long
The martial sword of mighty Tamburlaine,
Will now retain her old inconstancy   30
And raise our honors to as high a pitch
In this our strong and fortunate encounter;
For so hath heaven provided my escape
From all the cruelty my soul sustain'd,
By this my friendly keeper's happy means,   35
That Jove, surcharg'd with pity of our wrongs,
Will pour it down in showers on our heads,
Scourging the pride of cursed Tamburlaine.

ORCANES.

I have a hundred thousand men in arms;
Some that in conquest of the perjur'd Christian,   40
Being a handful to a mighty host,
Think them in number yet sufficient
To drink the river Nile or Euphrates,
And for their power enow to win the world.

KING OF JERUSALEM.

And I as many from Jerusalem,   45
Judaea, Gaza, and Scalonians' bounds,
That on mount Sinai with their ensigns spread

25. of true] *O1*, *O3–4*; of all true   conquest *O2*.
O2.   46. Judaea] *O1–3*; *Iuda O4*.
31. honors] *O1–2*; honor *O3–4*.   46. Scalonians'] *O1–3*; *Sclauonians*
40. in conquest] *O1*, *O3–4*; in the   *O4*.

---

37. *it*] i.e., pity.
40. *Some . . . Christian*] The army of Orcanes includes the small rear
guard with which he defeated Sigismund. See Part II, II.iii.43, note.
44. *enow*] enough.
46. *Scalonians*] the men of Scalona (Ascalon).
47. *ensigns*] banners.

Look like the parti-colored clouds of heaven
That show fair weather to the neighbor morn.

KING OF TREBIZON.

And I as many bring from Trebizon,   50
Chio, Famastro, and Amasia,
All bord'ring on the Mare Major sea,
Riso, Sancina, and the bordering towns
That touch the end of famous Euphrates,
Whose courages are kindled with the flames   55
The cursed Scythian sets on all their towns,
And vow to burn the villain's cruel heart.

KING OF SORIA.

From Soria with seventy thousand strong
Ta'en from Aleppo, Soldino, Tripoli,
And so unto my city of Damasco,   60
I march to meet and aid my neighbor kings,
All which will join against this Tamburlaine
And bring him captive to your highness' feet.

ORCANES.

Our battle then in martial manner pitch'd,
According to our ancient use, shall bear   65
The figure of the semicircled moon,
Whose horns shall sprinkle through the tainted air
The poisoned brains of this proud Scythian.

CALLAPINE.

Well then, my noble lords, for this my friend
That freed me from the bondage of my foe,   70
I think it requisite and honorable
To keep my promise and to make him king,
That is a gentleman, I know, at least.

ALMEDA.

That's no matter, sir, for being a king,
For Tamburlaine came up of nothing.   75

KING OF JERUSALEM.

Your majesty may choose some 'pointed time,

---

52. *Mare Major sea*] Black Sea.
64. *battle*] army.   65. *use*] custom.
65–66. *bear. . . moon*] adopt a crescent-shaped battle formation.
74. *That's no matter*] i.e., gentility is of no importance.

Performing all your promise to the full.

'Tis nought for your majesty to give a kingdom.

CALLAPINE.

Then will I shortly keep my promise, Almeda.

ALMEDA.

Why, I thank your majesty.   *Exeunt.*   80

[III.ii]

[*Enter*] Tamburlaine *with* Usumcasane *and his three sons* [Calyphas, Amyras, *and* Celebinus]; *four bearing the hearse of* Zenocrate, *and the drums sounding a doleful march; the town burning.*

TAMBURLAINE.

So burn the turrets of this cursed town,
Flame to the highest region of the air,
And kindle heaps of exhalations
That, being fiery meteors, may presage
Death and destruction to th'inhabitants!   5
Over my zenith hang a blazing star,
That may endure till heaven be dissolv'd,
Fed with the fresh supply of earthly dregs,
Threat'ning a death and famine to this land!
Flying dragons, lightning, fearful thunder-claps   10
Singe these fair plains and make them seem as black
As is the island where the Furies mask,
Compass'd with Lethe, Styx, and Phlegethon,
Because my dear Zenocrate is dead.

CALYPHAS.

This pillar plac'd in memory of her,   15
Where in Arabian, Hebrew, Greek, is writ:
"This town being burnt by Tamburlaine the Great
Forbids the world to build it up again."

---

2. *the . . . air*] See Part I, IV.ii.30, note.

3. *exhalations*] See Part I, I.ii.49–51, note.

6. *Over my zenith*] directly above me.

6. *blazing star*] comet. See notes on Part I, I.ii.49–51, and Part II, V.i.89.

12–13. *the island . . . Phlegethon*] i.e., Hades, ringed by the infernal rivers.

12. *Furies*] See Part I, II.vii.53, note.

12. *mask*] hide themselves, lurk.

AMYRAS.

    And here this mournful streamer shall be plac'd,
    Wrought with the Persian and Egyptian arms,   20
    To signify she was a princess born
    And wife unto the monarch of the East.

CELEBINUS.

    And here this table as a register
    Of all her virtues and perfections.

TAMBURLAINE.

    And here the picture of Zenocrate,   25
    To show her beauty which the world admir'd;
    Sweet picture of divine Zenocrate
    That, hanging here, will draw the gods from heaven
    And cause the stars fix'd in the southern arc,
    Whose lovely faces never any viewed   30
    That have not pass'd the center's latitude,
    As pilgrims travel to our hemisphere
    Only to gaze upon Zenocrate.
    Thou shalt not beautify Larissa plains
    But keep within the circle of mine arms.   35
    At every town and castle I besiege,
    Thou shalt be set upon my royal tent,
    And when I meet an army in the field
    Those looks will shed such influence in my camp
    As if Bellona, goddess of the war,   40
    Threw naked swords and sulphur balls of fire
    Upon the heads of all our enemies.
    And now, my lords, advance your spears again.
    Sorrow no more, my sweet Casane, now.

20. and Egyptian] *O1, O3–4*; and   39. Those] *Dyce*; Whose *O1–4*.
the Egyptian *O2*.

---

   19. *streamer*] pennon.
   20. *Wrought*] embroidered.
   23. *table*] tablet.
   29–33. *cause . . . Zenocrate*] wishing to behold the portrait of Zenocrate,
the southern stars, whose beauty is known only to those who have crossed
the equator (*the center's latitude*), will make a pilgrimage into our northern
latitudes.
   40. *Bellona*] the Roman goddess of war.
   41. *sulphur . . . fire*] Primitive incendiary bombs were made of sulphur,
saltpeter, resin, etc. Compare Part I, V.i.310–311.

Boys, leave to mourn. This town shall ever mourn,   45
Being burnt to cinders for your mother's death.

CALYPHAS.

If I had wept a sea of tears for her,
It would not ease the sorrow I sustain.

AMYRAS.

As is that town, so is my heart consum'd
With grief and sorrow for my mother's death.   50

CELEBINUS.

My mother's death hath mortified my mind,
And sorrow stops the passage of my speech.

TAMBURLAINE.

But now, my boys, leave off and list to me
That mean to teach you rudiments of war.
I'll have you learn to sleep upon the ground,   55
March in your armor thorough watery fens,
Sustain the scorching heat and freezing cold,
Hunger and thirst, right adjuncts of the war,
And after this to scale a castle wall,
Besiege a fort, to undermine a town,   60
And make whole cities caper in the air.
Then next the way to fortify your men;
In champion grounds what figure serves you best,
For which the quinque-angle form is meet,
Because the corners there may fall more flat   65
Whereas the fort may fittest be assail'd,

48. sorrow] *O1, O3–4*; sorrowes 58. thirst] *O4*; cold *O1–3.*
O2. 64. which] *Rob.*; with *O1–4.*
56. thorough] *O2–4*; throwe *O1.*

---

56. *thorough*] through.
63–64. *In . . . meet*] "I'll teach you what figure is best for flat country,
and also for which kinds of country (other than flat) the quinque-angle is
suited" (Kocher, p. 216).
63. *champion*] level and open.
63. *figure*] shape of fort.
65–67. *the . . . desperate*] If the fort has the shape of an irregular pentagon,
its acuter (or *sharpest*) and therefore weaker angles can be sited where other
factors make *th'assault . . . desperate* for the assailers, while its obtuser (or
more flat) and therefore stronger angles can be sited where the ground is
more favorable to the assailers.
66. *Whereas*] where.

And sharpest where th'assault is desperate;
The ditches must be deep, the counterscarps
Narrow and steep, the walls made high and broad,
The bulwarks and the rampires large and strong,   70
With cavalieros and thick counterforts,
And room within to lodge six thousand men.
It must have privy ditches, countermines,
And secret issuings to defend the ditch.
It must have high argins and covered ways   75
To keep the bulwark fronts from battery,
And parapets to hide the musketeers,
Casemates to place the great artillery

---

68. the counterscarps] *O1–2*; and   78. great] *O1–3*; greatst *O4*.
counterscarps *O3–4*.

---

68. *counterscarps*] the walls of the ditch facing the fort. Obviously, it was desirable that these should be *steep* (l. 69). But the whole outermost ring of defense was sometimes given the name "counterscarp." Accordingly, in saying that the counterscarps should be *Narrow* (l. 69), Tamburlaine was probably thinking more especially of the *covered way* (l. 75), which ran around the outer brink of the ditch and which received its name from the fact that it was protected from enemy fire by the *argin* (l. 75), an earthwork high enough to cover defending infantry. See Kocher, pp. 215–216.

70. *bulwarks*] large projecting earthworks erected at the angles of the fort. From these, heavy guns could sweep the whole length of the wall (called the *curtain* [l. 80]) as far as the adjacent bulwarks. The effect of such fire is described in ll. 79–82. See Kocher, pp. 213–214.

70. *rampires*] ramparts, immense heaps of earth supporting the walls from behind. A rampart would be at least thirty feet deep at its top and would stand about five feet lower than the wall it supported. The extra five feet of wall formed a *parapet* (l. 77). See Kocher, pp. 214–215.

71. *cavalieros*] mounds for heavy guns.   71. *counterforts*] braces, buttresses.

73. *privy ditches*] additional ditches running along the middle of the main ditches as obstacles to infantry attack and to undermining. See Kocher, p. 215.

73. *countermines*] underground tunnels as far as possible beneath the ditch and circling the walls. From these, the enemy's mining operations could be detected and intercepted. See Kocher, p. 215.

74. *secret issuings*] small doorways permitting the defenders to send forces into the ditch to drive out any besiegers who might make their way there. See Kocher, p. 215.

75. *argins . . . ways*] See note on l. 68.   77. *parapets*] See note on l. 70.

78. *Casemates*] chambers in the walls and bulwarks down near the bottom of the ditch. The *great artillery* placed in them came into play after the enemy had effected an entry into the ditch. See Kocher, p. 215.

And store of ordnance, that from every flank
May scour the outward curtains of the fort, 80
Dismount the cannon of the adverse part,
Murder the foe, and save the walls from breach.
When this is learn'd for service on the land,
By plain and easy demonstration
I'll teach you how to make the water mount, 85
That you may dry-foot march through lakes and pools,
Deep rivers, havens, creeks, and little seas,
And make a fortress in the raging waves,
Fenc'd with the concave of a monstrous rock,
Invincible by nature of the place. 90
When this is done, then are ye soldiers
And worthy sons of Tamburlaine the Great.

CALYPHAS.

My lord, but this is dangerous to be done;
We may be slain or wounded ere we learn.

TAMBURLAINE.

Villain, art thou the son of Tamburlaine, 95
And fear'st to die, or with a curtle-axe
To hew thy flesh and make a gaping wound?
Hast thou beheld a peal of ordnance strike
A ring of pikes, mingled with shot and horse,
Whose shattered limbs, being toss'd as high as heaven, 100
Hang in the air as thick as sunny motes,
And canst thou, coward, stand in fear of death?
Hast thou not seen my horsemen charge the foe,
Shot through the arms, cut overthwart the hands,

82. the walls] *Dyce*; their walles   91. ye] *O1–2*; you *O3–4*.
O1–4.   96. a] *O1, O3–4*; the *O2*.
90. by nature] *O1–3*; by the nature
O4.

---

80. *curtains*] See note on l. 70.
81. *adverse part*] opposing side, enemy.
98. *peal of ordnance*] discharge of cannon.
99. *A . . . horse*] a ring of pikemen, closely flanked by infantry carrying
small firearms and by cavalry. See Kocher, p. 211.
101. *sunny motes*] particles of dust in the sunlight.
104. *overthwart*] across.

Dyeing their lances with their streaming blood,   105
And yet at night carouse within my tent,
Filling their empty veins with airy wine,
That being concocted turns to crimson blood,
And wilt thou shun the field for fear of wounds?
View me, thy father, that hath conquered kings,   110
And with his host march'd round about the earth,
Quite void of scars and clear from any wound,
That by the wars lost not a dram of blood,
And see him lance his flesh to teach you all.

                                                          He cuts his arm.

A wound is nothing, be it ne'er so deep.   115
Blood is the god of war's rich livery.
Now look I like a soldier, and this wound
As great a grace and majesty to me
As if a chair of gold enamelled,
Enchas'd with diamonds, sapphires, rubies,   120
And fairest pearl of wealthy India,
Were mounted here under a canopy,
And I sat down cloth'd with the massy robe
That late adorn'd the Afric potentate
Whom I brought bound unto Damascus' walls.   125
Come, boys, and with your fingers search my wound,
And in my blood wash all your hands at once,
While I sit smiling to behold the sight.
Now, my boys, what think you of a wound?

CALYPHAS.

I know not what I should think of it.   130
Methinks 'tis a pitiful sight.

CELEBINUS.

'Tis nothing. Give me a wound, father.

111. his] *O1–2*; this *O3–4*.   123. the] *O1*; a *O2–4*.
111. march'd] *O3–4*; martch *O1–2*. 129. you] *O1, O3–4*; ye *O2*.
113. dram] *O1, O3–4*; drop *O2*.   132. 'Tis] *O1, O3–4*; This *O2*.

107–108. *Filling . . . blood*] An allusion to the current saying, "Good
wine makes good blood" (Tilley, W 461).
108. *concocted*] digested.
116. *the . . . livery*] the rich uniform worn by those who serve Mars.
120. *Enchas'd*] adorned. See Part I, I.ii.96, note.
124. *the Afric potentate*] Bajazeth, so called from his African conquests.

AMYRAS.

    And me another, my lord.

TAMBURLAINE.

    Come, sirrah, give me your arm.

CELEBINUS.

    Here, father, cut it bravely, as you did your own.   135

TAMBURLAINE.

    It shall suffice thou dar'st abide a wound.

    My boy, thou shalt not lose a drop of blood

    Before we meet the army of the Turk;

    But then run desperate through the thickest throngs,

    Dreadless of blows, of bloody wounds, and death;   140

    And let the burning of Larissa walls,

    My speech of war, and this my wound you see

    Teach you, my boys, to bear courageous minds

    Fit for the followers of great Tamburlaine!

    Usumcasane, now come let us march   145

    Towards Techelles and Theridamas

    That we have sent before to fire the towns,

    The towers, and cities of these hateful Turks,

    And hunt that coward, faint-heart runaway,

    With that accursed traitor, Almeda,   150

    Till fire and sword have found them at a bay.

USUMCASANE.

    I long to pierce his bowels with my sword

    That hath betrayed my gracious sovereign,

    That curs'd and damned traitor, Almeda.

TAMBURLAINE.

    Then let us see if coward Callapine   155

    Dare levy arms against our puissance,

    That we may tread upon his captive neck

    And treble all his father's slaveries.   *Exeunt.*

---

147. the] *O1–2, O4; not in O3.*   *O2.*
150. accursed] *O1, O3–4;* cursed   152. his] *O1, O3–4;* the *O2.*

---

135. *bravely*] well.
149. *runaway*] i.e., Callapine.
151. *at a bay*] at bay.

[III.iii]
[*Enter*] Techelles, Theridamas, *and their train*[, Soldiers *and* Pioners].

THERIDAMAS.

　　Thus have we march'd northward from Tamburlaine
　　Unto the frontier point of Soria,
　　And this is Balsera, their chiefest hold,
　　Wherein is all the treasure of the land.

TECHELLES.

　　Then let us bring our light artillery,　　　　　　　5
　　Minions, falc'nets, and sakers, to the trench,
　　Filling the ditches with the walls' wide breach,
　　And enter in to seize upon the gold.
　　How say ye, soldiers, shall we not?

SOLDIERS.

　　Yes, my lord, yes, come, let's about it.　　　　　10

THERIDAMAS.

　　But stay a while; summon a parle, drum.
　　It may be they will yield it quietly,
　　Knowing two kings, the friends to Tamburlaine,
　　Stand at the walls with such a mighty power.

Summon the battle. [*Enter*] Captain *with his wife* [*Olympia*] *and Son*
[*above*].

CAPTAIN.

　　What require you, my masters?　　　　　　　　15

THERIDAMAS.

　　Captain, that thou yield up thy hold to us.

CAPTAIN.

　　To you! Why, do you think me weary of it?

TECHELLES.

　　Nay, captain, thou art weary of thy life

0.1. Soldiers *and* Pioners] *this edn.*;　12. quietly] *O1–3*; quickely *O4*.
not in O1–4.　　　　　　　　　　13. friends] *O3–4*; friend *O1–2*.
2. point] *O1–2*; port *O3–4*.　　14.2. *above*] *Rob.*; *not in O1–4.*
9. ye] *O1, O3*; you *O2, O4*.　　17. do you] *O1, O3–4*; do thou *O2*.

　0.1. *Pioners*] trench-diggers.
　3. *Balsera*] See note on Part II, Characters of the Play, l. 22.
　3. *hold*] stronghold, fort. So also in l. 16.
　6. *Minions . . . sakers*] small pieces of ordnance.

If thou withstand the friends of Tamburlaine.

THERIDAMAS.

These pioners of Argier in Africa, 20
Even in the cannon's face, shall raise a hill
Of earth and faggots higher than thy fort,
And over thy argins and covered ways
Shall play upon the bulwarks of thy hold
Volleys of ordnance, till the breach be made 25
That with his ruin fills up all the trench;
And, when we enter in, not heaven itself
Shall ransom thee, thy wife, and family.

TECHELLES.

Captain, these Moors shall cut the leaden pipes
That bring fresh water to thy men and thee, 30
And lie in trench before thy castle walls
That no supply of victual shall come in,
Nor any issue forth but they shall die;
And therefore, captain, yield it quietly.

CAPTAIN.

Were you, that are the friends of Tamburlaine, 35
Brothers to holy Mahomet himself,
I would not yield it; therefore do your worst.
Raise mounts, batter, intrench, and undermine,
Cut off the water, all convoys that can,
Yet I am resolute; and so farewell.   [_Exeunt above._] 40

THERIDAMAS.

Pioners, away, and where I stuck the stake
Intrench with those dimensions I prescribed.
Cast up the earth towards the castle wall,
Which, till it may defend you, labor low,
And few or none shall perish by their shot. 45

21. in] _O1–3_; to _O4._   35. the] _O1–3_; _not in O4._
33. any] _Rob._; _not in O1–4._   36. to] _O1, O3–4_; of _O2._
34. quietly] _O1–3_; quickely _O4._ 40. I am] _O1–3_; am I _O4._
35. Were you] _O1–2_; were all you   40. S.D. _Exeunt above_] _Rob._; _not in_
_O3–4._   _O1–4._

23. _argins . . . ways_] See Part II, III.ii.68, note.
24. _bulwarks_] See Part II, III.ii.70, note.
26. _trench_] the _ditches_ mentioned in l. 7.
39. _convoys_] supplies under escort.

PIONERS.

We will, my lord.   *Exeunt* [Pioners].

TECHELLES.

A hundred horse shall scout about the plains
To spy what force comes to relieve the hold.
Both we, Theridamas, will intrench our men,
And with the Jacob's staff measure the height   50
And distance of the castle from the trench,
That we may know if our artillery
Will carry full point-blank unto their walls.

THERIDAMAS.

Then see the bringing of our ordinance
Along the trench into the battery,   55
Where we will have gabions of six foot broad
To save our cannoneers from musket shot;
Betwixt which shall our ordnance thunder forth,
And, with the breach's fall, smoke, fire, and dust,
The crack, the echo, and the soldier's cry,   60
Make deaf the air and dim the crystal sky.

TECHELLES.

Trumpets and drums, alarum presently!
And, soldiers, play the men; the hold is yours!   [*Exeunt.*]

[III.iv]
                Enter the Captain *with his wife* [Olympia] *and* Son.

OLYMPIA.

Come, good my lord, and let us haste from hence

46. S.D. Pioners] *Rob.*; *not in O1–4.*   63. hold] *O3–4*; holds *O1–2.*
55. into] *O1–3*; vnto *O4.*   63. S.D. *Exeunt*] *Rob.*; *not in O1–4.*
56. gabions] *Cunn.*, conj. *Broughton*;   [III.iv]
Galions *O1–4.*   0.1. *the*] *O1–2*; *not in O3–4.*
62. alarum] *O1–2*; alarme *O3–4.*

---

50. *Jacob's staff*] an instrument used for the purposes Techelles mentions.
"Range-finding by means of the gunner's quadrant and similar instruments
was a well developed department of Renaissance gunnery" (Kocher,
pp. 219–220).

54. *ordinance*] ordnance.

55. *battery*] fortified position within which the guns are to be deployed.

56. *gabions*] "These consisted of earth packed into a circle of stakes set
in the ground and bound with osier twigs or similar materials" (Kocher,
p. 220).

62. *alarum*] call to arms.   62. *presently*] at once, immediately.

Along the cave that leads beyond the foe.
No hope is left to save this conquered hold.
CAPTAIN.
A deadly bullet gliding through my side
Lies heavy on my heart. I cannot live.   5
I feel my liver pierc'd, and all my veins,
That there begin and nourish every part,
Mangled and torn, and all my entrails bath'd
In blood that straineth from their orifex.
Farewell, sweet wife! Sweet son, farewell! I die.   10
                                                                    [*Dies.*]
OLYMPIA.
Death, whither art thou gone that both we live?
Come back again, sweet Death, and strike us both!
One minute end our days, and one sepulcher
Contain our bodies! Death, why com'st thou not?
Well, this must be the messenger for thee.   15
Now, ugly Death, stretch out thy sable wings
And carry both our souls where his remains.
Tell me, sweet boy, art thou content to die?
These barbarous Scythians, full of cruelty,
And Moors, in whom was never pity found,   20
Will hew us piecemeal, put us to the wheel,
Or else invent some torture worse than that;
Therefore die by thy loving mother's hand,
Who gently now will lance thy ivory throat
And quickly rid thee both of pain and life.   25
SON.
Mother, dispatch me, or I'll kill myself;
For think ye I can live and see him dead?
Give me your knife, good mother, or strike home;
The Scythians shall not tyrannize on me.
Sweet mother, strike, that I may meet my father.   30
                                                        She stabs him.

9. straineth] *O1, O3–4*; staineth   10.1. *Dies*] *Rob.*; *not in O1–4.*
O2.   28. home] *O1–3*; haue *O4.*

2. *cave*] underground passage.
9. *orifex*] orifice.
15. *this*] i.e., a knife. See l. 28.
21. *the wheel*] an instrument of torture.
29. *tyrannize*] inflict pain or torment.

OLYMPIA.

> Ah, sacred Mahomet, if this be sin,
> Entreat a pardon of the God of heaven
> And purge my soul before it come to thee.

> *Enter* Theridamas, Techelles, *and all their train.*

THERIDAMAS.

> How now, madam, what are you doing?

OLYMPIA.

> Killing myself, as I have done my son,   35
> Whose body, with his father's, I have burnt,
> Lest cruel Scythians should dismember him.

TECHELLES.

> 'Twas bravely done, and like a soldier's wife.
> Thou shalt with us to Tamburlaine the Great,
> Who, when he hears how resolute thou wert,   40
> Will match thee with a viceroy or a king.

OLYMPIA.

> My lord deceas'd was dearer unto me
> Than any viceroy, king, or emperor;
> And for his sake here will I end my days.

THERIDAMAS.

> But, lady, go with us to Tamburlaine,   45
> And thou shalt see a man greater than Mahomet,
> In whose high looks is much more majesty
> Than from the concave superficies
> Of Jove's vast palace, the empyreal orb,
> Unto the shining bower where Cynthia sits,   50
> Like lovely Thetis, in a crystal robe;
> That treadeth fortune underneath his feet
> And makes the mighty god of arms his slave;
> On whom Death and the Fatal Sisters wait

40. wert] *O1–3*; art *O4*.   41. thee with] *O1–3*; with thee *O4*.

48–51. *Than . . . robe*] i.e., than is to be found anywhere in the heavens.
Theridamas first refers to the *superficies* or surface of the immovable *empyreal*
orb or empyrean (see Part I, II.vii.15, note), as a vast concavity. It encloses
the eight moving spheres and the earth itself. The innermost of these moving
spheres is that of the moon, to which he then refers as *the shining bower where*
Cynthia sits.

51. *Thetis*] a sea goddess.   53. *god of arms*] Mars.
54. *Fatal Sisters*] See Part I, I.ii.174, note.

With naked swords and scarlet liveries;   55
Before whom, mounted on a lion's back,
Rhamnusia bears a helmet full of blood
And strows the way with brains of slaughtered men;
By whose proud side the ugly Furies run,
Hearkening when he shall bid them plague the world;   60
Over whose zenith, cloth'd in windy air,
And eagle's wings join'd to her feathered breast,
Fame hovereth, sounding of her golden trump,
That to the adverse poles of that straight line
Which measureth the glorious frame of heaven   65
The name of mighty Tamburlaine is spread;
And him, fair lady, shall thy eyes behold.
Come!

OLYMPIA.

Take pity of a lady's ruthful tears,
That humbly craves upon her knees to stay   70
And cast her body in the burning flame
That feeds upon her son's and husband's flesh.

TECHELLES.

Madam, sooner shall fire consume us both
Than scorch a face so beautiful as this,
In frame of which nature hath showed more skill   75
Than when she gave eternal chaos form,
Drawing from it the shining lamps of heaven.

THERIDAMAS.

Madam, I am so far in love with you
That you must go with us—no remedy.

OLYMPIA.

Then carry me, I care not, where you will,   80
And let the end of this my fatal journey
Be likewise end to my accursed life.

62. join'd] *O1, O3–4*; inioin'd *O2*.   63. of] *O1–3*; in *O4*.
63. Fame] *O1–2*; Fume *O3–4*.

57. *Rhamnusia*] Nemesis. See Part I, II.iii.37, note.
61. *zenith*] head, crest.
64. *straight line*] The *axletree of heaven* (Part I, IV.ii.50), on which all the
spheres were believed to revolve.
75. *frame*] fashioning, framing.

TECHELLES.

>No, madam, but the beginning of your joy.
>Come willingly, therefore.

THERIDAMAS.

>Soldiers, now let us meet the general,   85
>Who by this time is at Natolia,
>Ready to charge the army of the Turk.
>The gold, the silver, and the pearl ye got,
>Rifling this fort, divide in equal shares:
>This lady shall have twice so much again   90
>Out of the coffers of our treasury.   *Exeunt.*

[III.v]

[*Enter*] Callapine, Orcanes, Jerusalem, Trebizon, Soria, Almeda,
with their train [*and* Messenger].

MESSENGER.

>Renowned emperor, mighty Callapine,
>God's great lieutenant over all the world,
>Here at Aleppo, with an host of men,
>Lies Tamburlaine, this King of Persia,
>In number more than are the quivering leaves   5
>Of Ida's forest, where your highness' hounds
>With open cry pursues the wounded stag—
>Who means to girt Natolia's walls with siege,
>Fire the town, and overrun the land.

CALLAPINE.

>My royal army is as great as his,   10
>That, from the bounds of Phrygia to the sea
>Which washeth Cyprus with his brinish waves,
>Covers the hills, the valleys, and the plains.
>Viceroys and peers of Turkey, play the men.

86. time] *O1–2, O4*; times *O3*.   *O1–4*.
88. the silver] *O1, O3–4*; and   1. emperor, mighty] *O1–3*; Empe-
siluer *O2*.   rour, and mightie *O4*.
[III.v]   5. the] *O1, O3–4*; this *O2*.
0.2. *and* Messenger] *Rob.*; *not in*

6. *Ida*] presumably Mt. Ida near Troy; but Mt. Ida in Crete is also
possible.
8. *Natolia*] here evidently a city; elsewhere Asia Minor.
11. *Phrygia*] an inland country in western Asia Minor.

Whet all your swords to mangle Tamburlaine,   15
His sons, his captains, and his followers.
By Mahomet, not one of them shall live.
The field wherein this battle shall be fought
For ever term the Persians' sepulcher,
In memory of this our victory.   20

ORCANES.

Now he that calls himself the scourge of Jove,
The emperor of the world, and earthly god
Shall end the warlike progress he intends
And travel headlong to the lake of hell,
Where legions of devils, knowing he must die   25
Here in Natolia by your highness' hands,
All brandishing their brands of quenchless fire,
Stretching their monstrous paws, grin with their teeth
And guard the gates to entertain his soul.

CALLAPINE.

Tell me, viceroys, the number of your men,   30
And what our army royal is esteem'd.

KING OF JERUSALEM.

From Palestina and Jerusalem,
Of Hebrews three score thousand fighting men
Are come since last we showed your majesty.

ORCANES.

So from Arabia Desert, and the bounds   35
Of that sweet land whose brave metropolis
Re-edified the fair Semiramis,
Came forty thousand warlike foot and horse
Since last we number'd to your majesty.

KING OF TREBIZON.

From Trebizon in Asia the Less,   40
Naturalized Turks and stout Bithynians

15. your] *O1–3*; our *O4*.
21. the] *O1, O3–4; not in O2*.
26. your] *O1–3*; our *O4*.
27. brandishing their] *O1, O3–4;*

brandishing in their *O2*.
28. with] *O1, O3–4; not in O2*.
34. showed your] *O1–3*; shewed to your *O4*.

36. *metropolis*] Babylon, which Semiramis was supposed to have rebuilt.
40. *Asia the Less*] Asia Minor.
41. *stout*] bold.
41. *Bithynians*] Bithynia was a district in northern Asia Minor.

Came to my bands, full fifty thousand more,
That, fighting, knows not what retreat doth mean,
Nor e'er return but with the victory,
Since last we number'd to your majesty.   45

KING OF SORIA.

Of Sorians from Halla is repair'd,
And neighbor cities of your highness' land,
Ten thousand horse and thirty thousand foot,
Since last we number'd to your majesty;
So that the army royal is esteem'd   50
Six hundred thousand valiant fighting men.

CALLAPINE.

Then welcome, Tamburlaine, unto thy death.
Come, puissant viceroys, let us to the field,
The Persians' sepulcher, and sacrifice
Mountains of breathless men to Mahomet,   55
Who now with Jove opens the firmament
To see the slaughter of our enemies.

[*Enter*] Tamburlaine *with his three sons* [*Calyphas, Amyras, and* Cele-
binus], Usumcasane, *with other.*

TAMBURLAINE.

How now, Casane? See, a knot of kings,
Sitting as if they were a-telling riddles.

USUMCASANE.

My lord, your presence makes them pale and wan.   60
Poor souls, they look as if their deaths were near.

TAMBURLAINE.

Why, so he is, Casane; I am here.
But yet I'll save their lives and make them slaves.
Ye petty kings of Turkey, I am come,
As Hector did into the Grecian camp,   65

46. repair'd] *O1–3*; prepar'd *O4*.   57.2. *other*] *O1, O3–4*; *others O2*.
47.] *O1–3*; not in *O4*.   62. he] *O1–3*; it *O4*.

---

46. *Halla*] a town to the southeast of Aleppo.   57.2. *other*] others.
62. *he*] i.e., their death, Tamburlaine himself.
65–68. *As . . . fame*] There is no such episode in the *Iliad*. Marlowe could
have found it in "any one of several repetitions of the Trojan story, such
as Lydgate's *Troy Book*, in which (Bk. III, ll. 3755 *seq.*) it is treated at length"
(Ellis-Fermor).

To overdare the pride of Graecia
And set his warlike person to the view
Of fierce Achilles, rival of his fame.
I do you honor in the simile;
For, if I should, as Hector did Achilles,   70
The worthiest knight that ever brandish'd sword,
Challenge in combat any of you all,
I see how fearfully ye would refuse,
And fly my glove as from a scorpion.

ORCANES.

Now thou art fearful of thy army's strength,   75
Thou wouldst with overmatch of person fight.
But, shepherd's issue, base-born Tamburlaine,
Think of thy end; this sword shall lance thy throat.

TAMBURLAINE.

Villain, the shepherd's issue, at whose birth
Heaven did afford a gracious aspect   80
And join'd those stars that shall be opposite
Even till the dissolution of the world,
And never meant to make a conqueror
So famous as is mighty Tamburlaine,
Shall so torment thee and that Callapine,   85
That like a roguish runaway suborn'd
That villain there, that slave, that Turkish dog,
To false his service to his sovereign,
As ye shall curse the birth of Tamburlaine.

CALLAPINE.

Rail not, proud Scythian. I shall now revenge   90
My father's vile abuses and mine own.

84. is] *O1–3*; the *O4*.

---

74. *glove*] thrown down as a challenge to battle.
76. *overmatch*] unfair match.
80. *a gracious aspect*] Tamburlaine claims that at the moment of his birth the relative positions of the heavenly bodies as observed from the earth were such as astrologers hold to be favorable to the "native."
81–82. *And . . . world*] and brought into apparent proximity heavenly bodies whose extreme apparent divergence will now endure until the end of time (with the result that there will never be another Tamburlaine).
88. *false*] betray.
91. *abuses*] injuries, wrongs.

KING OF JERUSALEM.

> By Mahomet, he shall be tied in chains,
> Rowing with Christians in a brigandine
> About the Grecian isles to rob and spoil,
> And turn him to his ancient trade again.   95
> Methinks the slave should make a lusty thief.

CALLAPINE.

> Nay, when the battle ends, all we will meet
> And sit in council to invent some pain
> That most may vex his body and his soul.

TAMBURLAINE.

> Sirrah Callapine, I'll hang a clog about your neck for   100
> running away again. You shall not trouble me thus to come
> and fetch you.
> But as for you, viceroy, you shall have bits,
> And, harness'd like my horses, draw my coach;
> And, when ye stay, be lash'd with whips of wire.   105
> I'll have you learn to feed on provender
> And in a stable lie upon the planks.

ORCANES.

> But, Tamburlaine, first thou shalt kneel to us
> And humbly crave a pardon for thy life.

KING OF TREBIZON.

> The common soldiers of our mighty host   110
> Shall bring thee bound unto the general's tent.

KING OF SORIA.

> And all have jointly sworn thy cruel death,
> Or bind thee in eternal torments' wrath.

TAMBURLAINE.

> Well, sirs, diet yourselves; you know I shall have occasion
> shortly to journey you.   115

CELEBINUS.

> See, father, how Almeda the jailor looks upon us.

104. harness'd] *O1–2*; harnesse   108. thou shalt] *O1–3*; shalt thou
O3–4.   *O4*.
106. on] *O1, O3–4*; with *O2*.   111. the] *O1–2*; our *O3–4*.

---

93. *brigandine*] See Part II, I.iii.122, note.
96. *lusty*] vigorous.
100. *for*] as a precaution against.
115. *journey*] drive (as horses).

TAMBURLAINE.

    Villain, traitor, damned fugitive!
    I'll make thee wish the earth had swallowed thee.
    Seest thou not death within my wrathful looks?
    Go, villain, cast thee headlong from a rock,   120
    Or rip thy bowels and rend out thy heart
    T'appease my wrath, or else I'll torture thee,
    Searing thy hateful flesh with burning irons
    And drops of scalding lead, while all thy joints
    Be rack'd and beat asunder with the wheel;   125
    For, if thou livest, not any element
    Shall shroud thee from the wrath of Tamburlaine.

CALLAPINE.

    Well, in despite of thee he shall be king.
    Come, Almeda, receive this crown of me.
    I here invest thee King of Ariadan,   130
    Bordering on Mare Rosso, near to Mecca.

ORCANES.

    What! Take it, man.

ALMEDA.

    Good my lord, let me take it.

CALLAPINE.

    Dost thou ask him leave? Here, take it.

TAMBURLAINE.

    Go to, sirrah, take your crown, and make up the half 135
    dozen.
    So, sirrah, now you are a king you must give arms.

ORCANES.

    So he shall, and wear thy head in his scutcheon.

TAMBURLAINE.

    No, let him hang a bunch of keys on his standard to put
    him in remembrance he was a jailor; that, when I take 140
    him, I may knock out his brains with them, and lock you

121. and rend] *O1, O3*; and rent   135. to] *O1–3*; *not in O4.*
O2; or rend *O4.*   139. No] *O1, O3–4*; Go *O2.*

---

  131. *Mare Rosso*] the Red Sea.
  133. *Good . . . it*] Almeda asks Tamburlaine's permission.
  135. *Go to*] See Part I, IV.iv.53, note.
  137. *arms*] used punningly.

in the stable when you shall come sweating from my chariot.

KING OF TREBIZON.

Away, let us to the field that the villain may be slain.

TAMBURLAINE.

Sirrah, prepare whips and bring my chariot to my tent; 145
for, as soon as the battle is done, I'll ride in triumph
through the camp.

Enter Theridamas, Techelles, *and their train.*

How now, ye petty kings? Lo, here are bugs
Will make the hair stand upright on your heads,
And cast your crowns in slavery at their feet.   150
Welcome, Theridamas and Techelles, both.
See ye this rout, and know ye this same king?

THERIDAMAS.

Ay, my lord, he was Callapine's keeper.

TAMBURLAINE.

Well, now you see he is a king. Look to him, Theridamas,
when we are fighting, lest he hide his crown as the foolish 155
King of Persia did.

KING OF SORIA.

No, Tamburlaine, he shall not be put to that exigent, I
warrant thee.

TAMBURLAINE.

You know not, sir.
But now, my followers and my loving friends,   160
Fight as you ever did, like conquerors;
The glory of this happy day is yours.
My stern aspect shall make fair victory,
Hovering betwixt our armies, light on me,
Loaden with laurel wreaths to crown us all.   165

TECHELLES.

I smile to think how, when this field is fought

152. know ye] *O1–2*; know you   163. aspect] *O1–3*; aspects *O4*.
O3–4.   165. Loaden] *O1–2*; Laden *O3–4*.
154. you] *O1, O3–4*; ye *O2*.

148. *bugs*] bugbears.   149. *Will*] that will.
150. *cast*] make you cast.
155–156. *as . . . did*] See Part I, II.iv.

And rich Natolia ours, our men shall sweat
With carrying pearl and treasure on their backs.

TAMBURLAINE.

You shall be princes all, immediately.
Come, fight, ye Turks, or yield us victory.   170

ORCANES.

No, we will meet thee, slavish Tamburlaine.   *Exeunt.*

[IV.i]

Alarm. Amyras *and* Celebinus *issues from the tent where* Calyphas *sits asleep.*

AMYRAS.

Now in their glories shine the golden crowns
Of these proud Turks, much like so many suns
That half dismay the majesty of heaven.
Now, brother, follow we our father's sword
That flies with fury swifter than our thoughts   5
And cuts down armies with his conquering's wings.

CELEBINUS.

Call forth our lazy brother from the tent,
For, if my father miss him in the field,
Wrath, kindled in the furnace of his breast,
Will send a deadly lightning to his heart.   10

AMYRAS.

Brother, ho! What, given so much to sleep
You cannot leave it when our enemies' drums
And rattling cannons thunder in our ears
Our proper ruin and our father's foil?

CALYPHAS.

Away, ye fools, my father needs not me,   15
Nor you, in faith, but that you will be thought
More childish-valorous than manly-wise.
If half our camp should sit and sleep with me,
My father were enough to scare the foe.
You do dishonor to his majesty   20

12. You cannot] *O1–3*; Can you
not *O4.*

---

12. *You*] that you.   14. *proper*] own.
14. *foil*] defeat, repulse.

To think our helps will do him any good.

AMYRAS.

What, dar'st thou then be absent from the fight,
Knowing my father hates thy cowardice
And oft hath warn'd thee to be still in field,
When he himself amidst the thickest troops   25
Beats down our foes, to flesh our taintless swords?

CALYPHAS.

I know, sir, what it is to kill a man.
It works remorse of conscience in me.
I take no pleasure to be murderous,
Nor care for blood when wine will quench my thirst.   30

CELEBINUS.

O cowardly boy! Fie, for shame, come forth!
Thou dost dishonor manhood and thy house.

CALYPHAS.

Go, go, tall stripling, fight you for us both,
And take my other toward brother here,
For person like to prove a second Mars.   35
'Twill please my mind as well to hear both you
Have won a heap of honor in the field
And left your slender carcasses behind
As if I lay with you for company.

AMYRAS.

You will not go, then?   40

CALYPHAS.

You say true.

AMYRAS.

Were all the lofty mounts of Zona Mundi
That fill the midst of farthest Tartary
Turn'd into pearl and proffered for my stay,
I would not bide the fury of my father,   45

36. both you] *O1–3;* you both
O4.

---

26. *to . . . swords*] to plunge our hitherto unstained swords in flesh for
the first time.
33. *tall*] doughty, valiant. Calyphas speaks with some irony.
34. *toward*] promising, "hopeful."
42. *the . . . Mundi*] the northern end of the Ural chain.
45. *bide*] face.

When, made a victor in these haughty arms,
He comes and finds his sons have had no shares
In all the honors he propos'd for us.

CALYPHAS.

Take you the honor, I will take my ease.
My wisdom shall excuse my cowardice.   50
I go into the field before I need?

Alarm, and Amyras *and* Celebinus *run in.*

The bullets fly at random where they list;
And, should I go and kill a thousand men,
I were as soon rewarded with a shot,
And sooner far than he that never fights;   55
And, should I go and do nor harm nor good,
I might have harm which all the good I have,
Join'd with my father's crown, would never cure.
I'll to cards. Perdicas!

[*Enter* Perdicas.]

PERDICAS.

Here, my lord.   60

CALYPHAS.

Come, thou and I will go to cards to drive away the time.

[Calyphas *and* Perdicas *retire to the open tent.*]

PERDICAS.

Content, my lord, but what shall we play for?

CALYPHAS.

Who shall kiss the fairest of the Turks' concubines first, when
my father hath conquered them.

PERDICAS.

Agreed, i'faith.   *They play.*   65

CALYPHAS.

They say I am a coward, Perdicas, and I fear as little
their taratantaras, their swords, or their cannons as I do a

51.1. *run*] *O1, O3–4; runnes O2.*
53. should I] *O1–3;* I should *O4.*
56. nor harm] *O1, O3;* no harme
O2, O4.

59.1. *Enter* Perdicas] *Dyce; not in
O1–4.*
61.1. Calyphas ... *tent*] *this edn.;
not in O1–4.*

51. *I go*] do I look as if I would go.
52. *list*] like.
67. *taratantaras*] bugle calls.

naked lady in a net of gold, and, for fear I should be
afraid, would put it off and come to bed with me.

PERDICAS.

Such a fear, my lord, would never make ye retire.   70

CALYPHAS.

I would my father would let me be put in the front of
such a battle once to try my valor.   *Alarm.*
What a coil they keep! I believe there will be some hurt
done anon amongst them.

Enter Tamburlaine, Theridamas, Techelles, Usumcasane, Amyras,
Celebinus, leading the Turkish Kings [of Natolia, Jerusalem, Trebizon,
and Soria; *and* Soldiers].

TAMBURLAINE.

See now, ye slaves, my children stoops your pride   75
And leads your glories sheep-like to the sword.
Bring them, my boys, and tell me if the wars
Be not a life that may illustrate gods,
And tickle not your spirits with desire
Still to be train'd in arms and chivalry?   80

AMYRAS.

Shall we let go these kings again, my lord,
To gather greater numbers 'gainst our power,
That they may say it is not chance doth this
But matchless strength and magnanimity?

TAMBURLAINE.

No, no, Amyras, tempt not fortune so.   85
Cherish thy valor still with fresh supplies,
And glut it not with stale and daunted foes.
But where's this coward villain, not my son,
But traitor to my name and majesty?
                    He goes in and brings him out.
Image of sloth and picture of a slave,   90
The obloquy and scorn of my renown!

74.3. *and* Soldiers] *Dyce; not in O1–4.*   76. glories] *O1, O3–4;* bodies *O2.*
75. ye] *O1–3;* my *O4.*   82. 'gainst] *O1–3;* against *O4.*

73. *coil*] commotion.
75. *stoops*] bends, subdues.
78. *illustrate*] beautify, shed luster upon.

How may my heart, thus fired with mine eyes,
Wounded with shame and kill'd with discontent,
Shroud any thought may hold my striving hands
From martial justice on thy wretched soul?   95

THERIDAMAS.
Yet pardon him, I pray your majesty.

TECHELLES. USUMCASANE.
Let all of us entreat your highness' pardon.

TAMBURLAINE.
Stand up, ye base unworthy soldiers!
Know ye not yet the argument of arms?

AMYRAS.
Good my lord, let him be forgiven for once,   100
And we will force him to the field hereafter.

TAMBURLAINE.
Stand up, my boys, and I will teach ye arms,
And what the jealousy of wars must do.
O Samarcanda, where I breathed first
And joy'd the fire of this martial flesh,   105
Blush, blush, fair city, at thine honor's foil,
And shame of nature, which Jaertis' stream,
Embracing thee with deepest of his love,
Can never wash from thy distained brows.
Here, Jove, receive his fainting soul again,   110
A form not meet to give that subject essence

92. mine] *O1, O3–4*; my *O2*.
94. may] *O1, O3–4*; nay *O2*.
100. once] *O1, O3–4*; one *O2*.
102. ye] *O1–2*; you *O3–4*.

105. martial] *O1–2*;   materiall *O3–4*.
106. thine] *O1–3*; thy *O4*.
107. which] *Rob.*; with *O1–4*.

94. *Shroud*] shelter, harbor.   94. *may*] which may.
99. *argument of arms*] meaning of military life.
103. *the . . . wars*] military zeal.
105. *joy'd*] rejoiced at.   106. *foil*] disgrace.
107. *Jaertis*] Jaxartes, a river flowing from Tartary into the Caspian Sea.
109. *distained*] sullied, dishonored.
110–114. *Here . . . consists*] "Here Jove receive again the soul of Calyphas, a spirit (i.e. 'form' almost in the sense of 'idea') not worthy to be the immortal part (essence) of that subject whose mortal part (matter) is derived from the flesh of Tamburlaine—in whom moves an immortal spirit of the same mould as thine own" (Ellis-Fermor). The technical terms derive from sixteenth-century Aristotelian studies.

Whose matter is the flesh of Tamburlaine,
Wherein an incorporeal spirit moves,
Made of the mold whereof thyself consists,
Which makes me valiant, proud, ambitious,   115
Ready to levy power against thy throne,
That I might move the turning spheres of heaven,
For earth and all this airy region
Cannot contain the state of Tamburlaine.   [*Stabs* Calyphas.]
By Mahomet, thy mighty friend, I swear,   120
In sending to my issue such a soul,
Created of the massy dregs of earth,
The scum and tartar of the elements,
Wherein was neither courage, strength, or wit,
But folly, sloth, and damned idleness,   125
Thou hast procur'd a greater enemy
Than he that darted mountains at thy head,
Shaking the burden mighty Atlas bears,
Whereat thou trembling hidd'st thee in the air,
Cloth'd with a pitchy cloud for being seen.   130
And now, ye canker'd curs of Asia,
That will not see the strength of Tamburlaine
Although it shine as brightly as the sun,
Now you shall feel the strength of Tamburlaine
And, by the state of his supremacy,   135
Approve the difference 'twixt himself and you.
ORCANES.
Thou showest the difference 'twixt ourselves and thee,
In this thy barbarous damned tyranny.
KING OF JERUSALEM.
Thy victories are grown so violent

113. incorporeal] *O1–2*; incorporall   *in O1–4.*
O3–4.   134. you   shall]   *O1–2*;   shall   ye
119. S.D. *Stabs* Calyphas] *Dyce*; *not*   *O3–4.*

117. *spheres*] See Part I, II.vii.25, note.
123. *tartar*] deposit (as inside a wine cask).
124. *wit*] understanding.
127–130. *he . . . seen*] See Part I, II.vi.1–6, note.
128. *Atlas*] the Titan who was condemned to bear the heavens on his
head and hands.
130. *for*] for fear of.   136. *Approve*] find out by experience.

That shortly heaven, fill'd with the meteors   140
Of blood and fire thy tyrannies have made,
Will pour down blood and fire on thy head,
Whose scalding drops will pierce thy seething brains
And with our bloods revenge our bloods on thee.

TAMBURLAINE.

Villains, these terrors and these tyrannies   145
(If tyrannies war's justice ye repute)
I execute, enjoin'd me from above,
To scourge the pride of such as heaven abhors.
Nor am I made arch-monarch of the world,
Crown'd and invested by the hand of Jove,   150
For deeds of bounty or nobility.
But, since I exercise a greater name,
The scourge of God and terror of the world,
I must apply myself to fit those terms,
In war, in blood, in death, in cruelty,   155
And plague such peasants as resist in me
The power of heaven's eternal majesty.
Theridamas, Techelles, and Casane,
Ransack the tents and the pavilions
Of these proud Turks, and take their concubines,   160
Making them bury this effeminate brat,
For not a common soldier shall defile
His manly fingers with so faint a boy.
Then bring those Turkish harlots to my tent,
And I'll dispose them as it likes me best.   165
Meanwhile, take him in.

SOLDIERS.   We will, my lord.

                          [*Exeunt with the body of* Calyphas.]

144. bloods on] *O1, O3–4*; blood   158. Casane] *O1,   O3–4;   Vsum-*
on *O2*.   *Casane O2*.
145. Villains] *O1–3*; Villaine *O4*.   166.1. *Exeunt . . .* Calyphas]   *Dyce;*
156. resist in] *Dyce, conj. Broughton;* *not in O1–4*.
resisting *O1–4*.

---

140. *meteors*] a word used for atmospheric phenomena of every kind. For
the formation of the "meteors" in question here, compare Part II, III.ii.2–9;
and see note on Part I, I.ii.49–51.
    156. *peasants*] boors.
    163. *faint*] faint-hearted, spiritless.   165. *likes*] pleases.

KING OF JERUSALEM.

O damned monster, nay, a fiend of hell,
Whose cruelties are not so harsh as thine,
Nor yet impos'd with such a bitter hate!

ORCANES.

Revenge it, Rhadamanth and Aeacus,   170
And let your hates, extended in his pains,
Expel the hate wherewith he pains our souls!

KING OF TREBIZON.

May never day give virtue to his eyes,
Whose sight, compos'd of fury and of fire,
Doth send such stern affections to his heart!   175

KING OF SORIA.

May never spirit, vein, or artier feed
The cursed substance of that cruel heart;
But, wanting moisture and remorseful blood,
Dry up with anger and consume with heat.

TAMBURLAINE.

Well, bark, ye dogs! I'll bridle all your tongues   180
And bind them close with bits of burnish'd steel
Down to the channels of your hateful throats;
And, with the pains my rigor shall inflict,
I'll make ye roar, that earth may echo forth
The far-resounding torments ye sustain;   185
As when an herd of lusty Cimbrian bulls
Run mourning round about the females' miss
And, stung with fury of their following,
Fill all the air with troublous bellowing.
I will, with engines never exercis'd,   190
Conquer, sack, and utterly consume
Your cities and your golden palaces,

170. it] *O1–2; not in O3–4.*   184. ye] *O1–2;* you *O3–4.*

---

170. *Rhadamanth and Aeacus*] two of the three judges in Hades.
173. *virtue*] power.   175. *affections*] feelings.
176. *artier*] artery.   178. *remorseful*] compassionate.
186. *Cimbrian*] The Cimbri were an ancient Celtic people. Spenser, *The Faerie Queene*, I.viii.11, seems to have led Marlowe to associate them with bulls.
187. *females' miss*] loss of their females.
188. *their following*] the following of them (the females).

And, with the flames that beat against the clouds,
Incense the heavens and make the stars to melt,
As if they were the tears of Mahomet   195
For hot consumption of his country's pride.
And till by vision or by speech I hear
Immortal Jove say, "Cease, my Tamburlaine!"
I will persist a terror to the world,
Making the meteors, that like armed men   200
Are seen to march upon the towers of heaven,
Run tilting round about the firmament
And break their burning lances in the air
For honor of my wondrous victories.
Come, bring them in to our pavilion.   *Exeunt.* 205

[IV.ii]   [*Enter*] Olympia *alone.*

OLYMPIA.
Distress'd Olympia, whose weeping eyes
Since thy arrival here beheld no sun,
But, clos'd within the compass of a tent,
Hath stain'd thy cheeks and made thee look like death,
Devise some means to rid thee of thy life   5
Rather than yield to his detested suit
Whose drift is only to dishonor thee;
And since this earth, dew'd with thy brinish tears,
Affords no herbs whose taste may poison thee,
Nor yet this air, beat often with thy sighs,   10
Contagious smells and vapors to infect thee,
Nor thy close cave a sword to murder thee,
Let this invention be the instrument.

Enter Theridamas.

THERIDAMAS.
Well met, Olympia. I sought thee in my tent,
But when I saw the place obscure and dark   15

2. beheld] *O1, O3*; beholde *O2, O4*.   3. a] *O1, O3–4*; the *O2*.

---

194. *Incense*] set on fire.
202. *tilting*] engaging in combat for sport.
[IV.ii]
7. *drift*] purpose.   12. *close*] secret.

Which with thy beauty thou wast wont to light,
Enrag'd, I ran about the fields for thee,
Supposing amorous Jove had sent his son,
The winged Hermes, to convey thee hence.
But now I find thee, and that fear is past.   20
Tell me, Olympia, wilt thou grant my suit?

OLYMPIA.

My lord and husband's death, with my sweet son's,
With whom I buried all affections
Save grief and sorrow, which torment my heart,
Forbids my mind to entertain a thought   25
That tends to love, but meditate on death,
A fitter subject for a pensive soul.

THERIDAMAS.

Olympia, pity him in whom thy looks
Have greater operation and more force
Than Cynthia's in the watery wilderness,   30
For with thy view my joys are at the full,
And ebb again as thou depart'st from me.

OLYMPIA.

Ah, pity me, my lord, and draw your sword,
Making a passage for my troubled soul,
Which beats against this prison to get out   35
And meet my husband and my loving son.

THERIDAMAS.

Nothing but still thy husband and thy son!
Leave this, my love, and listen more to me.
Thou shalt be stately queen of fair Argier,
And, cloth'd in costly cloth of massy gold,   40
Upon the marble turrets of my court
Sit like to Venus in her chair of state,
Commanding all thy princely eye desires;
And I will cast off arms and sit with thee,
Spending my life in sweet discourse of love.   45

16. wast] *O1, O3–4*; was *O2*.   44. and] *O1, O3–4*; to *O2*.
22. son's] *O1–2*; son *O3–4*.

---

19. *Hermes*] Jove's herald and messenger.
23. *affections*] emotions.
30. *Cynthia's . . . wilderness*] i.e., the moon's power to govern the tides.

OLYMPIA.

No such discourse is pleasant in mine ears,
But that where every period ends with death,
And every line begins with death again.
I cannot love, to be an emperess.

THERIDAMAS.

Nay, lady, then, if nothing will prevail,　　　　　　50
I'll use some other means to make you yield.
Such is the sudden fury of my love,
I must and will be pleas'd, and you shall yield.
Come to the tent again.

OLYMPIA.

Stay, good my lord, and, will you save my honor,　　55
I'll give your grace a present of such price
As all the world cannot afford the like.

THERIDAMAS.

What is it?

OLYMPIA.

An ointment which a cunning alchemist
Distilled from the purest balsamum　　　　　　　60
And simplest extracts of all minerals,
In which the essential form of marble stone,
Tempered by science metaphysical
And spells of magic from the mouths of spirits,
With which if you but 'noint your tender skin,　　65
Nor pistol, sword, nor lance can pierce your flesh.

THERIDAMAS.

Why, madam, think ye to mock me thus palpably?

OLYMPIA.

To prove it, I will 'noint my naked throat,
Which when you stab, look on your weapon's point,
And you shall see't rebated with the blow.　　　　70

46. in] *O1–3*; to *O4*.　　　　　　will *O4*.
55. good] *O1, O3–4*; now *O2*.　64. mouths] *O1, O3–4*; mother *O2*.
55. and, will you] *O1–3*; if you　67. ye] *O1–2*; you *O3–4*.

---

61. *simplest extracts*] "What alchemy terms the elements, or elemental
parts, of the minerals." (Ellis-Fermor).
62. *form*] determinant principle.
63. *metaphysical*] supernatural.
70. *rebated*] blunted.

THERIDAMAS.

Why gave you not your husband some of it,
If you loved him, and it so precious?

OLYMPIA.

My purpose was, my lord, to spend it so,
But was prevented by his sudden end;
And for a present easy proof hereof,   75
That I dissemble not, try it on me.

THERIDAMAS.

I will, Olympia, and will keep it for
The richest present of this eastern world.   *She 'noints her throat.*

OLYMPIA.

Now stab, my lord, and mark your weapon's point,
That will be blunted if the blow be great.   80

THERIDAMAS.

Here then, Olympia.   *[Stabs her.]*
What, have I slain her? Villain, stab thyself!
Cut off this arm that murdered my love,
In whom the learned rabbis of this age
Might find as many wondrous miracles   85
As in the theoria of the world.
Now hell is fairer than Elysium;
A greater lamp than that bright eye of heaven,
From whence the stars do borrow all their light,
Wanders about the black circumference;   90
And now the damned souls are free from pain,
For every Fury gazeth on her looks.
Infernal Dis is courting of my love,
Inventing masks and stately shows for her,
Opening the doors of his rich treasury   95

---

75. hereof] *O1, O3–4*; thereof *O2.*   *O1–4.*
77. and will] *O1, O3–4*; and I wil   87. Elysium] *Rob.*; *Elisian O1–4.*
O2.   89. do borrow] *O1, O3–4*; borow
81. S.D. *Stabs her*] *Rob.*; *not in*   doo *O2.*

---

84. *rabbis*] scholarly authorities.
86. *theoria*] contemplation, survey.
88. *that . . . heaven*] the sun.
93. *Dis*] See Part I, II.vii.36–37, note.
94. *masks*] lavish entertainments, combining literary, musical, and
spectacular elements.

To entertain this queen of chastity,
Whose body shall be tomb'd with all the pomp
The treasure of my kingdom may afford.   *Exit, taking her away.*

[IV.iii]
[*Enter*] Tamburlaine, *drawn in his chariot by Trebizon and Soria with bits
in their mouths, reins in his left hand, in his right hand a whip with which he
scourgeth them*; Techelles, Theridamas, Usumcasane, Amyras, Celebinus; [Orcanes, King of] Natolia, *and* Jerusalem, *led by with five or
six common* Soldiers.

TAMBURLAINE.
   Holla, ye pampered jades of Asia!
   What, can ye draw but twenty miles a day,
   And have so proud a chariot at your heels,
   And such a coachman as great Tamburlaine,
   But from Asphaltis, where I conquer'd you,   5
   To Byron here, where thus I honor you?
   The horse that guide the golden eye of heaven
   And blow the morning from their nosterils,
   Making their fiery gait above the clouds,
   Are not so honored in their governor   10
   As you, ye slaves, in mighty Tamburlaine.
   The headstrong jades of Thrace Alcides tam'd,
   That King Aegeus fed with human flesh
   And made so wanton that they knew their strengths,

98. my] *O1, O3–4*; thy *O2*.   0.4. with] *O1–3*; not in *O4*.
[IV.iii]   10. in] *O1–3*; as *O4*.
0.2. *his left*] *O1, O3–4*; *their left O2*.

---

   1. *pampered ... Asia*] Golding's Ovid (1567) has "pampred Jades of
Thrace" (ix.238). Marlowe introduces *jades of Thrace* in l. 12 of the present
scene. For other possible borrowings from Golding by Marlowe, see M. M.
Wills, "Marlowe's Rôle in Borrowed Lines," *PMLA*, LII (1937), 902–905.
   5. *Asphaltis*] a bituminous lake near Babylon. See Part II, V.i; and
Seaton, pp. 25–26.
   6. *Byron*] a town near Babylon.
   7. *horse*] plural.
   8. *nosterils*] nostrils.
   10. *their governor*] their controller, the driver of the chariot they draw.
   12–14. *The ... strengths*] One of the labors of Hercules (Alcides) was to
capture the man-eating mares of Diomedes (Aegeus), a savage Thracian
king.

Were not subdu'd with valor more divine   15
Than you by this unconquered arm of mine.
To make you fierce and fit my appetite,
You shall be fed with flesh as raw as blood
And drink in pails the strongest muscadel.
If you can live with it, then live, and draw   20
My chariot swifter than the racking clouds;
If not, then die like beasts, and fit for naught
But perches for the black and fatal ravens.
Thus am I right the scourge of highest Jove;
And see the figure of my dignity,   25
By which I hold my name and majesty.

AMYRAS.

Let me have coach, my lord, that I may ride,
And thus be drawn with these two idle kings.

TAMBURLAINE.

Thy youth forbids such ease, my kingly boy.
They shall tomorrow draw my chariot,   30
While these their fellow-kings may be refresh'd.

ORCANES.

O thou that swayest the region under earth
And art a king as absolute as Jove,
Come as thou didst in fruitful Sicily,
Surveying all the glories of the land,   35
And as thou took'st the fair Proserpina,
Joying the fruit of Ceres' garden-plot,
For love, for honor, and to make her queen,
So for just hate, for shame, and to subdue
This proud contemner of thy dreadful power   40
Come once in fury and survey his pride,
Haling him headlong to the lowest hell.

---

27. have coach] *O1–2*; haue a
coch *O3–4*.
28. with] *O1–3*; by *O4*.

37. garden-plot] *O1, O3–4*; garded
plot *O2*.

---

21. *racking*] scudding before the wind.   24. *right*] indeed.
25. *see the figure*] behold in me the very image.
32. *thou*] i.e., Pluto, who carried off Proserpina in the circumstances
Orcanes describes.
37. *Joying*] enjoying.
37. *Ceres*] Proserpina's mother.   40. *contemner*] scorner.

THERIDAMAS.

    Your majesty must get some bits for these,
    To bridle their contemptuous cursing tongues
    That like unruly, never-broken jades   45
    Break through the hedges of their hateful mouths
    And pass their fixed bounds exceedingly.

TECHELLES.

    Nay, we will break the hedges of their mouths
    And pull their kicking colts out of their pastures.

USUMCASANE.

    Your majesty already hath devis'd   50
    A mean, as fit as may be, to restrain
    These coltish coach-horse tongues from blasphemy.

CELEBINUS.

    How like you that, sir king? Why speak you not?

KING OF JERUSALEM.

    Ah, cruel brat, sprung from a tyrant's loins!
    How like his cursed father he begins   55
    To practice taunts and bitter tyrannies!

TAMBURLAINE.

    Ay, Turk, I tell thee, this same boy is he
    That must, advanc'd in higher pomp than this,
    Rifle the kingdoms I shall leave unsack'd,
    If Jove, esteeming me too good for earth,   60
    Raise me to match the fair Aldebaran,
    Above the threefold astracism of heaven,
    Before I conquer all the triple world.
    Now fetch me out the Turkish concubines.

53. speak you] *O1, O3–4*; speake ye   61. match] *O1–2*; march *O3–4*.
O2.   62. Above] *O1–3*; about *O4*.
57. same] *O1–3*; *not in O4*.

46. *the . . . mouths*] i.e., their teeth. So also in l. 48.
49. *their kicking . . . pastures*] i.e., their over-active tongues out of their mouths.
51. *mean*] means.
61. *Aldebaran*] a bright star in the constellation Taurus.
62. *threefold astracism*] constellation consisting of, or dominated by, three stars.
63. *triple world*] i.e., composed of Europe, Asia, and Africa. Compare Part I, IV.iv.74; and l. 118 of the present scene.

I will prefer them for the funeral   65
They have bestowed on my abortive son.

The Concubines *are brought in.*

Where are my common soldiers now that fought
So lion-like upon Asphaltis' plains?

SOLDIERS.

Here, my lord.

TAMBURLAINE.

Hold ye, tall soldiers, take ye queens apiece—   70
I mean such queens as were kings' concubines.
Take them; divide them, and their jewels too,
And let them equally serve all your turns.

SOLDIERS.

We thank your majesty.

TAMBURLAINE.

Brawl not, I warn you, for your lechery,   75
For every man that so offends shall die.

ORCANES.

Injurious tyrant, wilt thou so defame
The hateful fortunes of thy victory,
To exercise upon such guiltless dames
The violence of thy common soldiers' lust?   80

TAMBURLAINE.

Live continent then, ye slaves, and meet not me
With troops of harlots at your slothful heels.

CONCUBINES.

O pity us, my lord, and save our honors!

TAMBURLAINE.

Are ye not gone, ye villains, with your spoils?

They run away with the Ladies.

KING OF JERUSALEM.

O merciless, infernal cruelty!   85

TAMBURLAINE.

"Save your honors!" 'Twere but time indeed,

72. their] *O1, O3–4; not in O2.*   81. continent] *Rob.*; content *O1–4.*

---

65. *prefer*] promote.
70. *tall*] valiant, brave.
70, 71. *queens*] Tamburlaine puns on "queens" and "queans" (meaning "whores").

Lost long before you knew what honor meant.

THERIDAMAS.

It seems they meant to conquer us, my lord,
And make us jesting pageants for their trulls.

TAMBURLAINE.

And now themselves shall make our pageant,   90
And common soldiers jest with all their trulls.
Let them take pleasure soundly in their spoils
Till we prepare our march to Babylon,
Whither we next make expedition.

TECHELLES.

Let us not be idle then, my lord,   95
But presently be prest to conquer it.

TAMBURLAINE.

We will, Techelles. Forward then, ye jades!
Now crouch, ye kings of greatest Asia,
And tremble when ye hear this scourge will come
That whips down cities and controlleth crowns,   100
Adding their wealth and treasure to my store.
The Euxine sea, north to Natolia;
The Terrene, west; the Caspian, north-northeast;
And, on the south, Sinus Arabicus
Shall all be loaden with the martial spoils   105
We will convey with us to Persia.
Then shall my native city, Samarcanda,
And crystal waves of fresh Jaertis' stream,
The pride and beauty of her princely seat,
Be famous through the furthest continents,   110
For there my palace royal shall be plac'd,
Whose shining turrets shall dismay the heavens
And cast the fame of Ilion's tower to hell.
Thorough the streets, with troops of conquered kings,
I'll ride in golden armor like the sun,   115

87. you] *O1, O3–4;* ye *O2.*   114. Thorough] *O1–2;* Through
105. all] *O1–3; not in O4.*   *O3;* & through *O4.*

89. *make . . . pageants*] make mocking spectacles of us.
89, 91. *trulls*] strumpets.   94. *expedition*] haste.
96. *presently*] quickly.   96. *prest*] ready.
104. *Sinus Arabicus*] the Red Sea.
113. *Ilion*] Troy.   114. *Thorough*] through.

And in my helm a triple plume shall spring,
Spangled with diamonds, dancing in the air,
To note me emperor of the three-fold world;
Like to an almond tree ymounted high
Upon the lofty and celestial mount   120
Of ever-green Selinus, quaintly deck'd
With blooms more white than Erycina's brows,
Whose tender blossoms tremble every one
At every little breath that thorough heaven is blown.
Then in my coach, like Saturn's royal son   125
Mounted his shining chariot gilt with fire,
And drawn with princely eagles through the path
Pav'd with bright crystal and enchas'd with stars,
When all the gods stand gazing at his pomp,
So will I ride through Samarcanda streets,   130
Until my soul, dissevered from this flesh,
Shall mount the milk-white way and meet Him there.
To Babylon, my lords, to Babylon!   *Exeunt.*

Finis Actus Quarti.

[V.i]

Enter the Governor of Babylon *upon the walls with* [Maximus *and*] *others.*

GOVERNOR OF BABYLON.

What saith Maximus?

MAXIMUS.

My lord, the breach the enemy hath made

121. ever-green] *Rob.*; euery greene *O1–4.*
122. brows] *O1, O3–4*; bowes *O2.*
124. that thorough] *O1–3*; from *O4.*

126. chariot] *Dyce*; chariots *O1–4.*
[V.i]
0.1. Maximus *and*] *Rob.*; *not in O1–4.*

119–124. *Like . . . blown*] apparently borrowed by Marlowe from Spenser, *The Faerie Queene*, I.vii.32; Marlowe's alexandrine (l. 124) corresponds with that which concludes Spenser's stanza. But the first three books of *The Faerie Queene* were not published until 1590; so if Marlowe was the borrower he had presumably seen Spenser's poem in manuscript.
121. *Selinus*] a Sicilian town.
122. *Erycina*] Venus, who had a famous temple on Mt. Eryx in Sicily.
125. *Saturn's royal son*] Jupiter.   128. *enchas'd*] adorned.

Gives such assurance of our overthrow
That little hope is left to save our lives
Or hold our city from the conqueror's hands.   5
Then hang out flags, my lord, of humble truce,
And satisfy the people's general prayers,
That Tamburlaine's intolerable wrath
May be suppress'd by our submission.

GOVERNOR OF BABYLON.

Villain, respects thou more thy slavish life   10
Than honor of thy country or thy name?
Is not my life and state as dear to me,
The city and my native country's weal,
As anything of price with thy conceit?
Have we not hope, for all our battered walls,   15
To live secure and keep his forces out,
When this our famous lake of Limnasphaltis
Makes walls afresh with everything that falls
Into the liquid substance of his stream,
More strong than are the gates of death or hell?   20
What faintness should dismay our courages
When we are thus defens'd against our foe
And have no terror but his threat'ning looks?

Enter another [Citizen], *kneeling to the* Governor.

FIRST CITIZEN.

My lord, if ever you did deed of ruth,
And now will work a refuge to our lives,   25
Offer submission, hang up flags of truce,
That Tamburlaine may pity our distress
And use us like a loving conqueror.
Though this be held his last day's dreadful siege,
Wherein he spareth neither man nor child,   30
Yet are there Christians of Georgia here,
Whose state he ever pitied and reliev'd,

6. out] *O1*; our *O2–4*.   23.1. Citizen] *Rob.*; *not in O1–4*.
14. of] *O1–3*; in *O4*.   32. he] *O1, O3–4*; was *O2*.

14. *As . . . conceit*] as anything that may be of value in your estimation.
17. *Limnasphaltis*] See Part II, IV.iii.5, note.
21. *faintness*] weakness.

Will get his pardon if your grace would send.

GOVERNOR OF BABYLON.

How is my soul environed,
And this eterniz'd city, Babylon,   35
Fill'd with a pack of faint-heart fugitives
That thus entreat their shame and servitude!

[*Enter a second* Citizen.]

SECOND CITIZEN.

My lord, if ever you will win our hearts,
Yield up the town, save our wives and children;
For I will cast myself from off these walls   40
Or die some death of quickest violence
Before I bide the wrath of Tamburlaine.

GOVERNOR OF BABYLON.

Villains, cowards, traitors to our state,
Fall to the earth and pierce the pit of hell,
That legions of tormenting spirits may vex   45
Your slavish bosoms with continual pains!
I care not, nor the town will never yield
As long as any life is in my breast.

Enter Theridamas *and* Techelles, *with other Soldiers.*

THERIDAMAS.

Thou desperate governor of Babylon,
To save thy life, and us a little labor,   50
Yield speedily the city to our hands,
Or else be sure thou shalt be forc'd with pains
More exquisite than ever traitor felt.

GOVERNOR OF BABYLON.

Tyrant, I turn the traitor in thy throat,
And will defend it in despite of thee.   55
Call up the soldiers to defend these walls.

TECHELLES.

Yield, foolish governor! We offer more

37.1. *Enter . . .* Citizen] *Dyce; not in*   39. town, save] *O1–3*; towne, and
O1–4.   saue *O4.*
38. you] *O1, O3–4*; ye *O2.*

33. *Will*] who will.
35. *eterniz'd*] immortalized.

Than ever yet we did to such proud slaves
As durst resist us till our third day's siege.
Thou seest us prest to give the last assault,   60
And that shall bide no more regard of parley.

GOVERNOR OF BABYLON.
Assault and spare not! We will never yield!
                    Alarm, and they scale the walls. [*Exeunt above.*]

Enter Tamburlaine, [*drawn in his chariot by the* Kings of Trebizon *and*
Soria;] *with* Usumcasane, Amyras, *and Celebinus, with others; the two
spare* Kings[, Orcanes of Natolia, *and* Jerusalem].

TAMBURLAINE.
The stately buildings of fair Babylon,
Whose lofty pillars, higher than the clouds,
Were wont to guide the seaman in the deep,   65
Being carried thither by the cannon's force,
Now fill the mouth of Limnasphaltis' lake
And make a bridge unto the battered walls.
Where Belus, Ninus, and great Alexander
Have rode in triumph, triumphs Tamburlaine,   70
Whose chariot wheels have burst th'Assyrians' bones,
Drawn with these kings on heaps of carcasses.
Now in the place where fair Semiramis,
Courted by kings and peers of Asia,
Hath trod the measures, do my soldiers march,   75
And in the streets, where brave Assyrian dames
Have rid in pomp like rich Saturnia,

62.1. *Exeunt above*] *this edn.*; *not in*   62.2–3. *drawn . . . Soria*] *Dyce*; *not in*
O1–4.   *O1–4.*

---

60. *prest*] ready.
61. *bide . . . regard*] await no further consideration.
69. *Belus*] the legendary founder of Babylon.
69. *Ninus*] the reputed founder of Nineveh. His wife, Semiramis, was
supposed to have rebuilt Babylon. See Part II, III.v.36–37.
69. *Alexander*] Alexander the Great, who conquered Babylon in the
fourth century B.C.
71. *burst*] broken.   72. *with*] by.
73. *Semiramis*] See note on l. 69.
75. *measures*] grave or stately dances.
76. *brave*] finely arrayed, splendid.
77. *Saturnia*] Juno.

With furious words and frowning visages
My horsemen brandish their unruly blades.

Enter Theridamas *and* Techelles, *bringing the* Governor of Babylon.

Who have ye there, my lords?   80

THERIDAMAS.

The sturdy governor of Babylon,
That made us all the labor for the town
And us'd such slender reck'ning of your majesty.

TAMBURLAINE.

Go, bind the villain! He shall hang in chains
Upon the ruins of this conquered town.   85
Sirrah, the view of our vermilion tents
Which threaten'd more than if the region
Next underneath the element of fire
Were full of comets and of blazing stars,
Whose flaming trains should reach down to the earth,   90
Could not affright you. No, nor I myself,
The wrathful messenger of mighty Jove,
That with his sword hath quail'd all earthly kings,
Could not persuade you to submission,
But still the ports were shut. Villain, I say,   95
Should I but touch the rusty gates of hell,
The triple-headed Cerberus would howl
And wake black Jove to crouch and kneel to me;
But I have sent volleys of shot to you,
Yet could not enter till the breach was made.   100

GOVERNOR OF BABYLON.

Nor if my body could have stopp'd the breach
Shouldst thou have enter'd, cruel Tamburlaine.
'Tis not thy bloody tents can make me yield,

83. of] *O1–3*; for *O4*.   101. breach] *O1, O3–4*; brcath *O2*.
98. wake] *O1–3*; make *O4*.

---

87. *region*] See Part I, IV.ii.30, note.
89. *comets*] These were believed to be flaming masses of exhalation at the uttermost limits of the atmosphere and to presage great disasters. See Heninger, pp. 87–91.
93. *quail'd*] overpowered.
95. *ports*] gates.
97. *Cerberus*] See Part I, I.ii.161, note.
98. *black Jove*] Pluto. Compare Part II, IV.iii.32–33.

Nor yet thyself, the anger of the Highest,
For, though thy cannon shook the city walls,   105
My heart did never quake or courage faint.

TAMBURLAINE.

Well, now I'll make it quake. Go, draw him up,
Hang him up in chains upon the city walls,
And let my soldiers shoot the slave to death.

GOVERNOR OF BABYLON.

Vile monster, born of some infernal hag   110
And sent from hell to tyrannize on earth,
Do all thy worst! Nor death, nor Tamburlaine,
Torture, or pain can daunt my dreadless mind.

TAMBURLAINE.

Up with him, then! his body shall be scarr'd.

GOVERNOR OF BABYLON.

But, Tamburlaine, in Limnasphaltis' lake   115
There lies more gold than Babylon is worth,
Which, when the city was besieg'd, I hid.
Save but my life and I will give it thee.

TAMBURLAINE.

Then for all your valor you would save your life?
Whereabout lies it?   120

GOVERNOR OF BABYLON.

Under a hollow bank, right opposite
Against the western gate of Babylon.

TAMBURLAINE.

Go thither, some of you, and take his gold.

                    [*Exeunt some Attendants.*]

The rest forward with execution.
Away with him hence, let him speak no more.   125
I think I make your courage something quail.

          [*Exeunt Attendants with the* Governor of Babylon.]

When this is done, we'll march from Babylon
And make our greatest haste to Persia.
These jades are broken-winded and half tir'd;

---

105. city] *O1–3; not in O4.*   *not in O1–4.*
107. him] *O1, O3–4;* it *O2.*   126.1. *Exeunt . . . Babylon]*   *Dyce;*
114. scarr'd] *O1–2;* seard *O3–4.*   *not in O1–4.*
123.1. *Exeunt . . . Attendants]*   *Dyce;*

Unharness them, and let me have fresh horse.   130
So, now their best is done to honor me,
Take them and hang them both up presently.

KING OF TREBIZON.

Vile tyrant! Barbarous, bloody Tamburlaine!

TAMBURLAINE.

Take them away, Theridamas. See them dispatch'd.

THERIDAMAS.

I will, my lord.   135

[Exit with the Kings of Trebizon *and* Soria.]

TAMBURLAINE.

Come, Asian viceroys, to your tasks a while,
And take such fortune as your fellows felt.

ORCANES.

First let thy Scythian horse tear both our limbs,
Rather than we should draw thy chariot
And like base slaves abject our princely minds   140
To vile and ignominious servitude.

KING OF JERUSALEM.

Rather lend me thy weapon, Tamburlaine,
That I may sheathe it in this breast of mine.
A thousand deaths could not torment our hearts
More than the thought of this doth vex our souls.   145

AMYRAS.

They will talk still, my lord, if you do not bridle them.

TAMBURLAINE.

Bridle them, and let me to my coach.

They bridle them. [*The* Governor of Babylon *appears hanging in chains
on the walls. Enter* Theridamas.]

AMYRAS.

See now, my lord, how brave the captain hangs.

TAMBURLAINE.

'Tis brave indeed, my boy. Well done!
Shoot first, my lord, and then the rest shall follow.   150

135.1. *Exit* . . . Soria] *Rob.*; *not in*   147.1–2. *The* . . . Theridamas] *Dyce*;
O1–4.   *not in O1–4.*

132. *presently*] immediately.
137. *take* . . . *felt*] share the fate of your fellow kings.
140. *abject*] degrade, abase.   148, 149. *brave*] excellent(ly).

THERIDAMAS.

Then have at him, to begin withal.   *Theridamas shoots.*

GOVERNOR OF BABYLON.

Yet save my life, and let this wound appease
The mortal fury of great Tamburlaine.

TAMBURLAINE.

No, though Asphaltis' lake were liquid gold
And offer'd me as ransom for thy life,   155
Yet shouldst thou die. Shoot at him all at once.   *They shoot.*
So now he hangs like Bagdet's governor,
Having as many bullets in his flesh
As there be breaches in her battered wall.
Go now, and bind the burghers hand and foot,   160
And cast them headlong in the city's lake.
Tartars and Persians shall inhabit there,
And, to command the city, I will build
A citadel, that all Africa,
Which hath been subject to the Persian king,   165
Shall pay me tribute for in Babylon.

TECHELLES.

What shall be done with their wives and children, my lord?

TAMBURLAINE.

Techelles, drown them all, man, woman, and child.
Leave not a Babylonian in the town.

TECHELLES.

I will about it straight. Come, soldiers.   *Exit.* 170

TAMBURLAINE.

Now, Casane, where's the Turkish Alcoran
And all the heaps of superstitious books
Found in the temples of that Mahomet
Whom I have thought a god? They shall be burnt.

USUMCASANE.

Here they are, my lord.   175

TAMBURLAINE.

Well said. Let there be a fire presently.
In vain, I see, men worship Mahomet.

---

151. *have . . . withal*] I shall attack him, for a start.
157. *Bagdet*] Baghdad.
171. *Alcoran*] See Part I, III.iii.76, note.

My sword hath sent millions of Turks to hell,
Slew all his priests, his kinsmen, and his friends,
And yet I live untouch'd by Mahomet. 180
There is a God, full of revenging wrath,
From whom the thunder and the lightning breaks,
Whose scourge I am, and Him will I obey.
So, Casane, fling them in the fire!
Now, Mahomet, if thou have any power, 185
Come down thyself and work a miracle.
Thou art not worthy to be worshipped
That suffers flames of fire to burn the writ
Wherein the sum of thy religion rests.
Why send'st thou not a furious whirlwind down 190
To blow thy Alcoran up to thy throne,
Where men report thou sitt'st by God himself?
Or vengeance on the head of Tamburlaine
That shakes his sword against thy majesty
And spurns the abstracts of thy foolish laws? 195
Well, soldiers, Mahomet remains in hell;
He cannot hear the voice of Tamburlaine.
Seek out another godhead to adore—
The God that sits in heaven, if any god,
For He is God alone, and none but He. 200

[*Enter* Techelles.]

TECHELLES.

I have fulfill'd your highness' will, my lord.
Thousands of men, drown'd in Asphaltis' lake,
Have made the water swell above the banks,
And fishes, fed by human carcasses,
Amaz'd, swim up and down upon the waves, 205
As when they swallow asafoetida
Which makes them fleet aloft and gasp for air.

---

183. will I] *O1–2*; I wil *O3–4*.   *O1–4*.
190. send'st] *O1–2*; sends *O3–4*.   204. fed] *Rob.*; feed *O1–4*.
192. sitt'st] *O1–2*; sits *O3–4*.   205. upon] *O1–2*; *not in O3–4*.
193. head] *O1–3*; blood *O4*.   207. gasp] *O1, O3–4*; gape *O2*.
200.1. *Enter* Techelles] *Rob.*; *not in*

---

206. *asafoetida*] a resinous gum used in cookery and in medicine.
207. *fleet*] float.

TAMBURLAINE.

    Well, then, my friendly lords, what now remains
    But that we leave sufficient garrison
    And presently depart to Persia   210
    To triumph after all our victories?

THERIDAMAS.

    Ay, good my lord, let us in haste to Persia;
    And let this captain be remov'd the walls
    To some high hill about the city here.

TAMBURLAINE.

    Let it be so. About it, soldiers.   215
    But stay, I feel myself distempered suddenly.

TECHELLES.

    What is it dares distemper Tamburlaine?

TAMBURLAINE.

    Something, Techelles, but I know not what.
    But forth, ye vassals; whatsoe'er it be,
    Sickness or death can never conquer me.   *Exeunt.* 220

[V.ii]

    Enter Callapine, Amasia, [Captain,] *with drums and trumpets.*

CALLAPINE.

    King of Amasia, now our mighty host
    Marcheth in Asia Major where the streams
    Of Euphrates and Tigris swiftly runs;
    And here may we behold great Babylon
    Circled about with Limnasphaltis' lake   5
    Where Tamburlaine with all his army lies,
    Which being faint and weary with the siege,
    We may lie ready to encounter him
    Before his host be full from Babylon,
    And so revenge our latest grievous loss,   10
    If God or Mahomet send any aid.

KING OF AMASIA.

    Doubt not, my lord, but we shall conquer him.

212. in] *O1–2*; *not in O3–4.*   0.1. Captain] *Dyce 2*; *not in O1–4.*
[V.ii]   4. may we] *O1–3*; we may *O4.*

---

216. *distempered*] sick, ailing, disordered.

The monster that hath drunk a sea of blood
And yet gapes still for more to quench his thirst
Our Turkish swords shall headlong send to hell;   15
And that vile carcass drawn by warlike kings
The fowls shall eat; for never sepulcher
Shall grace that base-born tyrant Tamburlaine.

CALLAPINE.

When I record my parents' slavish life,
Their cruel death, mine own captivity,   20
My viceroys' bondage under Tamburlaine,
Methinks I could sustain a thousand deaths
To be reveng'd of all his villainy.
Ah, sacred Mahomet, thou that hast seen
Millions of Turks perish by Tamburlaine,   25
Kingdoms made waste, brave cities sack'd and burnt,
And but one host is left to honor thee,
Aid thy obedient servant, Callapine,
And make him after all these overthrows
To triumph over cursed Tamburlaine.   30

KING OF AMASIA.

Fear not, my lord. I see great Mahomet
Clothed in purple clouds, and on his head
A chaplet brighter than Apollo's crown,
Marching about the air with armed men
To join with you against this Tamburlaine.   35

CAPTAIN.

Renowned general, mighty Callapine,
Though God himself and holy Mahomet
Should come in person to resist your power,
Yet might your mighty host encounter all
And pull proud Tamburlaine upon his knees   40
To sue for mercy at your highness' feet.

CALLAPINE.

Captain, the force of Tamburlaine is great,
His fortune greater, and the victories
Wherewith he hath so sore dismay'd the world

---

18. that] *O1, O3–4;* this *O2.*   36. S.P. CAPTAIN] *Dyce 2; not in*
28. Aid] *O1–2;* And *O3–4.*   *O1–4.*

---

19. *record*] call to mind.

Are greatest to discourage all our drifts.   45
Yet, when the pride of Cynthia is at full,
She wanes again, and so shall his, I hope;
For we have here the chief selected men
Of twenty several kingdoms at the least.
Nor ploughman, priest, nor merchant stays at home;   50
All Turkey is in arms with Callapine;
And never will we sunder camps and arms
Before himself or his be conquered.
This is the time that must eternize me
For conquering the tyrant of the world.   55
Come, soldiers, let us lie in wait for him,
And, if we find him absent from his camp,
Or that it be rejoin'd again at full,
Assail it and be sure of victory.   *Exeunt.*

[V.iii]   [*Enter*] Theridamas, Techelles, Usumcasane.

THERIDAMAS.

Weep, heavens, and vanish into liquid tears!
Fall, stars that govern his nativity,
And summon all the shining lamps of heaven
To cast their bootless fires to the earth
And shed their feeble influence in the air.   5
Muffle your beauties with eternal clouds,
For Hell and Darkness pitch their pitchy tents,
And Death, with armies of Cimmerian spirits,
Gives battle 'gainst the heart of Tamburlaine.
Now in defiance of that wonted love   10
Your sacred virtues pour'd upon his throne,
And made his state an honor to the heavens,
These cowards invisibly assail his soul
And threaten conquest on our sovereign.
But, if he die, your glories are disgrac'd,   15

13. invisibly] *O1, O3–4*; inuincible
O2.

---

45. *drifts*] purposes.   47. *his*] his pride.
49. *several*] different.
54. *eternize*] immortalize.   58. *Or that*] before.
[V.iii]
4. *bootless*] unavailing.   8. *Cimmerian*] black, infernal.

Earth droops and says that hell in heaven is plac'd.

TECHELLES.

O, then, ye powers that sway eternal seats
And guide this massy substance of the earth,
If you retain desert of holiness,
As your supreme estates instruct our thoughts,   20
Be not inconstant, careless of your fame.
Bear not the burden of your enemies' joys,
Triumphing in his fall whom you advanc'd,
But, as his birth, life, health, and majesty
Were strangely bless'd and governed by heaven,   25
So honor, heaven, till heaven dissolved be,
His birth, his life, his health, and majesty!

USUMCASANE.

Blush, heaven, to lose the honor of thy name,
To see thy footstool set upon thy head;
And let no baseness in thy haughty breast   30
Sustain a shame of such inexcellence,
To see the devils mount in angels' thrones,
And angels dive into the pools of hell;
And, though they think their painful date is out
And that their power is puissant as Jove's,   35
Which make them manage arms against thy state,
Yet makes them feel the strength of Tamburlaine,
Thy instrument and note of majesty,
Is greater far than they can thus subdue.
For, if he die, thy glory is disgrac'd,   40
Earth droops and says that hell in heaven is plac'd.

[*Enter* Tamburlaine, *drawn by the captive Kings*, Amyras, Celebinus, *and* Physicians.]

TAMBURLAINE.

What daring god torments my body thus

31. inexcellence] *O1, O3–4*; in-   41.1–2. *Enter . . .* Physicians] *Dyce*;
excellencie *O2*.   *not in O1–4.*

19. *desert of holiness*] that which deserves religious worship.
20. *estates*] ranks, authorities.
31. *Sustain . . . inexcellence*] put up with so vile a shame.
34. *they*] the devils.
38. *note*] distinguishing feature, sign.

And seeks to conquer mighty Tamburlaine?
Shall sickness prove me now to be a man,
That have been term'd the terror of the world? 45
Techelles and the rest, come, take your swords,
And threaten him whose hand afflicts my soul.
Come, let us march against the powers of heaven
And set black streamers in the firmament
To signify the slaughter of the gods. 50
Ah, friends, what shall I do? I cannot stand.
Come, carry me to war against the gods,
That thus envy the health of Tamburlaine.
THERIDAMAS.
 Ah, good my lord, leave these impatient words
 Which add much danger to your malady. 55
TAMBURLAINE.
 Why, shall I sit and languish in this pain?
 No, strike the drums, and, in revenge of this,
 Come, let us charge our spears and pierce his breast
 Whose shoulders bear the axis of the world,
 That, if I perish, heaven and earth may fade. 60
 Theridamas, haste to the court of Jove;
 Will him to send Apollo hither straight
 To cure me, or I'll fetch him down myself.
TECHELLES.
 Sit still, my gracious lord; this grief will cease
 And cannot last, it is so violent. 65
TAMBURLAINE.
 Not last, Techelles? No, for I shall die.
 See where my slave, the ugly monster, Death,
 Shaking and quivering, pale and wan for fear,
 Stands aiming at me with his murdering dart,
 Who flies away at every glance I give, 70
 And, when I look away, comes stealing on.

64. cease] *O1–2, O4*; case *O3*.

---

49. *streamers*] pennons.
58. *charge*] level.
58–59. *his . . . world*] Atlas' breast. See Part I, II.i.11, note.
62. *Apollo*] As the god who warded off evil, he came to be regarded as
a god of medicine.
64. *grief*] pain.

Villain, away, and hie thee to the field!
I and mine army come to load thy bark
With souls of thousand mangled carcasses.
Look, where he goes! But see, he comes again   75
Because I stay. Techelles, let us march
And weary Death with bearing souls to hell.

PHYSICIAN.

Pleaseth your majesty to drink this potion
Which will abate the fury of your fit
And cause some milder spirits govern you.   80

TAMBURLAINE.

Tell me, what think you of my sickness now?

PHYSICIAN.

I view'd your urine, and the hypostasis,
Thick and obscure, doth make your danger great.
Your veins are full of accidental heat,
Whereby the moisture of your blood is dried.   85
The humidum and calor, which some hold
Is not a parcel of the elements
But of a substance more divine and pure,
Is almost clean extinguished and spent,
Which, being the cause of life, imports your death.   90
Besides, my lord, this day is critical,

73. bark] *O1–2*; back *O3–4*.   85. moisture] *O1–2, O4*; moister
82. hypostasis] *Rob.*; Hipostates   *O3*.
O1–4.

---

76. *stay*] delay.
78–99. *Pleaseth . . . all*] "As a result of his intense passion (and . . . as a
result of the position of his stars), Tamburlaine has occasioned in his body
an excess of febrile heat. This 'accidental heat' parches his arteries and
dries up in his blood the radical moisture (*humidum*) which is necessary for
the preservation of his natural heat (*calor*). The depletion of his *humidum*
and *calor* (whose admixture in the blood gives rise to the *spirits*) prevents
his soul's functions, stops his bodily activities, and thereby causes his
death" (Parr, p. 19).
82. *hypostasis*] sediment. Tamburlaine's physician follows Hippocrates in
regarding a *Thick and obscure* (l. 83) hypostasis as extremely dangerous. See
Parr, pp. 12–13.
87. *parcel*] part.
91. *critical*] "Critical days, the history of which goes back to Hippocrates
and Galen, were in general medical practice the days when the malignancy
of a disease was suddenly and swiftly altered for better or for worse. . . .
[The] mediaeval astrologers erected elaborate systems by which a disease

Dangerous to those whose crisis is as yours.
Your artiers, which alongst the veins convey
The lively spirits which the heart engenders,
Are parch'd and void of spirit, that the soul,   95
Wanting those organons by which it moves,
Cannot endure by argument of art.
Yet, if your majesty may escape this day,
No doubt but you shall soon recover all.

TAMBURLAINE.

Then will I comfort all my vital parts   100
And live, in spite of death, above a day.

Alarm within. [*Enter a* Messenger.]

MESSENGER.

My lord, young Callapine, that lately fled from your
majesty, hath now gathered a fresh army, and, hearing your
absence in the field, offers to set upon us presently.

TAMBURLAINE.

See, my physicians, now, how Jove hath sent   105
A present medicine to recure my pain.
My looks shall make them fly, and, might I follow,
There should not one of all the villain's power
Live to give offer of another fight.

USUMCASANE.

I joy, my lord, your highness is so strong,   110
That can endure so well your royal presence,

101.1. *Enter a* Messenger] *Rob.; not*   104. upon] *O1, O3–4;* on *O2.*
in *O1–4.*

---

could be diagnosed, attended, and healed according to the positions and
influences of the planets during these critical days. Wise mediaeval physicians believed implicitly that any alteration of the qualities of a man's body
was dependent upon the stars; Renaissance treatises on this subject give
abundant evidence that the tradition carried over into Elizabethan times"
(Parr, p. 20).
    93. *artiers*] arteries.   96. *organons*] instruments.
    99. *all*] completely.
    104. *presently*] immediately.
    106. *recure*] cure.
    111–112. *That . . . enemy*] Theridamas contrasts the contentment which
his leader's presence inspires in him with the dismay which it will inspire
in their foe.

Which only will dismay the enemy.

TAMBURLAINE.

I know it will, Casane. Draw, you slaves!
In spite of death, I will go show my face.

Alarm. Tamburlaine *goes in, and comes out again with all the rest.*

Thus are the villains, cowards, fled for fear,   115
Like summer's vapors vanish'd by the sun;
And, could I but a while pursue the field,
That Callapine should be my slave again.
But I perceive my martial strength is spent.
In vain I strive and rail against those powers   120
That mean t'invest me in a higher throne,
As much too high for this disdainful earth.
Give me a map. Then let me see how much
Is left for me to conquer all the world,
That these my boys may finish all my wants.   125

One brings a map.

Here I began to march towards Persia,
Along Armenia and the Caspian Sea,
And thence unto Bithynia, where I took
The Turk and his great empress prisoners.
Then march'd I into Egypt and Arabia,   130
And here, not far from Alexandria,
Whereas the Terrene and the Red Sea meet,
Being distant less than full a hundred leagues,
I meant to cut a channel to them both
That men might quickly sail to India.   135
From thence to Nubia near Borno lake,
And so along the Ethiopian sea,
Cutting the tropic line of Capricorn,
I conquered all as far as Zanzibar.
Then, by the northern part of Africa,   140
I came at last to Graecia, and from thence
To Asia, where I stay against my will;
Which is from Scythia, where I first began,

128. unto] *O1–3*; to *O4*.   143. began] *O1–3*; begun *O4*.

---

112. *only*] alone.   116. *vanish'd*] made to vanish.
132. *Whereas*] where.
136–139. *From . . . Zanzibar*] Tamburlaine here accepts Techelles'
conquests as his own. See Techelles' report, Part II, I.iii.186–205, and notes.

Backward and forwards near five thousand leagues.
Look here, my boys, see what a world of ground   145
Lies westward from the midst of Cancer's line
Unto the rising of this earthly globe,
Whereas the sun, declining from our sight,
Begins the day with our antipodes.
And shall I die, and this unconquered?   150
Lo, here, my sons, are all the golden mines,
Inestimable drugs and precious stones,
More worth than Asia and the world beside;
And from th'Antarctic Pole eastward behold
As much more land, which never was descried,   155
Wherein are rocks of pearl that shine as bright
As all the lamps that beautify the sky.
And shall I die, and this unconquered?
Here, lovely boys, what death forbids my life,
That let your lives command in spite of death.   160

AMYRAS.

Alas, my lord, how should our bleeding hearts,
Wounded and broken with your highness' grief,
Retain a thought of joy or spark of life?
Your soul gives essence to our wretched subjects,
Whose matter is incorporate in your flesh.   165

CELEBINUS.

Your pains do pierce our souls. No hope survives,
For by your life we entertain our lives.

TAMBURLAINE.

But, sons, this subject, not of force enough
To hold the fiery spirit it contains,
Must part, imparting his impressions   170

147. this] *O1–3*; the *O4*.

---

162. *grief*] suffering.
164–165. *Your . . . flesh*] Your soul has bequeathed to us the spirit that
animates us, our bodies being similarly part of your flesh. As in Part II,
IV.i.110–114, Marlowe uses technical terms derived from sixteenth-century
Aristotelian studies. See Ellis-Fermor.
167. *entertain*] maintain.
168–171. *But . . . breasts*] My substance, however, not strong enough to
retain my fiery spirit, must disintegrate, dividing the power of that spirit
(*his impressions*) equally between you. See Ellis-Fermor.

By equal portions into both your breasts.
My flesh, divided in your precious shapes,
Shall still retain my spirit, though I die,
And live in all your seeds immortally.
Then now remove me, that I may resign   175
My place and proper title to my son.
First, take my scourge and my imperial crown,
And mount my royal chariot of estate,
That I may see thee crown'd before I die.
Help me, my lords, to make my last remove.   180

THERIDAMAS.

A woeful change, my lord, that daunts our thoughts
More than the ruin of our proper souls.

TAMBURLAINE.

Sit up, my son; let me see how well
Thou wilt become thy father's majesty.   *They crown him.*

AMYRAS.

With what a flinty bosom should I joy   185
The breath of life and burden of my soul,
If not resolv'd into resolved pains
My body's mortified lineaments
Should exercise the motions of my heart,
Pierc'd with the joy of any dignity!   190
O father, if the unrelenting ears
Of death and hell be shut against my prayers,
And that the spiteful influence of heaven
Deny my soul fruition of her joy,
How should I step or stir my hateful feet   195
Against the inward powers of my heart,
Leading a life that only strives to die,
And plead in vain unpleasing sovereignty?

171. into] *O1–3*; vnto *O4*.   188. lineaments] *O1–2*; laments
174. your] *O1–3*; our *O4*.   *O3–4*.
186. breath] *O1–3*; breach *O4*.

176, 182. *proper*] own.
185–190. *With . . . dignity*] "How hard a heart I should have if I could
enjoy my life and the possession of my soul and if my body were not dissolved
in extreme pain (l. 187) and sympathetically afflicted (l. 188) and could
still direct the movements of a heart that was touched to joy by such things
as earthly dignities" (Ellis-Fermor).

TAMBURLAINE.

Let not thy love exceed thine honor, son,
Nor bar thy mind that magnanimity   200
That nobly must admit necessity.
Sit up, my boy, and with those silken reins
Bridle the steeled stomachs of those jades.

THERIDAMAS.

My lord, you must obey his majesty,
Since fate commands and proud necessity.   205

AMYRAS.

Heavens witness me with what a broken heart
And damned spirit I ascend this seat,
And send my soul, before my father die,
His anguish and his burning agony.

TAMBURLAINE.

Now fetch the hearse of fair Zenocrate.   210
Let it be plac'd by this my fatal chair
And serve as parcel of my funeral.

USUMCASANE.

Then feels your majesty no sovereign ease,
Nor may our hearts, all drown'd in tears of blood,
Joy any hope of your recovery?   215

TAMBURLAINE.

Casane, no. The monarch of the earth
And eyeless monster that torments my soul
Cannot behold the tears ye shed for me,
And therefore still augments his cruelty.

TECHELLES.

Then let some god oppose his holy power   220
Against the wrath and tyranny of Death,
That his tear-thirsty and unquenched hate
May be upon himself reverberate!

They bring in the hearse [of Zenocrate].

202. those] *O1–2*; these *O3–4*.   223.1. *of* Zenocrate] *Dyce*; *not in*
203. those] *O1–2*; these *O3–4*.   *O1–4.*

---

200. *magnanimity*] fortitude.
203. *steeled stomachs*] obdurately proud spirits.
208. *send*] may the heavens send.   212. *parcel*] part.
215. *Joy*] enjoy.   223.1. *hearse*] coffin.

TAMBURLAINE.

Now, eyes, enjoy your latest benefit,
And, when my soul hath virtue of your sight,   225
Pierce through the coffin and the sheet of gold
And glut your longings with a heaven of joy.
So reign, my son. Scourge and control those slaves,
Guiding thy chariot with thy father's hand.
As precious is the charge thou undertak'st   230
As that which Clymene's brainsick son did guide,
When wand'ring Phoebe's ivory cheeks were scorch'd,
And all the earth, like Aetna, breathing fire.
Be warn'd by him, then; learn with awful eye
To sway a throne as dangerous as his;   235
For, if thy body thrive not full of thoughts
As pure and fiery as Phyteus' beams,
The nature of these proud rebelling jades
Will take occasion by the slenderest hair
And draw thee piecemeal like Hippolytus   240
Through rocks more steep and sharp than Caspian clifts.
The nature of thy chariot will not bear
A guide of baser temper than myself,
More than heaven's coach the pride of Phaëton.
Farewell, my boys! My dearest friends, farewell!   245
My body feels, my soul doth weep to see

231. Clymene's] *O2*; *Clymeus O1*,   232. Phoebe's] *O1–3*; *Phœbus O4*.
O3–4.   240. thee] *O1–3*; me *O4*.

224–227. *Now . . . joy*] For the last time in his life, Tamburlaine gazes
upon her coffin. After his death, his soul will exercise the power of vision
now lodged only in his physical organs of sight. He will then behold Zenocrate's spirit.
231. *Clymene's brainsick son*] See Part I, IV.ii.49, and note.
232. *Phoebe*] the moon.
234. *awful*] awe-inspiring.
237. *Phyteus*] Apollo (Pythius), the sun-god.
239. *take . . . hair*] a variant of the proverb, "Take Time (occasion) by
the forelock, for she is bald behind" (Tilley, T 311).
240. *Hippolytus*] He was driving along the seacoast, when Poseidon sent
a bull out of the water. The horses panicked, upset the chariot, and dragged
Hippolytus along the ground until he was dead.
241. *clifts*] cliffs.
244. *Phaëton*] See Part I, IV.ii.49, note.

Your sweet desires depriv'd my company,
For Tamburlaine, the scourge of God, must die.   [*Dies.*]

AMYRAS.

Meet heaven and earth, and here let all things end,
For earth hath spent the pride of all her fruit,   250
And heaven consum'd his choicest living fire.
Let earth and heaven his timeless death deplore,
For both their worths will equal him no more.   [*Exeunt.*]

FINIS

248. S.D. *Dies*] *Rob.*; *not in O1–4.*   253. S.D. *Exeunt*] *Dyce* 2; *not in O1–4.*

252. *timeless*] untimely.

Appendix

Chronology

Approximate years are indicated by *, occurrences in doubt by (?).

Political and Literary Events	*Life and Major Works of Marlowe*
1558 Accession of Queen Elizabeth I. Robert Greene born. Thomas Kyd born.	
1560 George Chapman born.	
1561 Francis Bacon born.	
1564 Shakespeare born.	Christopher Marlowe born at Canterbury; baptized February 26.
1570 Thomas Heywood born.*	
1572 Thomas Dekker born.* John Donne born. Massacre of St. Bartholomew's Day.	
1573 Ben Jonson born.*	
1576 The Theatre, the first permanent public theater in London, established by James Burbage. John Marston born.	
1577 The Curtain theater opened. Holinshed's *Chronicles of England, Scotland and Ireland*.	

Drake begins circumnavigation of the earth; completed 1580.

1578

John Lyly's *Euphues: The Anatomy of Wit.*

1579

John Fletcher born.
Sir Thomas North's translation of Plutarch's *Lives.*

Enters as scholar at King's School, Canterbury.

1580

Thomas Middleton born.

Enters Corpus Christi College, Cambridge.

1583

Philip Massinger born.

1584

Francis Beaumont born.*

Receives Cambridge B.A.

1585

Engages in secret government service.*

1586

Death of Sir Philip Sidney.
John Ford born.

DIDO, QUEEN OF CARTHAGE (with Nashe).*

1587

The Rose theater opened by Henslowe.
Execution of Mary, Queen of Scots.
Drake raids Cadiz.

Receives Cambridge M.A. upon intervention of the Privy Council.
TAMBURLAINE, Parts I and II.*

1588

Defeat of the Spanish Armada.

1589

Greene's *FRIAR BACON AND FRIAR BUNGAY.**
Kyd's *THE SPANISH TRAGEDY.**

Imprisoned in Newgate for a street fight.

1590

Spenser's *Faerie Queene* (Books I–III) published.
Sidney's *Arcadia* published.
Shakespeare's *HENRY VI*, Parts I–III,* *TITUS ANDRONICUS.**

*THE JEW OF MALTA.**

1591

Shakespeare's *RICHARD III.**

1592

Shakespeare's *TAMING OF THE SHREW** and *THE COMEDY OF ERRORS.**

Death of Greene.

Summoned on a charge of assault. In government service at the siege of Rouen (?).

THE MASSACRE AT PARIS,* DOCTOR FAUSTUS,* EDWARD II.*

1593

Shakespeare's *LOVE'S LABOR'S LOST;* Venus and Adonis* published. Theaters closed on account of plague.

Summoned to appear before the Privy Council, May 18, on a charge of heresy.

Killed by Ingram Frizer in a tavern at Deptford, May 30.

1594

Shakespeare's *TWO GENTLE-MEN OF VERONA;* The Rape of Lucrece* published.

Shakespeare's company becomes Lord Chamberlain's Men.

Death of Kyd.

1595

The Swan theater built.

Sidney's *Defense of Poesy* published. Shakespeare's *ROMEO AND JULIET,* A MIDSUMMER NIGHT'S DREAM,* RICHARD II.**

Raleigh's first expedition to Guiana.

All Ovid's Elegies published (translation).*

1596

Spenser's *Faerie Queene* (Books IV–VI) published.

Shakespeare's *MERCHANT OF VENICE,* KING JOHN.**

James Shirley born.

1597

Bacon's *Essays* (first edition).

Shakespeare's *HENRY IV*, Part *I.**

1598

Demolition of The Theatre.

Shakespeare's *MUCH ADO ABOUT NOTHING,* HENRY IV,* Part II.*

Hero and Leander published.

Jonson's *EVERY MAN IN HIS HUMOR* (first version).

Seven books of Chapman's translation of Homer's *Iliad* published.

1599

The Paul's Boys reopen their theater.

The Globe theater opened.

Shakespeare's *AS YOU LIKE IT*,* *HENRY V, JULIUS CAESAR.**

Marston's *ANTONIO AND MEL-LIDA*,* Parts I and II.

Dekker's *THE SHOEMAKERS' HOLIDAY.**

Death of Spenser.

1600

Shakespeare's *TWELFTH NIGHT.**

The Fortune theater built by Alleyn.

The Children of the Chapel begin to play at the Blackfriars.

Lucan's First Book Translated Line for Line published.

1601

Shakespeare's *HAMLET*,* *MERRY WIVES OF WINDSOR.**

Insurrection and execution of the Earl of Essex.

Jonson's *POETASTER.*

1602

Shakespeare's *TROILUS AND CRESSIDA.**

1603

Death of Queen Elizabeth I; accession of James VI of Scotland as James I.

Florio's translation of Montaigne's *Essays* published.

Shakespeare's *ALL'S WELL THAT ENDS WELL.**

Heywood's *A WOMAN KILLED WITH KINDNESS.*

Marston's *THE MALCONTENT.**

Shakespeare's company becomes the King's Men.

1604
Shakespeare's *MEASURE FOR MEASURE*,* *OTHELLO*.*
Marston's *THE FAWN*.*
Chapman's *BUSSY D'AMBOIS*.*

1605
Shakespeare's *KING LEAR*.*
Marston's *THE DUTCH COURTESAN*.*
Bacon's *Advancement of Learning* published.
The Gunpowder Plot.

1606
Shakespeare's *MACBETH*.*
Jonson's *VOLPONE*.*
Tourneur's *REVENGER'S TRAGEDY*.*
The Red Bull theater built.
Death of John Lyly.

1607
Shakespeare's *ANTONY AND CLEOPATRA*.*
Beaumont's *KNIGHT OF THE BURNING PESTLE*.*
Settlement of Jamestown, Virginia.

1608
Shakespeare's *CORIOLANUS*,* *TIMON OF ATHENS*,* *PERICLES*.*
Chapman's *CONSPIRACY AND TRAGEDY OF CHARLES, DUKE OF BYRON*.*
Dekker's *Gull's Hornbook* published.
Richard Burbage leases Blackfriars theater for King's company.
John Milton born.

1609
Shakespeare's *CYMBELINE*;*
Sonnets published.
Jonson's *EPICOENE*.

1610
Jonson's *ALCHEMIST*.

Chapman's *REVENGE OF BUSSY D'AMBOIS.**
Richard Crashaw born.

1611
Authorized (King James) Version of the Bible published.
Shakespeare's *THE WINTER'S TALE,* THE TEMPEST.**
Beaumont and Fletcher's *A KING AND NO KING.*
Middleton's *A CHASTE MAID IN CHEAPSIDE.**
Tourneur's *ATHEIST'S TRAGEDY.**
Chapman's translation of *Iliad* completed.

1612
Webster's *THE WHITE DEVIL.**

1613
The Globe theater burned.
Shakespeare's *HENRY VIII* (with Fletcher).
Webster's *THE DUCHESS OF MALFI.**
Sir Thomas Overbury murdered.

1614
The Globe theater rebuilt.
The Hope theater built.
Jonson's *BARTHOLOMEW FAIR.*

1616
Publication of Folio edition of Jonson's *Works.*
Chapman's *Whole Works of Homer.*
Death of Shakespeare.
Death of Beaumont.

1618
Outbreak of Thirty Years War.
Execution of Raleigh.

1620
Settlement of Plymouth, Massachusetts.

1621
Middleton's *WOMEN BEWARE
WOMEN.**
Robert Burton's *Anatomy of Melancholy* published.
Andrew Marvell born.

1622
Middleton and Rowley's *THE
CHANGELING.**
Henry Vaughan born.

1623
Publication of Folio edition of
Shakespeare's *COMEDIES, HIS-
TORIES, AND TRAGEDIES.*

1625
Death of King James I; accession of
Charles I.
Death of Fletcher.

1626
Death of Tourneur.
Death of Bacon.

1627
Death of Middleton.

1628
Ford's *THE LOVER'S MELAN-
CHOLY.*
Petition of Right.
Buckingham assassinated.

1631
Shirley's *THE TRAITOR.*
Death of Donne.
John Dryden born.

1632
Massinger's *THE CITY MADAM.**

1633
Donne's *Poems* published.
Death of George Herbert.

1634
Death of Chapman, Marston, Web-
ster.*
Publication of *THE TWO NOBLE*

KINSMEN, with title-page attribution to Shakespeare and Fletcher.
Milton's *Comus*.

1635
Sir Thomas Browne's *Religio Medici*.

1637
Death of Jonson.

1639
First Bishops' War.
Death of Carew.*

1640
Short Parliament.
Long Parliament impeaches Laud.
Death of Massinger, Burton.

1641
Irish rebel.
Death of Heywood.

1642
Charles I leaves London; Civil War breaks out.
Shirley's *COURT SECRET*.
All theaters closed by Act of Parliament.

1643
Parliament swears to the Solemn League and Covenant.

1645
Ordinance for New Model Army enacted.

1646
End of First Civil War.

1647
Army occupies London.
Charles I forms alliance with Scots.
Publication of Folio edition of Beaumont and Fletcher's *COMEDIES AND TRAGEDIES*.

1648
Second Civil War.

1649
Execution of Charles I.

1650
Jeremy Collier born.

1651
Hobbes' *Leviathan* published.

1652
First Dutch War began (ended 1654).
Thomas Otway born.

1653
Nathaniel Lee born.*

1656
D'Avenant's *THE SIEGE OF RHODES* performed at Rutland House.

1657
John Dennis born.

1658
Death of Oliver Cromwell.
D'Avenant's *THE CRUELTY OF THE SPANIARDS IN PERU* performed at the Cockpit.

1660
Restoration of Charles II.
Theatrical patents granted to Thomas Killigrew and Sir William D'Avenant, authorizing them to form, respectively, the King's and the Duke of York's Companies.

1661
Cowley's *THE CUTTER OF COLEMAN STREET*.
D'Avenant's *THE SIEGE OF RHODES* (expanded to two parts).

1662
Charter granted to the Royal Society.

1663
Dryden's *THE WILD GALLANT*.
Tuke's *THE ADVENTURES OF FIVE HOURS*.

1664
Sir John Vanbrugh born.

Dryden's *THE RIVAL LADIES.*
Dryden and Howard's *THE INDIAN QUEEN.*
Etherege's *THE COMICAL RE-VENGE.*

1665
Second Dutch War began (ended 1667).
Great Plague.
Dryden's *THE INDIAN EMPEROR.*
Orrery's *MUSTAPHA.*

1666
Fire of London.
Death of James Shirley.